I GOT
PRO
from
MY
FATHER

No Weapon Shall "Prosper"

Tonya R. Love

Weapon Shall "Prosper"

Copyright © Tonya R. Love

ISBN: 978-0-9984230-1-2

Published: 17th January 2017

Publisher: Tonyarepslove

E-book edition available.

The right of Tonya R. Love to be identified as author of this Work has been asserted by her in accordance with sections 77 and 78 of the Copyright, Designs and Patents Act 1988.

All rights reserved. No part of this publication may be reproduced, stored in retrieval system, copied in any form or by any means, electronic, mechanical, photocopying, recording or otherwise transmitted without written permission from the publisher. You must not circulate this book in any format.

Scripture quotations marked (NIV) are taken from the Holy Bible, New International Version®, NIV®. Copyright © 1973, 1978, 1984, 2011 by Biblica, Inc.™ Used by permission of Zondervan. All rights reserved worldwide. Also taken from the Holy Bible, English Standard Version® (ESV®) Copyright © 2001 by Crossway, a publishing ministry of Good News Publishers. All rights reserved. ESV® Text Edition: 2016

To find out more about this Author and upcoming books, music, and videos, go online to Tonyarepslove on Facebook, YouTube, Twitter @Tonyarepslove, and tonya_reps_love on Instagram.

This book is dedicated to the loving memory of my son Prosper

Table of Contents

Acknowledgements: 7

The Prologue: 8

Chapter One: Prophecy Inspired by God (PROSPER) 14

Chapter Two: Relocate & Renew (PROSPER) 27

Chapter Three: Omit Men's Laws & Tradition (PROSPER) 36

Chapter Four: Sacrifice of One's Independence (PROSPER) 52

Chapter Five: Praise God through Tribulations (PROSPER) 74

Chapter Six: Eat Only from the Tree of Life (PROSPER) 89

Chapter Seven: Rest and Reap (PROSPER) 157

About the Author: 232

The Prophet's Prayer

As I sit here contemplating what to write, I must pause and pray,

"Holy Spirit guide me through the Word of God,
and let your wisdom light the way.

Lord, give me revelation; something mere man can never ever teach.

Anoint my words with power so that many lost
and dying souls may be reached.

Yes, I pray for discernment, and that you take the blinders off of my eyes.

Let me see Satan for who he really is; beyond
his lying wonders and disguise.

God please don't forget your mercy, love and tender grace,

For I need these to fall back on when the world spits in my face.

I pray for a measure of faith, no wait, a measure of faith times two;

like Elisha, I need a double portion if I want to make it through.

I pray most of all, for your truth; because I know it will set your people free.

With You and Your attributes in me, I will be the
prophet you have destined me to be."

Acknowledgements

First and foremost, I would like to thank God for not allowing any 'Weapon Formed Against Me' to Prosper in my life and especially while writing this book.

I would like to thank my children Chandreka, Ezekiel, Ciera, and Nathaniel for believing in God's word even when they couldn't believe in me. Special thanks to my son, Prosper, who has transitioned to heaven, who was the living symbol, and promise of God's word for making me want to prosper in the calling of God.

I include my husband, Bennie Davis, Aka Novacane, for causing me to grow and mature in God.

I am grateful to my mother for introducing me to God and encouraging my relationship with him.

There is my Aunt Rita, who has also gone to be with the Lord, for being the best spiritual mother anyone could ask for.

I owe a special thanks to all the preachers who spoke God's word into my life and ministered to my many needs: Apostle Darryl McCoy, Apostle Linda Thompson, Pastor Johnnie Griffin, Pastor Greg Henry, Pastor Eric Osborne and Bishop TD Jakes, who actually preached at my dad's funeral) Joseph Prince. Joel Osteen who I watched religiously on TBN.

I thank Vinnie Kaufman Sr., who believed in me and my story and dedicated his knowledge and funds to help me get my story to the public.

I appreciate my editor Lance Knight for making himself readily available to me day or night.

Thanks to my book designer Debbi Stocco for her talent and the quality of work and professionalism, and to Donnell D. Bennett, my professional photographer for the beautiful photos.

The Prologue

I DEBATED MANY years about writing this story, my story. A story that would entail the many facets of the hardships, trials, tribulations, and manifestations of my life; emotionally, physically, mentally, sexually, and yes even spiritually. Most people who have encountered me, and know even bits and pieces of my life's journey, seem to always compare my life to the Biblical story of Job. The Bible describes Job as a faithful and loving servant of Almighty God, a man who was blessed beyond the wildest imagination, a man who bore many difficulties in life; from losing his estate, his health, and the sudden death of all of his children. A man of integrity who loved and respected Almighty God, a man The Almighty honored, and could boast about. A man Satan placed a wager against, and vowed to prove to the Almighty, that if handed enough adversities, would curse God. A man that God had so much faith in, that He accepted Satan's wager, with the one stipulation of not taking his life.

Job and I shared a lot of similarities, in that through the course of the many afflictions, and torments, life could throw my way, I kept my perpetual love and faith in God. I didn't understand my suffering, but then I really didn't know or understand God, outside of what religion taught me about Him. Religion taught me to believe that I had to make myself worthy of His love; that I had to follow certain rituals and keep certain laws to obtain His favor. Religion fooled me into thinking that the God of the Bible no longer exist. His miracles, blessings, gifts and other attributes that make Him sovereign, loving, forgiving and all powerful, were merely meant for the people of the Bible days. So when I began to search out God for myself and tried to make sense of all the outrageous difficulties I was experiencing, it was no wonder that I began to study the life of Job.

During the course of my studying, I realized that although Job suffered as I did, his story wasn't all that much like mine. He, unlike me, was wealthy, educated, and held a great deal of positive influence on his family and community, and disparate from me, Job had experienced the goodness and favor of God for the most part of his life. But more importantly, Job never had a God given mission or prophecy that God vowed to develop and that Satan vowed to destroy. To me Job seemed to only suffer because he had an immense love for God; not for any particular sin that He had committed, in essence his suffering was for the sole purpose of bringing glory to God. My life sufferings would come from an array of conflicting contributions, such as allowing the wrong people into my life; some pain I ignorantly created for myself and others I know were strategically sent from Satan just as he did with Job, to get me to question my love for, and faith in, God. It would take me the majority of my life to try to comprehend the ways of God, and until this very day I still don't understand everything. As the Bible clearly declares in **Isaiah 55:9, "As the Heavens are higher than the Earth so are My ways and My thoughts higher than yours."**

Still, my life would often be spent pondering these questions, "What was the message that God was trying to teach me through my suffering, trials and tribulations, or better yet, what was God using them for that He could teach the world, why would God allow such suffering in the lives of the people He claims to love so much? How can one person's suffering contribute to the betterment of the one suffering, let alone others?

I can remember the prophecies spoken by a variety of preachers of various churches, in different cities and states. In fact, they played in the back of my mind constantly; a worldwide ministry that would one day help change the world for the better. It seemed simple, I would literally preach one day, or my writings would minister to people through my poetry, songs, or books. I never understood that ministry could not come without misery. I could not write anything with substance or meaning without learning the meaning, and developing substance. I would have to learn to trust that God would navigate me through the darkness in order for me to be able to understand and appreciate HIS light. God had to not only teach me about faith, HE had to develop and exercise my faith in order for me to complete His assignment and His will in my life. So one day while reading my Bible God spoke to my heart and said that I should study the lives and promises of three characters from the Bible, and learn from them, because my life would be fashioned after theirs in some way or the other.

The first person God had me to study about was **Sarah**, a woman of old age, who God would literally have to give a miracle to in order to achieve a specific purpose through her life. I could relate to this great woman of faith because just as with her, in my lack of patience in waiting for God to perform His promise, I would do countless numbers of imprudent things to try to hurry the promises of God, and inadvertently make things worse. Also as well as her, I would suffer from feelings of inadequacies and low self-esteem, believing God could choose a better source or person by which to fulfill his mission.

David was the second person God said I should study; our lives were really parallel in a lot of areas. David and I were both considered to be a couple of *nobodies* that God desired to use; people who literally came from nothing, and whose families often undermined and esteemed us as unworthy of God's favor. But the Bible describes him as having a heart after God's own, a person who in spite of his sins was totally in love with God. This was also a similarity that David and I shared. Like David my relationship with God began at a young age, and it was a relationship that I would make mistakes in, but never walk away from. Secondly, like David, I would be faced with giants and battles in my life, yet my intimate and deep love for God would come flowing out beautifully from my heart as inspirational poetry. David and I both would suffer the loss of our children. David and I would seek love in all the wrong places, though we knew God was the ultimate source of love. We would suffer greatly from our mistakes and the betrayal of those who were close to us.

Last but not least, God told me to study the life of a person I most recognize in myself, and that is **Joseph** the son of Jacob. Joseph and I shared in the fact that God began dealing with us as youngsters by giving us dreams that we couldn't understand, nor ever fathom. We were both the black sheep of our families because people could not understand or appreciate the call of God on our lives. I experienced the same kind of hurt and betrayal Joseph had received from his own family members due to their built up resentment and jealousy of the favor of God on our lives. I, as well as Joseph, would experience many hardships, including being incarcerated, both physically and spiritually for a time as Joseph had been, and would be used in that time of confinement to minister to others. The most important factor that Joseph and I shared is the fact that I too would be given the opportunity to forgive my family and others for their hurt and betrayal, realizing as He did, that even though they did hurt me and cause me a lot of distress. In the end it is what God allowed for His specific purpose, and that all things that were meant to be bad toward me, God turned around and used for my good as it is written, **Genesis 50:20 NIV, "You intended to harm me, but God intended it for the good to accomplish what is done, the saving of many lives."**

My hope is that just as I have learned from the characters above, that God allows us to go through and experience certain things not just for ourselves, but so that others can learn from our stories. They will recognize that they are not alone and that their stories may be similar to that of some others whose lives can testify to the faithfulness, love, and power of God; a God who doesn't show favoritism or doesn't rate us on the standards of gender, age, race, education, religious beliefs, economics ranks, or influence. A God who seeks imperfect people through whom to do a perfect work. My prayer is that through my many miseries, which include but are not limited to, molestation, physical and spiritual rape, domestic violence, abandonment, homelessness, jail, poverty, witchcraft, suicide attempts and ultimately, the death of my youngest child, Prosper, will bloom into the world wide ministry God spoke into and over my life. My truth was hidden in the pages of the Bible, in the lives of **Sarah**, **Joseph** and **David**, and hopefully you will find your truth in the pages of this book and in my life.

Prepare yourself for the journey of a lifetime, a journey that will astonish your mind, challenge your heart, and revitalize your spirit. Some of the details in this book may exceed most people's definition of 'normal', and in fact may be difficult to believe. My life was never normal, and now that I look back on it, neither was it meant to be. I had to seek counseling before I could take this flight back into my past, reliving the horrors and hurts that God had delivered me from. A trip back and forth between the natural and supernatural realms that both conveyed their goodness and evil attributes in my life. I had to mentally equip myself for the ridicule, laughter, disbelief, judgments, and criticisms of those who know me and from absolute strangers. But this is my God given assignment and I am merely a living and willing vessel whom He decided to use for His sole purpose. In time I learned that the story was never really about Sarah, David, Joseph or even myself, the story was always, and will continue to be bigger than any of us because all of our stories are about the God that we all love and serve; and we are all just His humble children. Our lives and our stories were all written, produced, and directed by our Heavenly Father for one reason and one reason only: TO BRING GOD GLORY. As it is written **Isaiah 43:7, "Everyone who is called by my name whom I created for my glory, whom I formed and made." (NIV), and Psalms 111:2-3, "How amazing are the deeds of the Lord! All who delight in Him should ponder them. Everything He does reveals His glory and majesty."**

Allow us to pray… Heavenly Father we come before you as humbled vessels with thanksgiving in our hearts to our mighty and sovereign God who created us for His glory. We are as clay in the hands of the Potter, we surrender our will and allow you to mold and shape us into the fashion that is suited for you. Father this story, though mine is not about me or anything that I went through, it is about the God who brought me through triumphantly by His Word. May my problems, trials and tribulations decrease as your answers, power and love are increased and edified within each page of this book. Allow your Holy Spirit to minister and heal through my life and the words you gave me to those who are hurting and suffering in one way or another. May my life be a testimony to all those who read this book, and may all those who believe in You forever stand on the promises in your Word, no matter what comes against them. It is written in **Numbers 23:19, 20, KJV, "God is not a man, that He should lie or a son of a man that He should change His mind. Has He said and will He not do it or as He spoken and will He not make it good."** Beloved I pray that you Prosper in all things and be in health just as thy soul Prospers in Jesus name amen.

Chapter One

Prophecy Inspired by God (PROSPER)

GOD CREATED THE heavens and the earth. Now the earth was formless and empty, darkness was over the surface of the deep, as the Spirit of the Almighty God was hovering over the face of the waters and then my heavenly Father said, "Let there be light", and there was light. Can you imagine for a moment a world full of emptiness, darkness, and nothingness? I can, because I was a shadow of that fallen world and just like that meaningless and bare world, I was internally hollow and vacant, and nothing but the spoken Word of God could ever fill my void. Of course I didn't recognize or accept this truth until many hurtful, heart wrenching, soul aching years later.

I often find myself pondering the thoughts of my Lord as He faithfully speaks light into what seems to be an impossible situation. I wonder why He cared about us so much that He would bless us mere humans with such a measure of his majestic splendor and glory. More importantly, I wonder when He would speak his power changing Word into my personal world. How dark would my world have to be before He would take the time to hover over my situation? How long would I remain blinded and terrorized by the sounds of the blackness?

The truth is, that darkness comes in many forms. There is a *natural darkness* where an area or space has little or no light. Then there is a *spiritual darkness* where something is hidden from our knowledge. Finally, there is a *time or specific situation of darkness* that is characterized by tragedy, or unhappiness; my world just happened to be a combination of the three.

As I reflect on my catastrophic life's memories, I come to realize that I was born with an array of ominous clouds over my head, and that those clouds were assigned to follow me and pour out their hail of living hell and horror into my world. What I didn't know was that these showers of affliction and pain would flood not only into my life, but also in the lives of those who were very near and dear to me. Even at birth I rained on my mother' and dad's parade when I abruptly intruded into their weekly routine of Sunday Dates and decided that I wanted to be born while he and she were in attendance to a movie on her birthday. Just like the rain, my mother reminds me of how I could not have come at a more inconvenient, time. There she was nineteen years of age and she was giving birth to her third child on her birthday. A day that was supposed to be fun and exciting, a day that was meant to honor her was snatched away by another crumb snatcher they couldn't afford to take care of.

So what do you name a baby that you barely wanted or could afford, who has intruded on your birthday; an individual who would forever share your special day? If it had been up to my dad I would have left the hospital with a name that fails to describe me or one that I could never had lived up to; that being the female version of Bernard, Bernadette, which means 'brave as a bear'. My mother, thank The Father, chose to go against my very abusive and controlling dad's wishes, and tricked him into naming me Tonya which means 'praiseworthy'. I personally believe it was prophetically inspired by God, as the Father could see through the clouds and see the light from his Son that waited patiently to one day brighten my dark and gloomy life. Although the truth in my name would one day declare its victory over the many battles in my life, I would never experience its definition of being praiseworthy until the Father was assured that I would remain humble, and realize that He is the only reason and source to any amount of recognition, appreciation or success that would one day surpass the level of loneliness and failure that tried to become my norm. In essence I had to be humbled, lest I stumble over a *cliff we call pride.*

Pride was one area I felt like I never had any issues with, but of course pride won't allow you to admit to pride. Like every other human being besides our first parents, Adam and Eve, my Genesis began in my mother's womb a dark and empty place. I was a formless, helpless, and innocent fetus that depended solely on My Creator to sustain me until my time of birth. Like every other person who travels through their mother's dark birth canal, whose umbilical cord is cut off and is birthed into God's creation, I inadvertently became a sinner and independent from my Creator. The sources of light that he created such as the moon, stars and sun shined brilliantly in and throughout the earth, but failed to yield some light into my very pathetic and unilluminated life. My life from birth had developed into a spiritual graveyard. Everything around me was dead, even I was a dead girl walking in confusion and a collision of life's catastrophes. Little did I know that all the crying and praying to the One who is the real source of light, would eventually ignite and cause a combustion of heat that would burn away the things that held me back from all my Creator has designed for me, yes I remember the day God first spoke light into my darkness.

I was just seventeen in February of 1992 when a very close friend of mine invited me to attend her church. A month prior I had given birth to my second child, a son whom I named Ezekiel.

I remember as though it were yesterday, physically sitting in that unfamiliar place, but mentally confined to the same place of torment and confusion that I had become enslaved by. I tried hard not to concentrate on this beautiful baby boy I had just given birth to, the same baby whose life I had just tried to end. My desire was to forget the haunting memories of the abuse and abandonment that tormented my mind and caused me countless nights of sleeplessness. I tried desperately hard to conceal the fact that I had these twisted, illusive, and evil thoughts, invading my mind and confiscating my very soul.

Although the mood in the church could be termed as joyous and grateful, my emotions would not allow me to set aside the burdens I was currently facing, neither could I ignore the memories of the mental institution that had become my residence in the previous month. So there I was trying so hard to suppress my tears, control my emotions, and contain my distorted thoughts. But it would be to no avail, because the moment the pastor began to preach the sermon he entitled "Thanksgiving," I simply became disoriented and drained, to say the least.

"Thanksgiving?" I said to myself. This is the month of February and even if we were in November I doubt if I would have had anything for which I could be grateful, not even life.

As the pastor began to reiterate over and over the need to always be grateful to God, no matter what the circumstances were, my mind was forced to replay my life's horrific scenes over and over in my head. Undoubtedly, I could not control the emotions that seemed to multiply and intensify, and of course I began to whimper quietly, but not for long because that soft whimpering would soon escalate into an emotional bawling experience as the pastor's spirit began to connect to mine. It seemed as though he could look into and feel everything that was going on in my life. My past, present, and future might have been hidden from me, but God allowed this anointed and very prophetically ordained man to see into the depths of my life. Everything about me was divulged to him and my life lay naked and vulnerable before his eyes. The abandonment, all sorts of abuse, the betrayals, and even the attempted suicide while pregnant with my son, had all been revealed to him. How could someone I never met know so much about me, and why was he crying so profusely, as if he could feel my pain? It was inexplicable to a girl who thought no one ever loved or cared about her.

I remember while he was approaching me with tears in his eyes, compassion in his voice, and our spirits bonding to one another, the statement that would flow from his lips and ultimately alter my life forever.

"God loves you," he stated while grasping my hand and trying to pull me into the middle of the aisle in order to embrace me as if he were demonstrating God's affection toward me for Him. I could barely see through the shower of tears that fell from my eyes, let alone hold my head up to look at him, or anyone else for that matter. My spirit, my heart, my mind, and my flesh were all shattered, and nothing but the grace of God could mend these fragmented pieces.

"I see suicide demons all around you," Were the next shocking words to come from his mouth, and the fragmented pieces began to break down further into the lowest denominator possible.

How could he know? There was no way possible for this man, whom I had never seen before, to have that very private and intimate information about me, but he was just beginning to touch the surface of what the Lord had to say to me through his vocal cords?

"You have been through so much for somebody your age, and you don't understand why you have to go through the things you do. Sometimes you feel as if the weight of the world is upon your shoulders. The trials that you have been through have been more than people twice your age have endured. You feel alone and neglected, and that nobody loves you. But God wants to ensure you that He loves you and that you are the apple of His eye. I see your mother has played a very devastating role in your life. You have felt so much abandonment, abuse and neglect from her, and you can't understand why she doesn't love you."

Crying hysterically, he continued, "I feel the pain and the abuse of the men who have touched you, manipulated you and abused you for their selfish desires, but I can see God has blessed you with unique and special gifts."

He raised my hands and anointed them with oil. "You have a worldwide ministry living on the inside of you and that is why the devil fights you so much and desires to kill you, so that he can destroy the ministry that waits to be birthed from your spirit. I can see that you write, and the biggest ministry ever is the Bible, for it was written and can get into places that human beings cannot. I can see your life changing, and affecting others who will go through some of the same kinds of trials and tribulations that you have, and will face during your lifetime. Know that God is with you. Know that He will never leave you, and that as sure as I stand here as a prophet under the anointing of The Almighty, every word that I have spoken will come to pass. God will begin to use you prophetically, and break through the boundaries of religion and tradition in order to develop a sacred relationship with you. God has given you the spirit and cry of Hannah. Dedicate back to Him everything that He is going to birth through you.

I immediately collapsed onto the floor because of the heaviness of his words on my heart; I could no longer stand or bear to hear him.

"You were chosen from your mother's womb to allow God to be glorified through your life, for God has sworn by Himself that although Satan will fight you violently, he will not prevail. God will get the glory from your life. All you have to do is trust in God, stand on His word, and lean not on your own understanding, for God is willing and able to do just what He said. This prophecy will not die; it shall surely come to pass."

It Shall Come to Pass

God shall bring it to pass

Whether He takes His time or works fast

He shall bring it to pass

Everything that is His desire will become His task…

We don't understand everything that we go through

But I am here to declare that there is hope for you

God spoke this in His word and he cannot lie

He promised to work it out for both you and I

Remember God's promises are always yeah and amen

On His word alone you can surely stand

Never worry about what the devil says about you

But know that every word God promised has to come true

Simply believe His word and keep your faith

And God will stand by every promise that He has made

But if your mind wanders and turns to doubt

Open your Bible and witness many promises coming about

Yes, many witnesses, each with their own story to tell

How the word of God is spirit and life and cannot fail

First let us examine Abraham and Sarah, a couple of old age

They lived a very abundant life but had no kids in which to raise

However, God promised them a son through whom He would bless

The descendants of this seed who followed in God's righteousness

Years upon years had gone by, turning Sarah's faith to doubt

She conceived in her own mind a way to bring God's promises about

She did not pray, fast, or seek God in one way or another

All she knew was that she was barren but ready to be a mother

One day she suggested her husband have sex with her slave

But if you read the word of God that is not the orders that God gave

Abraham, however, obeyed the voice of his wife; we can't say why

Maybe he was also starting to doubt or just tired of her cries

However their decision was made

But this story is so far from done

The slave conceived from Abraham,

But the child was not God's chosen one

God was not pleased so he allowed resentment
to occur between Sarah and her slave

Thereby forcing Sarah to be remorseful for the decision she had made

But God who is faithful and cannot lie also blessed Sarah's womb

A promise she laughed at one day had to come true

So, yes, their battle with being barren was finally won

Isaac, meaning laughter, is what they named their promised son

Of course, my facts of God's faithfulness do not stem from one story

Let us visit a young lad named Joseph whose life also testifies of God's glory

Joseph was a young boy tremendously loved by his natural father

To his older, but immature and jealous brothers, this became a bother

Our heavenly Father also loved Joseph and began showing him dreams

His dreams were of him being honored above his family and so it seemed

    Arrogance from Joseph rendered the brothers to
    come up with a Satan-inspired scheme

    But a Satan-inspired scheme is rendered powerless
    to God's word is this poetry's theme

    Yet conspiring to murder Joseph was a manipulative
    thought shared by his brothers

    Mere men do not have the ability to murder
    God's will as they would soon discover

What the devil planned for evil was all along part of God's plan

Sparing Joseph's life, they sold him as a slave to Pharaoh's right hand man

Even though Joseph became a slave, God's hand remained evident in his life

And everything was going well until he was tempted by his master's wife

Joseph humbly honored God and did everything his master demanded

When he repeatedly refused her advances, she could not stand it

Her feelings were hurt and her pride and lust were crushed

She had to make certain that Joseph would keep his mouth shut

    Joseph innocently ran from her temptations but
    mistakenly leaves his garments behind

Feeling rejected she does the first deceitful thing to come to mind

Something inside of her turns her heated lust into a cold - hearted rage

Help! She cried and everyone in the palace could hear the screams she gave

Accusing Joseph of attempted rape, she screams her untruths

But who can deny her when she holds his garments as if they were proof

Angry from betrayal her husband throws an innocent Joseph into jail

But God's anointing remains with Joseph and
God won't allow His anointing to fail

Again and again, Satan uses people in an effort to hinder Joseph's dreams

Dreams of being in a position of honor fade as hell reigns supreme

First the betrayals by his brothers and now innocent and in prison

However, Joseph did not focus on the negatives
but serving God became his mission

Joseph prophesied, interpreted dreams and
spoke wisdom to all who would listen

Forgiving, and merciful he was a great example of the so called Christian

Allowing God to use him and his gifts, Joseph
continuously watched others being blessed

On the contrary, he also witnessed others who weren't so fortunate

I am sure Joseph pondered over his childhood dreams time and time again

Reminding him constantly that this life of
betrayal was not all God had for him

And he was right. God would change Joseph'
life suddenly and without notice

But he had to remain faithful to God, keep his integrity, and stay focused

The interpretation of Pharaoh's dream also
allowed Joseph's dream to be birthed

And just as God promised, He brought him honor and raised his worth

King David is another example of the faithfulness of God's Word

For he was one of the greatest kings to grace this earth

But as a young shepherd, no one noticed the greatness that he possessed

They ignorantly judged his outside to determine his worthiness

But the Creator, who searches the heart rather than the appearance of a man

Knew the shepherd boy reverenced and loved
him more than the average man

God knew that David would be a man after God's heart

Although he would make mistakes, from God
or his Word he would never part

David's triumph over Goliath was just an example that God was with him

For this is just one of many battles that God would allow David to win

Royalty bestows David as God changes shepherd boy into a legendary king

The king who was anointed to battle and yes to write psalms, dance and sing

A mighty man strong enough to fight battles,
yet gentle enough to write poems

The level of his anointing in his book of Psalms is still awesomely shown

Whenever we are faced with various situations,
there is a psalm that we can recite

Aligned with faith in God's word it's bound to change your life

Now that I have shared examples from the
Bible, I will share those of my own

I testify about it continuously, especially in my songs, books, or poems

He promised me peace in each and every area of my life

He promised this to a person who was abused
as a child and became a battered wife

Prosperity he promised to an individual who
thought poverty was her middle name

Prosperity he delivered to me, while putting my demons to an open shame

Prosperity not just in a form of money, but success
over every obstacle that stood in my way

I triumphed over my own sinful mistakes but
continuously made mistakes along the way

But I kept it close to my heart every dream and
word He spoke into my very being

Sometimes I couldn't understand the visions
the prophecy or their meanings

So I began to ask God for wisdom understanding and divine revelations

He began to simplify Himself and His Word and sent forth confirmations

I wish I could tell you that my transformation happened overnight

But the truth is I was weak and spiritually childish most of my adult life

God, who is a sensitive, caring and loving Father,
chastised me when He needed to

On the other hand, there is not one trial that I had
in which He did not see me through

The gifts of writing, prophecy and the revelation
of knowing who God really is

Will be passed down from generation to generation starting with my kids

A gift that would minister to many people who have
or will experience the same situations I faced

A gift that will inspire people to lay down their
religious ways and seek God face to face

More importantly, a gift that would shatter every
curse of the enemy and set my family free

A gift that would allow me to awaken and become
the person that God has destined me to be

Prosperity he promised to a woman who felt like
she was the black sheep of her family

Through all my trials and failures, The Father saw that I could stand to be

Blessed, and blessing me was all along a part of His perfect plan

I was an individual who grew up in foster homes and was homeless at times

I even made my bed in jail both physically and in my mind

Prosperity he promised to a high school dropout
and a divorced mother of five

Prosperity in every aspect He anointed me
with through His son Jesus Christ

A promise not be a bench warmer but to unveil
the ministry He placed inside of me

That will one day reveal the

Prophetic, anointed writer that represents His Royalty

Chapter Two

Relocate & Renew (PROSPER)

For those of you who are familiar with the Bible, the book of Mark, Chapter 4, describes Jesus telling the parable of a farmer who sows seeds in different types of ground, and the response each seed makes in accordance to the ground in which it was sown.

Now a parable is nothing more than an allegorical story designed to illustrate or teach some truth or spiritual lesson. In this particular parable the different hypothetical situations are about a farmer who represents God (we must keep in mind that God uses people as vessels in which to speak and operate through, so the sower can be anyone.

The seed represents the Word of God and the soil is in representation of the condition of the person's heart in which the Word is sown. There are four basic soil (heart) conditions and Jesus thoroughly explains how each one responds differently to the same Word given by the same Sower.

The First soil is not even soil at all; it is described as wayside, or highway because it is basically made out of a hard substance such as concrete. We all know that it is impossible to plant anything in concrete, likewise, God is saying that some people's hearts have become so hardened that it is basically impossible to plant the seed of His Word in their hearts.

Now this person's heart can be hardened by any number of things such as unbelief, hurt, lack of understanding, sin, denial, and pride, among other things.

The second heart or soil that Jesus describes is what I like to call the shallow heart. It is a soil that has a little soil under the surface but is covered in stones. So though it may be possible for the seed to germinate and begin to grow, the sun will eventually cause it to wither away before it has a chance to reach maturity. This particular illustration is in reference to a person who hears the word, believes it at first, but eventually trials, tribulations and maybe even persecution causes the word to wither away because the word was not fully embedded in the heart.

The next soil that He explains about are the seeds that fell amongst thorns I refer to this illustration as the crowded heart, because the thorns here represent the cares of the world that often choke the life out of the seed before it has a chance to reach maturity. This is an example of a heart that wants and believes God's word but is still easily influenced by the world.

Last but not least is the good ground that some seeds had the opportunity to fall upon. This of course is an example of a good heart that hears the word, believes it and allows it to be nurtured by obtaining the understanding of it, learning to confess it with faith, and has the wisdom to practice it in their daily lives until they reach the spiritual maturity that will enable God to develop that seed into spiritual fruit.

So why have I sidetracked from my story to share and explain this parable of the sower, seed, and soil you might be asking yourself. The reason is that after I had received the prophecy (seed of God's Word) through Apostle McCoy (sower), the condition of my heart had to be questioned. Which of these four scenarios given in the parables best describes my heart at a time in my life when I barely knew, understood or even loved myself, let alone this higher majestic Supreme Being that I could not see? Well a good indication of the condition of my heart, though wounded, must have been good because God's word, this prophecy, the one that is being unfolded and revealed even as I write this book, is the seed that I held onto like my only and last hope, and in deed it was.

My heart wasn't considered good soil because I was a good person, or because I was some sort of saint, it wasn't good because of my educational background or influence. I wasn't a faithful tither. I made mistake after mistake, and some things that I did, though I am not proud of them now, were deliberate and spiteful. Yet my heart was considered good soil simply because I believed. I didn't understand this God or His ways but I chose to believe in Him and study and develop a personal relationship with Him. My heart was considered good because, though I didn't know anything about religions, I was always ready to go beyond religion and its traditions, to develop a spiritual union with my Creator. My heart was considered good because over the course of time I learned to confess God's word. Later I would teach His word to my children when trials, tribulations and persecutions arose. God saw that my heart was good and that my relationship with him could not be compromised by money, fame, or idols of any sort. My heart was good because my heart fell in love with God and I learned to put him first in everything. A good heart simply requires faith, **Hebrews 11:6 says, "Without faith it is impossible to please God."**

This made me the perfect target for the devil, because he did any and everything in his power to get me to denounce God, to get me to stop believing in His word, and to get me to think that the prophecy spoken over my life would never happen. Not only did he want me to believe that it would not happen he did everything to try and stop it. The level of his demonic twisted and evil mind should have made me throw in the towel a long time ago and the people he uses to do his bidding are often times the ones closest to you with the most influence on you.

So the question I asked God was, "Was I born with this good heart or did it have to be developed over time, as soil sometimes has to be toiled in order to prepare it for the garden of blessings God wants to plant? Will my heart endure seasons of summer heat with its fiery torments of trials and tribulations? Could it stand through winter where everything in my life seemed to wither and die? Would the season of spring, take my heart into new and unfamiliar territory? And what blessings or curses will fall on me in the season of fall. Yes, from the moment of conception our hearts and lives are designed to develop and grow in accordance with God's timing, which is figurative of the four seasons given to us in our literal year. In comparison to the figurative and literal seasons, I learned through the years how God created and ordained everything to work in its perfect timing. I didn't know it at the time, but even my summer, premature birth on my mother's birthday had its significance and its reason.

I was born the third child to my unmarried parents in the country hills of West Virginia, on a sweltering and humid summer night on June 30th, on my Mother's 19th birthday. My parents, though young, were very family oriented, church going people, whose lives depicted the very definition of dysfunction. My mother was from a huge family, and her mother was abusive to her and her siblings. My dad was born with Epilepsy, a dis-order his family would blame for his violent tendencies and outbreaks. I don't remember much about my dad before the age of eight, because I was often shifted from pillow to post, either with family members taking me in, and an undisclosed number of foster homes. Because my dad was violent with my mother; she would often have to seek a safe haven away from him. At one point my mother ended up leaving and relocating to a small city in Pennsylvania called Easton.

Easton is where my mind finds my first memories of my childhood. A childhood that consisted of a single mother with a mediocre job in the local hospital, and a tiny apartment full of furniture and toys. We didn't own a car, and literally had to walk everywhere, but my older brother, younger sister and I didn't complain because we were happy, well at least they were. I, on the other hand, appreciated all the extras my mother gave and did for us, but ended up feeling like I got the short end of the stick when it came to receiving my mother's love and affection. In one instance I recall getting hit by a car and having to go the hospital. After being released from the hospital my mother took me home and beat me with an extension cord. As a matter of fact, it seemed as if my mother was always whipping me for one reason or another, even if it wasn't my fault, which is why I learned to keep things to myself, including the fact that our babysitter and her boyfriend were molesting me.

My mother was a very strict and tidy person. I recall a day that she was mopping our kitchen floor, and being especially thirsty, I was begging for a drink of water. My mom got so mad at me that she forced me to drink almost an entire ice cold pitcher of water until I threw up; and again I got a whipping. I *walked on eggshells* around my mom, tried not to squirm when she was straightening my hair so that I wouldn't get hit with the hot comb, tried to not my get clothes dirty, even tried to eat all the food my mom placed before me despite the fact my mom wasn't a great cook, but still the whippings continued and nothing or no one could dissuade them.

I remember I used to cry and scream for God to help me during the course of my beatings, and it's no wonder I thought God had answered my prayers, when my father came knocking on our door one day, because when he arrived my beatings suddenly ceased.

Father, Dad, or Daddy were unfamiliar terms to my siblings and I, who were accustomed to having a one parent home, but his exuberant and adventurous presence was welcome in my life. After a few short months, dad and mom would remarry. They held a small ceremony in my mother's living room and afterwards we would relocate to West Virginia, otherwise known as hell.

A literal hell awaited us, but this time I would not experience it physically for myself. I was only the observer of the hell my dad would put my mother through, and strangely enough I found myself wanting to be her God, so as to rescue her from her tormentor, the same tormentor that rescued me from her.

The sound of my father cursing and fighting my mother still brings me to tears. I can remember so vividly seeing the results of his abuse all over my mother's face and body. I recall one time in particular when my father had blackened both of her eyes and then made her get up and prepare a big Sunday dinner for the next day. She was taking the boiled potatoes off of the stove and when my mother squeezed beside him while he was leaning in the kitchen doorway he threatened to put her head in the oven and turn it on. After my mother finished cooking dinner that night my father proceeded to beat her for so long that we couldn't keep our eyes open and we cried ourselves to sleep. The next morning, we woke up to dad yelling at my mom and throwing her into a tub of ice water. Mom was completely unconscious because she had tried to take her life by overdosing on his medicine, it was at that moment, when I saw my Father straddling my mother, shaking and slapping her, that clips of my memory came back to me. I saw this man before he was the same man who kicked in our door years ago, cut my mother's face all up and even slit her throat. As if that wasn't enough to traumatize me, this maniac threw her out of the window of our apartment from the third floor. It was nothing but the grace of God that gave my mother the strength to hold on the window panel until rescue and police got there to pull her back in. My love and respect for this man immediately turned into loathing and hatred. Night after night I had dreams of waking up to find my mother dead. The dreams seemed so real and vivid at times, that my siblings and I would often put our ears to our parents closed bedroom door in hopes of hearing just a peep out of our mother. My days and nights were filled with the terror of a new evil that would resurface throughout different phases in my life until it almost became my norm. A family curse, a learned behavior, or demonic inspiration; either way Domestic Violence and I were introduced.

Thankfully my mother would come to her senses and leave this man for good, but who knew she'd be leaving us as well.

It was at that last foster home in which we stayed in for five years, where another foster child remembered us from a previous foster home where I learned that we had often been in and out of the system, but I can honestly say I don't remember any other homes except that one. For the most part, things were great in that foster home, we lived in a huge house, had birthday celebrations, parties, attended church, and I have great memories of strangers who opened up their hearts and homes and treated us like family. It was there that I could divulge the secret of molestation I had experienced, and receive the counseling that I so badly needed, but I was careful not to tell of the present molestation my sister Ruth and I were then experiencing by my foster mother's 40-year-old son, Jake. I didn't want to risk us being moved, or maybe it was because I had trained my mind to wander and separate from my body; becoming simply anaesthetized to the experience until my sister rehashed the memories years later

While in the foster home I learned to cook, clean, and other responsibilities a young woman needed in order to make a good life for herself. After the death of Jake, who had been molesting us, things became rather normal, and I actually stopped anticipating my mother coming to get us and starting over with her and her new preacher husband, Ben. Starting over with her meant relocating and giving up the stability I had grown accustom to.

Stop the Silence

Listen closely, can you hear the dreadful overwhelming silence

It's the sound I hear regularly after a toll of domestic violence

I wonder as I lie here frightened and alone in my bed

Is this the day I might find either of my parents' dead?

What exactly will I find as I approach my parent's room

Tears begin to flow down as I wonder what was that boom?

I heard it so clearly last night and it still rings in my head

Oh my Lord help me was the last thing my mother said

I tiptoed down the hall afraid of what I might find

But I tell you it's the silence that's driving me out of my mind

I open my parent's door slowly hoping to get a holler or fuss

Sit down somewhere was the usual or stop bothering us

No!!! I screamed as I looked at them soaked in each other's blood

My emotions begin to tremble as my tears begin to flood

Why I wonder did they choose to ignore the obvious signs

One day a huge fight the next day they were fine

So now I'm wondering who exactly do I blame

I guess both my parents if I had to name a name Trish and Mark

Would be the cause of my dreadful hurting pain

Because they took domestic violence for granted and life for a game

They played it so often each one seeking to be a winner

Arguing and cursing was the usual each night at dinner

Jealousy was often a reason, but disrespect would be the cause

Because neither of them had it therefore they knew not what it was

To love honor and obey as the Bible clearly demands

My daddy showed honor for my mother by using the back of his hand

My mother was not perfect, she too had her faults

For she was not to obey a man at least that's what she been taught

Compromising was always an issue they each sought their own way

Self-gratification was their motive and for it their lives would they pay

One more opportunity to teach them right from now on will I pray

But it's too late and so very sad to say

Domestic violence has again won its own way

It doesn't care who it threatens, hurts, or kills

It appreciates your anger and your jealousy is its thrill

It thrives off of fear and control is its reward

It's not racially motivated so it gets the award

"Most likely to destroy a family with the use of its own members

Someone must have made this acceptable his name I can remember

Lucifer, Satan or sometimes he's called the devil

He is the mastermind of this scheme and domestic violence is his rebel…

Chapter Three

Omit Men's Laws & Tradition (PROSPER)

THE DAY MY mother came with her new preacher husband, Ben, to pick us up was scary and exciting at the same time. I can't remember the exact date, but I remember the feeling of anxiety and excitement as my sister Ruth and I awaited their arrival. After all, this would not be the first time we anticipated mom coming to get us, and then be severely let down when she didn't show up. To be honest I was kind of hoping that she would not come because we had the opportunity to be adopted by our foster mother, because the State of Pennsylvania was only giving mom this last and final chance to regain custody of us. It was obvious that my foster family shared my feelings and didn't want to see us leave either, none of us wanted to break the bonds of the family that we had become.

You can't begin to imagine the level of disappointment and fear when they arrived in their brown two door dodge. Mom looked different from what I was accustomed to. She wasn't wearing any makeup and she wore her once relaxed thick hair in a rather large jerry curl, but I was more focused on Ben. This new man that we just met was already married to my mother, which made him our stepdad. Once again we were driving with yet another man who would prove to me that hell isn't just a destination, it is a lifestyle.

When we got to Augusta, Georgia we moved into a small apartment. The first thing we noticed was that there wasn't a television in the house. The first night plays vividly in my mind. My mother cooked dinner; fried chicken, creamed corn and biscuits. I remember biting into the chicken and blood came seeping out of it, when I refused to eat it my mother got so angry that she braided five switches together, beat me until my clothes were torn off my back and my body was whelped up and bleeding, but I refused to shed a tear, and that made things worse. If Ben had not come into the room to intercede… Sadly, Ben would have to intervene more often than I care to admit. Later mom would destroy all the nice clothing my foster home mother bought for us, because their religion made it a sin for girls and women to wear pants. But I believe there was more to it than that. Mom knew how much we cherished the clothes our foster mother bought us and she took pride in destroying them that day because I had humiliated her by pointing out that her chicken was undone. I didn't mean any harm by it, I just didn't want to eat bloody chicken; but mom would never see it that way. I couldn't believe this woman who had not seen her children in over four years was capable of beating me almost to a bloody pulp, and I couldn't believe Ben would join in and assist in my future whippings, and they probably couldn't believe that I would stir up the nerve to fight back. Now as I look back on it, I felt as if this new home environment was nothing less than a cult. We were forced to attend church assemblies at least 4 times week. The congregation only consisted of some of the neighborhood teenagers and elderly people from the nursing home. To the outside world we seemed like the perfect family, but on the inside we were more dysfunctional than the families Ben ministered to.

The religion that they practiced was considered "Pentocostal" and our small church was just a small piece of this uniquely large organization of other churches that were under the umbrella and ruling of one man. Most of the people that were members of this southern regional congregation were military as Ben was once a part of the U.S. army. The most exciting thing about the organization with all of its so called Holiness members of submissive women, dominating men, and little obedient, modestly old fashion dressed children, was their quarterly fellowship meetings. (The children were not allowed to attend skating rings, movies, or even have a television in their home, because according to this religion, all of these things were considered evil.) These were meetings where all the churches from different regions of the world would come together and listen to a sermon by a chosen pastor, and then fellowship over a banquet of food made by the members. Later we would often participate in fun filled activities consisting anywhere from kick ball to a simple game of hide and seek. It didn't bother us at that time to wear our everyday uniforms, which was an old fashioned looking dress, because all the other women and children at the fellowship were dressed in unison.

In our everyday lives Ruth and I were often humiliated and embarrassed following their traditions of wearing these long ugly dresses to school every day, because kids would pick on us, so my sister and I started shoplifting for our school clothes. We didn't understand why we had to dress so old fashioned and cheap, seeing that my parents had saved enough money to move us out of the very small apartment into a nice three-bedroom house; where I finally got my own bedroom. Their so called religious traditions seemed to create more barriers and hostility than anything and our family never quite felt like family; we were missing that one thing that would bind us all together, because church wasn't doing anything other than devouring our time.

Although we went to church several times a week, and sometimes ate out on Sundays, our family never quite meshed, but Ben finally found the void that our family so desperately needed to bring us closer when he brought home Butch. Butch was my all white purebred pit bull puppy. Oh how I loved Butch, and Butch actually brought some sense of belonging to our very distant and dysfunctional atmosphere. Although Butch was a family pet, he and I became inseparable. I had taught Butch how to sit in a baby stroller, and would actually stroll him around the neighborhood. People got a kick out of how this obese, well behaved, fun loving dog, who was often most people's misconception of an endangerment to society in general, was capable of being trained by such a young adolescent as myself. I remember the day Butch caused me to question this so called God who they forced me to pray to and worship almost every day. I recall the feeling of ultimate let down the day Butch got run over by a car and my step dad acted like he was in no rush to get him to the vet, which was less than ten minutes from our house. Ben chose to ignore the urgency coming from the screaming, and crying Ruth and I did, instead he chose to use this as a time to show off his praying skills and his so called relationship with God. Watching my dog lie in our yard trying so hard to gasp for air and constantly spewing up the blood that kept lodging in his poor little lungs, was difficult to say the least. "Help him!" I shouted to Ben, and instead of putting him in our car and driving less than two blocks to the local vet, he bent over my dying dog and prayed over him. At that time, I was no more than thirteen years of age, and had absolutely no knowledge of real prayer or how it works. What I did know was that we needed a miracle and this God that I heard so many people testify about in church, was capable of giving my dog this miracle. After what seemed to be an eternity in my teenaged mind, Butch suddenly grew worse. Finally, my mother convinced Ben to take Butch to the vet. Ruth and I eagerly waited to find out if Butch would make it back home alive. Our faces dropped when our parents returned home looking distraught, it was apparent that I'd lost my best friend.

The fact that Butch was only a year old and died so suddenly made it that much more difficult to get over his death. I spent countless hours locked in my room, reliving Butch's final moments in my head. His gasping for air, his bloody mouth, and his heavy and very slow breathing, but the thing that seemed to torment me the most was that stupid prayer. I just wondered if Ben had of acted faster, and had not paused to pray over my dog, then maybe just maybe, my dog would have had a fighting chance. If only I could turn back the hands of time I would bring my dog back, because without him I was lost. A new resentment for Ben and prayer was established in my mind.

I didn't know the definition of depression back then, and if someone had diagnosed me with it I would have certainly denied it. Still I couldn't explain wanting to be alone and having a lack of interest in school, hobbies, or extracurricular activities. I was still forced to attend church the majority of my free time, I began to detest it that much more. My after-school energy and time was often spent caged up in my room, however this was at a point in my parent's lives when they had begun to rebel against some of the church's traditions, and started easing up on some of its rules and regulations. For instance, my mother had a job as a housekeeper, and pants were an ordinary part of her everyday uniform, so my mother began to bend a little bit when it came to our school wardrobe and we were finally allowed to wear pants. As exciting as that was, I think the fact that they purchased a television for our home brought about the most delight. It was hilarious watching them squirm to gather the television, pack it up, and hide it every time a member of the church came by for a visit. Eventually my parents figured out that it was easier to just leave the television in their bedroom and for a while my parents' bedroom became the place we would all gather around to watch whatever Ben felt was appropriate which was mostly sports. It was an average football Sunday that would prove that this want-to-be pastor had more sins to hide, sins that God would consider way more devious than a television set.

* * *

It all happened on a Sunday, the Lord's day, as some call it. The family conducted their usual ritual of attending Ben's boring and empty church service. Ruth found her way to a friend's house. Mom decided to run errands and do laundry, and I just wanted to go home and go to sleep. Normally I would have taken this time to take Butch for a walk, but Butch was no longer with us, and I was feeling loss. After trying to sleep to no avail and becoming restless while waiting for my mother to bring home something to eat, I decided to go into the kitchen to make a sandwich to tide me over. Ben walked in and asked if I wanted to watch television, he said he would bring the television out into the living room for me to enjoy. Of course I agreed, and after waiting for him to relocate the television he turned on a football game. Not knowing he was going to watch it with me I began to feel uncomfortable, but I tried not to make it so obvious, so I pretended to start yawning and acted like I was sleepy. "Well I guess I better go in my room and lay down, tell my mama to wake me up when she gets home," I said to him. "Alright," he answered. Minutes later I was in my bed staring at the ceiling when I get this knock on my door. "Yes?" I asked, and Ben proceeded to ask me to open the door, stating he wanted to talk to me. I opened the door halfway, still feeling awkward because of how uncomfortable he made me feel. When I opened the door he apologized for Butch dying and said he felt like I was pulling away from the family. He said he loved my mom and us girls and he wanted to try to show it more. Then he pushed my door all the way open and said he felt like the family should show more affection to one another, so could he start by giving me a hug. I responded yes, when my mom is here. He said it's just a simple hug and he walked up to me and wrapped his arms around me and brought my body in close to his and began rubbing his hands up and down my back putting his hands closer and closer to my rear end. I pushed against his chest trying to move away from him, but he would not let go. I began tearing up, thinking to myself this man is about to violate me. In frustration and anger I found the strength to push him away from me and I fled the house, hoping my mother was still at the laundromat that was in close proximity to our house.

I was grateful when I found my mom there still folding clothes. I blurted out what my stepdad did and how it made me feel. Mom immediately called her best friend, (we always referred to her as Aunt Rita.)

My aunt suggested we go and make a police report to see if charges against Ben could be pressed. It was another blow to find out that the police didn't think he had committed a crime, and there was nothing they could do in regards to our complaint. But I knew in the back of my mind that if I hadn't pushed him away from me, he would have taken things a lot further, and now that he wasn't going to be arrested he would have plenty of opportunity to do so.

My mother confronted Ben once again when we returned home. Their argument had carried into the middle of the night when mom finally made the decision that she wanted to leave him for good. The level of excitement that ran through me when mom told us of her decision was enormous. I felt like we were finally going to escape this in-the-closet child molester and his religious rules. We'd have our mother all to ourselves, but then again, leaving would mean that there would be no one to stop Mom from going overboard when it came to whipping me. I was caught between a rock and a hard place, and things were about to cave in on me.

When my mother came home from work the next day it was evident that she had an attitude with me. Even though I had not done anything wrong, mom started snapping at me, and some of the stuff that she was saying was making me feel like she felt I was trying to take her place and become the lady of the house. She implied that I wanted Ben and was coming on to him.

"Look," she said, as she swung my room door open, "Who told you to go in my kitchen and cook?" I'm thinking to myself, you work eight hours a day are we supposed to starve until you get home, but I knew better then to verbalize those thoughts, so I just said I don't know. "Well don't take your (she said the A curse word) back in my kitchen; you not grown,"' she replied. My mother didn't curse often but when she did I knew she meant business. I was really confused because just yesterday she was talking to us about leaving Ben, now she was screaming at me because I cooked dinner, and not particularly for Ben, I just fixed the food and left it there for anyone who desired to eat it. You would think she would be appreciative not having to cook after getting off work late. I asked her what me and Ruth were supposed to eat until she got home, because the little bit of food that we had in the house was frozen and required thawing out and cooking. "You heard what I said stay your (she used the curse word) out my kitchen and we not moving nowhere. This man done put me in a house and bought me a car, and I am not about to ruin it because you want to be fast." That's when it hit me like a ton of bricks; if I had any thoughts that things were going to get better for me, I was wrong. Mom made it official. I was at war with her and Ben. Everything I did or said was heavily scrutinized. Sometimes I got in trouble for absolutely no reason at all. My mom would just walk into my room to tell me how much she didn't like me or could not stand me. She wanted me to respond so she could have a reason to assault me. I would just sit there, stare at the wall and try to maintain my composure. I didn't cry because I did not want her to defeat me mentally, but then her verbal taunts and threats weren't enough and she began to physically taunt me. It's sad when the only person you have to call to rescue you from your tormentor is someone you know wants to violate your innocence sexually. Sometimes Ben would come into the room to get her, and all of a sudden they would get into it, and she would get mad at him for defending me. There are times that I am not proud of how my mother tried to bully me and I would fight her back and if Ben tried to help her, I would fight him too.

The relentless fights would get so violent that often times I would be removed from my home and placed in a juvenile detention center after my parents called and twisted their story. Other times I would be kept home from school until my bruises healed, those were the times I would run away and stay in abandoned buildings for days at a time.

Eventually I came to the conclusion that my best bet was to start socializing once again. I began walking through my predominately white neighborhood and since there were only a few African Americans in the neighborhood, we all pretty much knew each other, so I began to visit their houses more. One day while walking to one of my friend's house a guy named Stacey drove up and began conversing with me. I really didn't have that much experience with boys, except the time a so-called friend set me up to be raped several months after we had first moved to Augusta. Years earlier, a friend named Cheryl had come by and asked me to walk with her to the store. After briefly walking through the apartment complex she claimed she was suddenly tired and wanted to rest under this sort of open garaged area. After a few moments of resting, an apartment adjacent to the open area opened up, and surprisingly enough, an older teenage boy named Chad, who was obsessed over me, was standing at the door. Cheryl acted like she was shocked to know he lived there, but that did not prevent her from inviting him to come out and hang with us for a while. I participated in the small talk, but I was adamant that she and I continue our mission to the store. You see although he was a very attractive boy I was still very shy and wasn't sexually active yet. I wish I hadn't been so naïve. I should have put two and two together the moment she started making excuses for us to enter his apartment; the way she did it was so slick. "What does your apartment look like on the inside" she asked him. Chad replied, "go and see for yourself." I was nervous thinking about what could occur as she was entering his apartment and leaving me alone with him. She came back and said "well I guess it's alright, but what does your bedroom look like… I bet it's messy. You look like you would have a messy bedroom." "Ain't nothing messy about me little girl. You could have gone and checked out my bedroom too. I'm going to stay out here and keep Tonya company. A brief moment later she was back on the porch and she said to him Alright, not bad you got a nice room. I guess I underestimated you, Tonya do you want to see it she added. My stupid, gullible, self said sure why not, thinking he would stay on the porch and talk to her while I was in the house just as he had done with me. So I hurried into the house pushed his bedroom door opened peeked inside and was trying my best to get back out the door so Cheryl and I could finally finish our journey to the store. Before I could even turn around good Chad was approaching me. I tried hard to resist him, and I screamed for my friend, (she was long gone). Chad just picked me up over his shoulders and carried me to his bed. The pain was unbearable and blood was everywhere. I felt so ashamed. I knew I could never tell anybody what had happened to me. I knew my parents would definitely punish me, and all my friends would look at me differently. Weeks later Chad bragged about our encounter and a group of young men actually jumped me, beating me so badly that they left me with a blood clot in my eye because I would not adhere to their sexual advances.

So having Stacey, this older man, approach me years later was very intimidating for me, because my encounters with men were never positive, yet after recently losing my dad in an automobile accident I craved the love and affection of a man. Later in life I would come to realize that sex is not an indicator or reflection of love, but my young mind was manipulated into believing it was back then. For months I allowed Stacey to abuse my young body and take advantage of me sexually, but it was all I knew. Once we found out that I was pregnant things took a turn for the worse. I was looking for a father figure in Stacey, but he would prove himself not worthy to be a father figure to our own baby.

I never really had an opportunity to develop a relationship with my dad because of his inhumane abuse to my mother. Granted he had done some very sickening things to her and I should despise him, and at times I did, but it never stopped me from longing to have the intimacy that I shared with him. Besides he had never demonstrated any form of abuse towards me, and did not allow my mother to mistreat me either. In fact, he and my mother were discussing sending me to live with him before his life was taken in a car crash on October 5th, 1988. I had memories of dad severely beating my mother, but I also had good memories of him being an awesome father to his children. Dad would create scavenger hunts out in the woods and hide treasures for us to find, he would allow us to assist him in reconstructing his house, take us out in his truck and teach us how to drive, take us on dates to drive-in movies, restaurants among other things.

It didn't take much convincing by Stacey for me to make a simple decision of being violated by him, or risk being violated by Ben, or be home and hope my mom wasn't feeling like fighting me, but choosing Stacey still left me with consequences. My parents of course were very disappointed when I ended up pregnant, especially since I was pregnant from a man that was about six or seven years older than me, and they had me locked up for being rebellious. My mother sought to press charges against Stacey, but couldn't because I was of legal consent, so she and his mother sat down and came to the conclusion that they would assist me with the baby once she was born.

* * *

Although I was pregnant, things in my house were not getting any better, mom still didn't want me in her kitchen cooking or buying groceries for the house. Instead, she would wait until she got off of work and buy the groceries daily. It was one thing to starve when I was just feeding myself, but it was entirely different now that I was eating for two. Ultimately I started shoplifting groceries in order to eat. When I almost got caught by the store manager, I knew I didn't want to risk my freedom so I sought out my Aunt Rita for direction. Aunt Rita was like a mother to me. She started bringing me plates of food, almost daily, and my mom was not happy about it at all. My mother suspected my Aunt Rita of having reported her to family social services after they appeared at our house one day, to investigate claims of abuse and neglect. It was a big pain for my parents, but for me it was a blessing in disguise.

* * *

Named by her daddy's first cousin and born almost a year after my daddy's death, Chandreka became my world. She was that pure love I had always longed for, and I would do anything to protect her from experiencing any of the drama that I had gone through. Consequently, once I brought her home from the hospital I didn't allow her to have that much interaction with Ben. Being that I had babysat all the time or just hung out with some older friends who already had children, I really didn't need that much assistance from my mother either, besides assisting me financially, I basically cared for my baby on my own.

If I thought that my daughter's presence would change things in my house for the better, I was sadly mistaken. The fights seemed to escalate and Ben's secret sinful sexual desires became more apparent, I recall a time when a friend of mine named Anita was at my house visiting. Honestly we were going to go for a joy ride in my parent's car once they had fallen asleep, but either way Anita and I were in my room hanging out when she suddenly screamed. What happened I asked her, trying to figure out what all the fuss was about? Ben was at the window peeking in on us, she shouted. I immediately ran over to see for myself and sure enough I saw him running from my bedroom window to make it back into the house. I ran and told my mom, "You never believe me, but now I got a witness that your husband is a freak and now he is peeping in my window". By the time my mom grabbed her robe to come out and confront Ben he had locked himself in the bathroom and was pretending that he had been there the whole time. My mother banged on the bathroom door but Ben refused to open it so my mother grabbed a hammer and smashed the door in and an altercation occurred between them.

The altercation didn't seem to have frightened Anita and it was something I had grown accustom to, the only difference is that this time I wasn't their only prey. There was a point when their altercation found its way in my room where Anita was holding my screaming and terrified daughter in an attempt to keep her safe from all the ruckus, to my surprise Ben called Anita, the B word and demanded she leave our house. I thought for certain that Chandreka was going to end up getting hurt in all the scuffle, so without thinking, I immediately jumped into the fight to assist my mother and throw in some personal punches while I was at it. At some point during the fight a knife was drawn and Ben wound up being stabbed in the chest. We didn't call the police my mother was standing there with a bloody knife in her hand and although she had her ways, she was still my mother. I couldn't afford to risk losing her. Anita, who was the only one who knew how to drive a stick shift, ended up driving us to some pond to get rid of the knife. I never quite understood why that was necessary because I knew Ben didn't want this dark secret exposed.

Despite how severe the fight was I was surprised when my mother came home and actually nursed him putting bandages on the wound that she had caused to his chest. This further proved how really dysfunctional my family was.

*　*　*

By the time Chandreka was one years old I got pregnant by Stacey once again. When we found out I was pregnant this time, he had moved on to someone more his age. It was someone who had finished school and was in college preparing for a lucrative career, whereas I was still in high school, pregnant with my second baby.

Either way I didn't want to accept or respect the fact that he had moved on, because I felt like it was going to come between my children's relationship with their dad. After all my childish shenanigans I knew Stacey didn't want me, because I kept giving him more responsibilities by continuously getting pregnant… I decided to abort the baby.

I was almost eleven weeks pregnant when some of my much older neighbors, at that time, took me to the abortion clinic with the money from Stacey. These neighbors were a safe haven for me from the moment I found out I was pregnant with my first baby. A Mexican woman and her Caucasian, self-proclaimed, redneck husband's house, became my after school hang out spot. As strange as some people might think it is, these people opened their home to me, fed me, advised me, and taught me the meaning of genuine love within a family. It was this redneck man who foretold the date I was going to have Chandreka months before my sonogram was performed. I went into labor at their house after one of the best Mexican dishes I have ever tasted. I was shocked when it occurred on the exact date he said it would. I developed a reverence and confidence, in them which led me to trust them in keeping the secret of my abortion, and accompanying me to actually have the procedure done.

Once we made it into the abortion facility no one was allowed to accompany me in the procedure room. The procedure was to check the baby's heartbeat and give me a sonogram to see exactly how far I was and how the baby was positioned. While doing the sonogram they asked if I wanted to know the sex of my baby and I responded with a quiet no, because I was beginning to feel guilty for this life that I was about to take and I didn't want to make it any more personal. I just knew I could not let my mother find out I was pregnant again. A little part of me was hoping my daughter's dad would take me back once I got rid of the so called trophy as he would call it.

After the procedure they informed me I would bleed a little heavier than a heavy period, but I wasn't supposed to do anything physical, which meant taking care of my daughter, going to school, and doing my chores. Needless to say I suffered through my recovery process with complications, which I was forced to keep to myself, however that wouldn't stop me from getting pregnant again.

The Sixth Commandment

I'm an eight-week old fetus at least that's what people say

But the Lord tells me that I am a success to be born on a specific day

He comes to visit me often and assures me it won't be long

Before my body is complete and I meet my earthly home

He whispers my destiny softly and it settles deep within my heart

He takes pride in perfecting each and every one of my body parts

This place you're in is the womb of your natural mother

She will love you affectionately and treat you like none other

For you are the fruit of her womb her greatest pride and joy

It won't even matter to her whether you are a girl or boy

You'll continue to grow in her physically feeling the warmth of her love

This womb will practically keep you from
anything dangerous you could think of

The Lord explained this to me the way things were supposed to be

But, like everything perfect the devil desires to kill it viciously

For as soon as I was rest assured my life would begin its course

Something awful happened and it had the devil's force

Before I knew it something powerful was pulling at my limbs

Something humongous was sucking me up and pulling me deep within

I YELLED OUT FOR JESUS but He was already there bitterly crying

I said Lord what's happening He said my child your body is dying

But today I promise that you will meet me at my home

I will tell you the future of your life before your very throne

The Lord then told us about abortions and asked if we had any suggestions

Yes, we said Lord but first we have some questions

Is it true our own mothers could have thought of us so small

How is it they take for granted life the greatest gift of all?

Lord they say how mighty and awesome we could have been

If only people would realize that murder is a sin

Rest my children said God underneath my sacred wings

Rest in my peace and every good thing it shall bring

This I say with wrath to the people who dwell on the Earth

Take this thoughtful wisdom and everything that it's worth

For the blood of innocent babies cry out to me from the ground

How long will I quench my wrath and let their spirits down

For I knew them before you brought them into the world

It was I who would decide if they would be a boy or girl

Call them whatever you will to me it's all the same

But I the Lord will give them their eternal prophetic ordained name

For I knew them before they came forth out of thy womb

I loved them and planned their destiny before you dare did assume

That the life you're holding is yours for the taking

But I warn you my angels are writing names of every death you're making

Harden not your heart and take heed to this word

I assure you on judgment day no excuses will be

Their blood cries out to me how long shall I deny them

Their chance to confront their murders the one
who should have stuck by them

It's time to shout it from the roof tops so the world knows I demand this

I am a just God and will judge ye

THE SIXTH COMMANDMENT

(THOU SHALT NOT KILL)

Chapter Four

Sacrifice of One's Independence (PROSPER)

After finally accepting the fact that Stacey and I were not going to get back together, I decided to just concentrate on raising and protecting Chandreka, finishing school and not focus on boys for a while, so I continued hanging out at several of my neighbors' houses. One day while visiting my girlfriend, her older brother Juan, let it be known that he had taken a liking to me. He was a very attractive man and much older than I was. Legally we should have not been permitted to be together. I was a mere 16 years of age and he was in his early twenties, but unlike my daughter's dad he and I would share a deep love and devotion for one another.

When I was sexually involved with Stacey, it was never about physical or emotional satisfaction for me, the sexual encounters were more about deciding who I wanted to be violated by, either him or Ben. The choice was simple for me I was determined not to be home with Ben and not put my baby girl in harm's way, so even though I knew I was nothing more than another notch on Stacey's belt, I chose to continue the meaningless sex with him. This was fairly easy to do since I was already sexually numb from being sexually violated numerous times By then I had trained my body to disassociate itself from my brain, and sex meant nothing to me. That was before I met my oldest son's dad.

At sixteen years of age having your twenty-three-year-old boyfriend pick you up from school in the newest sports car, write you poetry, bring you flowers, and serenade you over the phone through the night, is quite over-whelming, especially when love has never been demonstrated to you. It wasn't just the fact that Juan would go above and beyond to shower me with gifts that made me become so infatuated with him, it was more the fact that he allowed me to have a voice. He showed me that I meant something more to him than mere sex; my opinions, feelings, safety and overall well-being mattered to him.

Besides the difference in our ages Juan and I had a great number of things in common; from our love of obtaining wisdom and knowledge, to our love and ability to express ourselves poetically. We were both very affectionate, loving and loyal people, who were looking for genuine love in our very dysfunctional lives. There was no limit to our determination to maintain the love we found in each other.

My parents didn't like the fact that I was dating another older man, and once again they tried to have him arrested for statutory rape just like they did with Stacey, but again, my age and consent made it impossible for them to do that. However, Juan wasn't the same sex-crazed user that my daughter's dad had been. He didn't sneak around and pick me up just to have sex with me and then drop me back off like a paid prostitute; and he didn't leave me with a feeling of emptiness. He was a gentleman and he showed me what it was to be treated like a lady even though I was only a teenager.

Juan was intrigued by my level of maturity and my devotion to my daughter at such a young age, but he was also very observant and knew that things in my house were not normal. He could see the tension between Ben and I and he noticed how I worked overtime to keep my daughter away from him. When he confronted me for answers on why I was so evasive with Ben I would try to change the subject because it wasn't anything I was proud of, or could explain.

After a while when my parents could tell that Juan and I were a legitimate couple and it was clear how much he loved me and my baby girl, they finally began easing up on allowing me to date him. One of the reasons could have been that Ben's church no longer existed and my parents were starting to drift away from their beliefs and from one another, but I like to think that another reason is that my mom wanted a man in the house, and around me so that she didn't have to worry about Ben trying to violate me again, but Juan, this new, incredibly strong man, couldn't be with me and protect me from anything or everybody including himself.

Obsession with Juan was inevitable as he took his stand as my friend and protector. I was completely and utterly in love with the idea of spending the rest of my life with him, so much so that I didn't take notice of the skeletons that began emerging from my parent's closet, let alone the ones that were beginning to materialize from his.

Adultery was a *femur size skeletal bone* that my parents tried to conceal not only from each other, but from our family and their church organization. I don't know which one of my parents began having the affairs first, but I do know that their affairs set in motion a downward spiraling effect on all of our lives. Once again the parents who were supposed to be drawing me closer to God were ultimately responsible for placing a wedge between us.

I recall the times my mother would make us all leave the house and tell us we couldn't return until a specific time. On one occasion I had quite a bit of company and everyone knew us as the so called church family, but it didn't stop her from putting everyone out, including my baby, so she could have sex with her lover. I also recall the times my stepdad would be sitting in his car and us catching him with pornography, time and time again. Their adultery caused more distress and chaos in my life because it introduced another reason for them to have these knock-down-drag-out altercations in front of my daughter, and it once again proved that my sick stepdad had a problem with lust.

After I called Juan, crying and disclosing the news about the latest fights in my home, and breaking down about how terribly uncomfortable I was in my home around Ben, Juan came, helped me pack my clothes, and moved me and my baby in with him at his stepmothers house. It was refreshing yet intimidating being around him twenty-four-seven, and looking to him to take care of all of mine and my daughters expenses. But it also meant that I wouldn't have my mother to transport my daughter to and from daycare while I attended school, it meant I couldn't see my friends at my leisure, it meant I was transitioning from an honor roll student to a possible high school dropout. Most importantly, it meant that I would finally peel off all of his layers and expose his dark side.

I should have known something was suspicious about him when he began picking me up from school in a variety of new cars. I should have paid attention to his large stacks of money, but instead I was mesmerized in how much he was spoiling me and my baby girl. I was naïve and believed him when he said he made his money from working, and selling drugs on the side. Even though that should have given me enough reason to vacate the relationship, it did the exact opposite.

The truth was that I loved the attention I was getting around school by dating this older, very attractive and well-built man with new cars and money. Many females were attracted to him, but who for some strange reason, had fallen in love with little ole me. At my age back then, I didn't know much about how to take care of a man. It was new for me to be living with him and his stepmother and to become this over-night make-believe wife. I felt as though I was playing house. I was suddenly responsible for cooking, cleaning, laundry and satisfying him sexually, except this was no ordinary game of house, and my daughter wasn't some rag doll I could toss to the side and pick back up whenever I got ready.

On the days he felt like driving me to school his stepmom would often babysit my daughter. It was nice to get away and be somewhat like a normal teenager and interact with people closer to my age, but it would be hard for me to concentrate on my advanced classes after constantly being awakened by my daughter who was missing my mother terribly. It was also hard to concentrate on my studies when I'd been up the night before, trying to accommodate him sexually and because of my lack of experience he was starting to be left unsatisfied, and he didn't have any problem criticizing me about it. Nevertheless, to *keep my man satisfied* he would spend countless hours violating my young body and making me do things I was not comfortable with. So it was no wonder that I would fall asleep during important events like my midterms, and be cranky and short with my peers and teachers.

It got to the point where I just began attending school just to cut class. I didn't want to be home all worn out with sex and household chores. I was literally too tired to participate in class. Of course cutting class led me to meet students that I never encountered before. I was typically a goody two shoes and was able to gravitate toward different groups and organizations within the school. My popularity came at a price though, because the year before I was just an ordinary girl. The thing that probably got me the most recognition was when I was pregnant with Chandreka and a so called, popular girl who was under the impression that her boyfriend was interested in me, began to bully me. Every single day this girl would follow me to my different classes and threaten to fight me after school. Every day I was terrorized in the hallways with promises of hurting me while I was pregnant with my daughter. I could not imagine why this girl had so much hate and envy towards me, she was the one with all the friends, the nice clothes, and the popular boyfriend. What made her think that he would want me, especially while I was pregnant? That was absolutely asinine to me, but her hatred for me would not diminish even when my mother came to the school to speak with her mom and the principal. I often heard people tell her to leave me alone, that I didn't bother anyone. Clearly I was pregnant, I had the stomach to prove it.

One day during a fire drill she approached me and as usual she came and threatened to fight me outside during the fire drill. We were escorted outside by a school official and while I was out there I suddenly became obsessed with her and I couldn't keep my eyes of her. I watched as she smiled and greeted friends, how she laughed and played around with different people, and I quickly became enraged. Who did she think she was, laughing and enjoying herself, but stealing my joy? I was already going through enough foolishness and dysfunction at home and now she was bringing dysfunction to my school.

In spite the fact that the bell had rung for us to return to class, my feet could not move and my eyes were fixed on this young lady who had morphed into this ugly monster. I felt this incredibly overwhelming urge to destroy it. With tears in my eyes I raced to get behind her, I followed her closely, and by the time we had made it back in the classroom, only she and one other student were standing there. I could no longer control myself as I started picking up and throwing books, desks and anything I could get my hands on at her. I backed her up in the corner just as she had done to me for the past several months and let out my pent-up rage and frustration on her. I didn't seem to tire from making her pay for all the hell and torture she had dragged me through. And because of the fact that I was pregnant, the school officials had no choice but to wait until I decided to stop on my own, because they were afraid to grab me and chance hurting my unborn child.

When my body was finally exhausted and drained I ended up collapsing onto the floor. I didn't think about the bodily harm the girl might have. I just felt peace, calm and serenity; the same feelings I had experienced after fighting with my parents. It was a release that I would constantly seek and obtain throughout my life. Needless to say, a year later the so called bullies in the school showed a deep respect for me. Everyone knew at this point that I was no pushover; and my popularity grew.

Although I had never skipped school before, it was rather exciting, hiding and just hanging out in the hallways; until I got caught. The aroma of marijuana and the scent of alcohol led to our being caught by one of the high school administrators. I remember how nervous I was for them to try to reach my mother. I also recall how relieved I was when their attempts failed and they informed me that I couldn't return to the school until she had a conference with my principal.

After school Juan came to pick me up as usual. Some of my new friends that I started cutting classes with, walked over to his car with me. I was a little surprised when he knew a certain male classmate of mine named, Howard, from his job. I didn't think Howard was old enough to work a full time job and still attend school, but it explained why he was cutting class along with me, but later on I found out that he and Juan were involved with way more than cutting class.

The fact that I could not return to school without my parents made it easy for me to just drop out. I basically accepted the role of housewife to Juan and he did a good job of providing for me. Chandreka and I had everything we needed, and plenty to splurge with, had Juan not been so tight fisted with his money. If he took me out to dinner and I couldn't eat it all, he would fuss about all the hungry people around the world and remind me of how he had just gotten me out of a home where I came close to starvation. That made me feel so guilty that I would force myself to eat all of whatever was put in front of me. I didn't understand his method of doing things and the way his brain worked. I could not figure out why he was so sparing with his money since he always had so much of it. Stacks of money were hidden all over his bedroom, and I was amazed at how disciplined he was to save so much. I often wondered why he never put any of it into a bank account, but soon enough that question was answered. Juan and Howard began hanging out all the time. Our intimate walks in the park and family time with my daughter started to include him more and more, and I was growing sick of it. Well at least that was the excuse I used when I began vomiting and feeling nauseous. I would often complain of dizziness and offer to stay home while they hung out, but Juan wasn't having it. Even the times that he told me his car was in the shop he still wanted to take me and my daughter on outings, and when we got too tired to walk he and Howard took turns carrying us.

Eventually Juan's stepmom suggested I go get a pregnancy test. She was a very superstitious woman and claimed that her dreams of fish meant someone was pregnant. Although I don't believe in superstition I decided to oblige her. To this day I cannot say whether it was a coincidence or not, but the pregnancy test turned out to be positive. Our reactions to the pregnancy test conflicted. He had wanted to have a baby with me from day one. I was a little more apprehensive, because I was already experiencing how difficult motherhood was with one child. All the same, he showed a sincere interest in my pregnancy, something Stacey never did. It was at this time in our lives that he would take me to go meet his real mother and the rest of his siblings who lived in a different city. It was during this trip that things about this strange ties between these men started to be revealed.

I was nervous about meeting the rest of his family, and I should have appreciated the fact that he asked Howard to tag along, instead I was upset and confused. I felt like they were spending entirely too much time together, and that their friendship started invading our relationship. On the way to

Atlanta Chandreka and I fell asleep in the back of the car. When she woke me up I noticed that the car wasn't moving, we were parked on the side of the highway and Juan and my classmate weren't in the car. When I looked out the back window I noticed that there were some people standing next to what seemed like a broken down car. I observed Juan and Howard running from the car with tools and other items in their hands. I couldn't make out exactly what it was because it was getting dark out. By the time they had approached the car they were breathing heavily as they put whatever items they had obtained in the trunk of the car. When I asked them what was going on Howard remained quiet, but Juan said some people who were stranded on the side of the rode needed help and they helped them; and that was that.

When we finally arrived in Atlanta we had a beautiful visit. It turned out that my nervousness was unmerited, and his family was actually rather accepting of me and my daughter, although they thought I was quite young to be in such a serious relationship. His family also appeared to be genuine, loving, respectful, and friendly with one another, which made it more difficult for me to want to leave their company. I felt comfortable in their home and I was reasonably disappointed when it was time for us to return back home.

It was long after midnight before we all got back on the road to go home. Again Chandreka and I snuggled in the back of the car to fall asleep. During the drive I overheard Howard tell Juan that the police were behind him, and asked what he should do. Juan gave him directions as to which way to proceed, and the police kept tagging along behind us. Before I knew what was happening we were speeding, and dodging in and out of traffic in an effort to make it back to Augusta and avoid the police. Thankfully we made it home without incident, but it left me to ponder who I was entrusting mine, my daughter's and unborn child's life with.

One particular day, while visiting my mom, I ran into an old friend of mine, Keisha and convinced her to accompany the three of us to the park while my mom took Chandreka to visit her dad and his family. The four of us decided it would be fun to get on a seesaw. Me and Juan sat on one side and she and Howard were on the other. For some strange reason Juan decided it would be funny to jump off the seesaw leaving me to fly into the air and bounce off the seesaw, landing hard on my rear end.

The pain was unbearable, and I was cramping. When I got home I noticed that there was a large clot of blood in my panties. I was anxious and didn't know what was going on with my body so I did something I never thought I would do. I confided in and sought help from my mother. Surprisingly, she suggested I go to the hospital. More shocking is the fact that she drove us there. After several test had been done Juan and I waited nervously anticipating the news of the fate of our unborn child. When the doctors came in and mentioned spontaneous abortion as my diagnosis, my adolescent mind didn't comprehend. Miscarriage. The doctor had to break it down to me in simpler terms. Either way he put it meant that I had lost my baby.

Instantly, a feeling of misery and despondency came over me. I was weighed down with the guilt of having taken my other baby's life when I'd had that abortion. I felt as though God was punishing me by taking this baby's life, the same baby I thought I didn't want, and now would never have.

After the miscarriage, I decided to move back home to my mother's house to try to recover properly this time, as I had not done when I'd had the abortion. My pregnancy symptoms never subsided, and I could not figure out why. The sleepiness and nausea caused me to become really irritable so that my level of tolerance and patience with people was edgy. The syndrome escalated even further, and before I knew it Ruth became the next victim of my rage.

Ruth might have been a few years younger, but she was more endowed physically than me and a lot more advanced socially and sexually. I believed in relationships and chose to be faithful to whomever I was seeing. There was a time when my sister and I were very close, especially in the foster home, because when we moved into a house full of strangers, she catered to me almost as if I was her mother. But our relationship had diminished since our mother regained custody of us. Honestly, I think my mother purposely put a wedge between us, because she was jealous of the fact that Ruth would look to me for love and guidance instead of her. Once my younger sister started developing physically she became overly confident in her sexuality and became very promiscuous and belittling of me. She and I were complete opposites, physically, mentally, and socially. For her that meant she was superior to me and she had no problem looking down on me, or saying downgrading things to me. Normally I ignored her and her immature, selfish rants, but every now and again she would push me into a corner and I would come out swinging. I've pulled knives on her, blacked her eye, and slung her against the wall several times for trying to bully me, but the day she physically threatened my daughter I took things to another level.

It was a day that Juan was trying to call and check on me, because I had just had the miscarriage. I was on the phone and in the middle of a conversation she just came and clicked the receiver right in my face. I gave her a crazy look and proceeded to call him back, but as soon as we were conversing she came storming out of her room and called me the word meaning female dog, and stated she needed to use the phone. I said, "When I'm finished talking then you are more than welcome to use it." Still this was not good enough for her, and after I tried for the third time to call Juan, she immediately hung up the phone. She called me that vulgar name again "Nobody cares about you talking to your boyfriend or about y'all's baby that y'all lost." I don't know why, but I just looked at her at that moment with such hurt and disgust. She didn't know what it was like to lose a baby and I hated how she was belittling my pain. I said to her with the straightest look on my face, "If you hang this phone up or call me that name again I am going to hurt you." Well obviously she didn't believe me because she did it again but I made sure to hold up my end of the bargain; I hit her across the head with a crowbar, "I told you not to call me names!" I kept yelling at her, "Why come you can't just leave me alone?" Then I noticed her head was bleeding and I knew I was going to have to face my mother. I didn't mean to hit her that hard, but she was constantly harassing me just like that girl in school, and I couldn't stand it anymore so I went outside to get some fresh air, leaving my baby sleeping on the couch. While I was out there Ruth locked me out of our house, walked over to where Chandreka was, and said she was going to hit her since she couldn't get to me. I saw her straddle my sleeping baby, acting as though she was going to hit her. Before I knew it I had punched in my mother's front window, reached through the broken glass and unlocked the door. Once I got in the house she had ran and hid in her bedroom. I just grabbed my daughter, put her in a stroller and left the house with my hand bleeding profusely.

I was halfway to Anita's house, when my mother pulled her car next to me. I already knew this was not going to be easy, or pretty for that matter. My mother just got out of the car and punched me dead in my mouth, knocking my front tooth out of my mouth. My daughter was screaming at the top of her lungs and I was trying to fight my mother back. Ben pulled up behind her and convinced me to get in the car with my baby. The police were called by my mother because she actually wanted me to go to jail for what I had done to my sister. I thought for sure I was going to jail, but one of the officers told my mother that he was going to take both of us to jail and call the Department of Children and Families to report child abuse. He said that I would probably lose my daughter and she would lose custody of me and my sister. Of course my mother decided not to press charges and to hide what she had done to my mouth she took me to the dentist to get my tooth fixed.

After I returned from the dentist things at home did not get any better. If I never had an intense hatred for everybody in that household I did now. I would continue to look to Juan to have even an inclination of some sort of peace and before I knew it, even he would abandon me and alter my life forever.

I reminisce about a time when he, Howard, and I were taking my daughter to the neighborhood tennis court for some quiet quality time away from all the hustle and bustle in the world. The tennis court was a place I visited often. Ever since we had gotten Butch I would take him there and play fetch with the balls we found while at the park. It was a place I walked to almost every day while pregnant with my daughter. There I wrote poetry in my journal because of its peace and serenity, But soon the tennis court became the place where my worst nightmare was realized.

Juan and Howard were enjoying a game of dominos. My baby girl was riding around on her little tricycle and I was watching two men play an intense game of tennis. I noticed that Juan and Howard seemed to be in a deep conversation and were addressing certain events that were written in the newspaper. Juan was trying to silence Howard, and seemed to be catching an attitude with him. Out of frustration Juan told me that he was ready to go; he came over and gathered my baby and her tricycle. He picked her up, put her on his shoulders and carried her bike in his free hand. I was walking alongside them when I noticed we had left Howard behind. I asked Juan what the problem was and what they were arguing about. When I looked back I noticed that he was no longer at the picnic table they were just playing dominos at, and then I heard his voice coming from the same area where the men were playing tennis. I looked over and was shocked to my very core. Howard had pulled a gun on them and was demanding their keys and money. Juan saw that I observed what was transpiring and tried to hurry us along down the road, but I couldn't stop looking back at those poor men who didn't deserve what was happening to them.

Howard eventually caught up with us in those people's stolen car. Juan insisted me and my daughter get in the car with them and out of fear or disbelief I obliged him and requested he take me straight home. Once he had dropped me off at my house he and Howard drove into the sunset and our relationship, as it was, drove off with them.

I don't know the events that transpired when the two of them got on the road and arrived in Atlanta, all I know is that they were both apprehended by the police and charged with crimes listed from traffic violations all the way to armed robbery, false imprisonment and an array of other charges that I had no idea he was involved in.

This was an extremely difficult time in my life because the man I thought was supposed to be my protector was no longer able or available to protect me. To make things worst I was still experiencing the symptoms of pregnancy from the miscarriage I recently had, so my neighbors once again came to my rescue and took me to the local Planned Pregnancy Center where I had the abortion previously, to take yet another pregnancy test.

The doctors were amazed when they got the results from the urine test. It indicated no pregnancy, but the blood test indicated I was several months along. After performing a sonogram, they figured I was pregnant with twins when I had lost one of them in that miscarriage. The other baby had survived and was growing normally and healthy inside of me. I wanted so much to share this experience with Juan, who desperately wanted a son to carry his name, but he would miss out on all the thrills and deals of my pregnancy… and over a decade of his son's life.

Juan made it a point not to have me present at any of his court appearances. Once I accidently walked in on one, I could clearly understand why. I had gone to the jailhouse for my usual weekly visit when they told me he was in court, which was within walking distance from the jail. When I entered the courtroom I observed him sitting at the defense table with his attorney, and a woman was on the stand. I was curious to know who the woman was because there were only men that were robbed that day at the tennis court. The woman was very emotional while giving her testimony and I could hardly make out her words, but after gathering herself together she was able to give a very distinct and precise testimony of having been robbed by Juan and Howard. I found out that they had several other witness in line to testify to the fact that they had been victimized by them as well.

When all was said and done they tried to give Juan eighty years behind bars for his crime spree and I felt as though a rug had been pulled from underneath me because after hearing his sentence I fell… and hard.

* * *

My parents had recently bought a mobile home to rent out as a source of extra income, but that trailer would become the place where my mom and her drug addicted boyfriend would reside, leaving me to stay home alone with Ben. Ruth was locked away in an all-girls institution in another city and I was forced to live with this man that constantly made me feel creepy. I don't know if I was more relieved or disgusted when I found out that Ben had moved a prostitute into the house. The way he conducted himself in this ordeal would prove even further this man was a man full of lies and hypocrisy.

My daughter was at her usual, getting into things, and no matter how much I tried to keep her away from my stepdad she loved going into his bedroom because it was where she remembered my mother being. It was one thing allowing her to be in there momentarily when my mom lived there, but now that my mom had moved out I was adamant about keeping her out of there. One day in particular she kept running back toward his room and every time I ran behind her to retrieve her and bring her back up front with me she would burst out laughing as if she and I were playing a game.

After a while I noticed that she didn't have her little sippy cup and I began to search all over the house for it. It dawned on me that there was a possibility that she may have lost it when she kept going back into Ben's room, so I went back there in an attempt to find it. When I turned the knob to enter into the room I noticed the door was locked. Now I was thinking I may have made a mistake and locked the door when I was trying to keep her out of it, but then I heard a noise coming from the room that startled me. I knocked on the door asking if someone was there, but no one answered, but my daughter was crying her eyes out and kept trying her best to get into that room. I decided to go outside to the front of the house so that I could peek through the window, and that's when I notice her.

She was a Caucasian woman who looked like she might be strung out on drugs and the first thing that came to my mind is that this woman had broken into the house. Frantically I ran to my neighbors with my daughter to call the police. Once the police met me back at the house the woman insisted that she was Ben's girlfriend and had his permission to be at the house. She called Ben at his job and he verified to the police that everything she said was correct.

I didn't know where this woman had come from and I didn't want my baby around her. She looked filthy and I could tell that she was a woman of the streets.

I decided I'd had enough and it was time to get my daughter out of that situation. I contacted an agency by the name of the Crisis Pregnancy Center and they assisted me with getting my own place. The only trouble was that I didn't have any income other than the little part time job I had at a local restaurant. My mother was getting a social security check for my sister and I because of my father's epilepsy and death, but she used that to support herself and her drug addicted boyfriend. The crisis pregnancy center helped me to get my food stamps and welfare check, they also found a one-bedroom apartment for me and furnished it so my daughter and I could have a safe place to lay our heads.

Not even a whole month passed before my apartment was broken into. The night that it happened I was lying in the bed with my daughter, I started dreaming about Juan who was still incarcerated at this time. In this dream Juan was knocking on my window to tell me to open the door, but then he changed into what is known as the grim reaper, and I became terrified of him. I was trying desperately not to allow him access to my place. Whether this was in the dream or not I cannot tell, but I heard people at the door and when I tried to get up to answer it something invisible was holding me down and would not allow me to get up. When I woke up the next morning I noticed the door was kicked in and barely hanging on its hinges. I didn't know it then, but as I looked back I understood God was protecting me from waking up and walking in on someone who could have possibly hurt me and my children.

After the initial shock had worn off I called my mother to tell her what had transpired. I told her I didn't feel safe staying there with my daughter and asked if we could move into the trailer with her. She didn't even have to think about it, she responded rather quickly that her boyfriend didn't want anyone staying with them. To be honest I wasn't shocked but I knew it meant I had to go back to my stepdad's house.

I had been at Ben's house all of two weeks before I realized I could not dwell in that situation much longer either. I enjoyed the independence I'd experienced having my own place. I was never really the party type so it wasn't about having wild parties or boys coming over, I actually enjoyed the one on one time with my baby, and started developing a rudimentary relationship with this supreme being known as God.

It was suggested that I temporarily move into a homeless shelter in order to expedite the housing application I had recently submitted. The moment my daughter's grandmother found out I was planning to move my baby in with me she came and asked me for temporary custody (not court ordered) of her until I got in my place.

The Salvation Army was the shelter my friends recommended me to stay in because it was supposed to be the cleanest and safest of all the other shelters. Despite the praise that came from the people who suggested it as my new temporary home I despised the place, it seemed that the majority of the people who were staying there were drug users and battered women. I didn't feel like I could relate to these people because I didn't feel like I had anything in common with them. That is until I met my friend Dawn.

Dawn was a young Caucasian girl who became like a sister to me. She had two girls from an African American man who was currently in jail, just as my boyfriend was. Dawn and I became inseparable and we made a vow to one another that whoever got their place first would let the other come live with them. I had put in my application months before Dawn did and I thought for certain that I would be the one that the housing authority would call first for an apartment.

Things didn't work out that way, and to make things even worse, a girl who was a personal friend of mine put her application in after my friend Dawn did and even she got her place before I did. I didn't know what the problem was or who to seek out for help, so my Aunt Rita who is known for her writing abilities encouraged me to let my voice be heard by writing a letter to the local news station. Meanwhile I moved in with a couple who took compassion on me, but I ignorantly and selfishly took advantage of their kindness by running up their phone bill in an effort to keep in contact with Juan who was now in Prison. So once again I was homeless until Dawn opened her home to me.

Things were perfect between my friend and I until someone reported her for having unauthorized residents in her home. My daughter and I barely associated with anyone or went anywhere, but to this day I believe prejudice played a big part in why we were reported. Clearly I was going to have to surrender yet another safe haven and head back to Ben's house.

It was getting closer to the time for me to give birth to my unborn child and I had absolutely nothing ready for him. My Aunt Rita finally began to really sympathize with my situation and invited me to move into her two bedroom, two-bath home where she and her husband lived with no children.

My aunt was a real neat and tidy person, she was a fabulous homemaker and interior decorator, and she took me under her wing, teaching me the majority of what I know today as a woman. Still I couldn't stop thinking about how I had ruined my children's lives. I didn't understand why I was going to have to go through this delivery without Juan, and I certainly didn't know how I was going to take care of my babies.

It got so drastic that all I could do was cry hysterically all day long without ceasing. I would visit the mirrors in the bathroom and question God about who I was and how come I had to go through so much hell. A mother cannot love anyone as much as she loves her children and I wanted to love and protect them, but didn't think I was worthy enough to have even been blessed with them.

I didn't know how to pray. I just called out to God and said I didn't want to know this God that my mom or stepdad served. I wanted to know the God of the Bible, His faithfulness, agape love, almighty power, and miracles. I was in need of Him and His attributes but I wasn't sure if He heard the cries of a lost, neglected, abused and sinful little girl who was trying to find her way in a very big and confusing world.

I remember the day I came to my breaking point and I just didn't want to live anymore. I felt certain that I was doing my children and myself a dishonor by taking up air and space. So there I was sitting on my Aunt's couch crying profusely as I had every waking moment for the past month or so, when a very valuable crystal fell off of her entertainment center and broke unto the floor. Her entertainment center was at least twenty feet or so away from the couch when the crystal figurine came tumbling down. I was nowhere near it and oddly as it seemed, I couldn't figure what had caused it to fall but I knew my Aunt was going to be rather annoyed with me.

I was expecting my Aunt to have a negative reaction to losing her sacred peace of crystal, but I didn't expect her to become so furious with me and tell me I was no longer welcome in her home. I don't know if she thought I was lying or if the little figurine meant more than me being homeless with my baby being due shortly. She told me that I could stay the weekend and she would take me back to the shelter on Monday

Whether my Auntie knew it or not I'd felt like she was my last hope and that hope was just flushed down the toilet because of some materialistic thing that could be replaced. If I ever doubted my value in life this was a time that it was clear to me that I wasn't worth anything to anybody.

I locked myself in the attached bathroom staring at myself in the mirror with disgust and hatred. I was tired of living my life in one dark tunnel after the next. Light seem to be evading me so I decided to make darkness my permanent rest, and take my life right there and then.

I wanted to fall asleep peacefully and never wake up again, so I decided the best method was to take a bottle of pain medicine that was in her medicine cabinet. After taking the pills I decided to read a book hoping it would take my mind off of things. Since my Aunt was a very spiritual woman she only had spiritual books around her house so the book that most grabbed my curiosity was a book by Jimmy Swaggart called, "Questions and Answers about The Bible". While reading the book I noticed that a bluish light in the shape of an angel silhouette appeared at the foot of the bed. It was bright but not to the point to where it startled me… just enough for me to undoubtedly notice it.

I was not frightened by the presence of the angel, because I had seen one before when I was younger and living in West Virginia while visiting my mom's sister. At that time, I was outside playing with my cousins. I remember looking into the sky and it was as if God opened my eyes temporarily into the spiritual world, I saw an angel ascending back into the clouds with a very distinct smile on his face, one that I will never forget. The angel that appeared to me that day in my Aunt's house brought peace into the room and into my spirit, which I had never experienced before. I thought I may have been imagining things seeing this bluish silhouette, so out of disbelief I kept getting up and turning on the light, hoping I could see the angel more clearly, but every time the light went on the angel would disappear and every time I turned the light off it would reappear. After a while I just allowed him to sit on the edge of the foot of my bed until I fell asleep.

Sometime during the middle of the night something whispered in my ear I heard it telling me to go wake my Aunt and tell her what I had done.

I knocked on her door and made the confession to taking the pills. She immediately called the EMTs, who transported me and my unborn child to the labor and delivery division of the hospital.

Once at the hospital my stomach was pumped to help get rid of the drugs in my system. Getting my stomach pumped was a humiliating and painful experience because they were forcing tubes down my nose and throat. During the procedure one of the nurse's realized that I was pregnant and became so upset that she actually teared up and had to leave the room to compose herself. I knew I wanted to commit suicide and end my life but I really never fathomed the homicide I was committing against my innocent, unborn baby. Thankfully they were able to save both our lives, but I wasn't out of danger yet because I kept trying to go into premature labor. I didn't realize how serious my condition was until they locked me up in a mental institution.

Being locked away was probably the best thing that could have happened to me at that time, because it gave me a chance to speak to someone about everything I had been going through. It also enabled me to get the help I needed in order to take care of my baby. The staff was endearing and compassionate towards me and my situation; they actually surprised me with a baby shower and bought him tons of new gifts. I was grateful to know that whenever he was born he would have the things he needed, including a roof over his head. Because I was still legally under age my mother had to assume legal custody of me; but her boyfriend would change that.

After being released from the hospital's mental ward I probably went a week or two before I went into labor with my son. There was a young attractive doctor who had offered me a place on his couch, but I declined. I guess I didn't want to trust a stranger but I would soon come to regret that decision. It was an early Saturday morning when my water broke while staying with my mom and her boyfriend at his place, because they had moved out of the trailer. Mom didn't have transportation at that time and was waiting for her ride to come pick her up and said I would have to wait to ride along with her.

For hours I was in labor after my water had broken, and I could feel the pressure of my baby's head between my legs. By the time we got to the hospital we didn't even have time to fill out any paperwork. They decided to try to take me directly into labor and delivery, but it was to no avail, I was giving birth to my son on the elevator. Once in my recovery room I contacted Juan in jail to tell him of his son's birth. Juan thought I would name our son after him but I decided to grab a Bible and name him after whatever book I turned to and his name ended up being Ezekiel. Naming my son after this character in the Bible, I became intrigued to know more about him and decided to use the rest of my hospital stay reading up on him, consequently I learned more about God as well.

On the last day in the hospital I was preparing to go back home to my mother's home when she came in and told me that I needed to work out a change of plans. She informed me that her boyfriend didn't want me in his house anymore. He said all I did was stay in my room all day and that I wasn't friendly. I didn't understand why she would not defend me in that situation, knowing my history with Ben and knowing her boyfriend would say vulgar inappropriate things about mine and my sister's body parts, so it was normal for me not to want to have interaction with everyone especially my mother's mates. I wasn't interested in what he had to say about me, all I knew is that I was back at square one, better known as Ben's house.

I tried my best to settle back into my old bedroom with both of my children, but I couldn't escape the fact that Ben had this known prostitute still residing in the house. I felt the need to keep me and my children physically clear of her as much as I possibly could, but I could not protect them from the stench of crack being smoked in the home. Pam, my stepdad's girlfriend wasn't the only drug addicted person whose negative lifestyle would begin to intertwine with mine and even though I tried different ways to make things better they just kept getting worse.

I allowed my best friend, to move in with me and my stepdad and although the suggestion came out of her need to find shelter for her and her new baby, I was hoping she could help shelter me from all the negativity I was experiencing, but both of us would need shelter from her drug addicted, abusive, boyfriend who had no problem coming to the house and beating her up in front of me and the children. It was the first time I had witnessed a man beat a woman since watching my dad beat mom, but I was older although I wasn't an adult and I loved this girl like family so without thinking I stood up to this man who was almost twice our age and defended her honor. He told me one day after chasing him away with a crowbar that someone was going to beat my" A". Who knew he could see into my future?

After they rekindled their relationship, I knew it wasn't safe for my babies to be in that home any longer. So I contacted my friend Dawn and thankfully she suggested I and the kids move back in with her until my apartment came through.

This time when I moved back into Dawn's house she had made some very significant changes into her life and started attending church as her Sunday ritual. On my first weekend back at her house she invited me to attend a service with her. It was at this service when the man of God, Apostle Darryl McCoy, called me out from among the congregation after I tried to conceal myself and my tears while he was preaching a sermon about Thanksgiving and how we should always be thankful. At the time I didn't think I had anything to be thankful for because I was alone, homeless, and not feeling loved. I had been and still was, going through so much at such a young age. Through the anointing he prophesied into my life about me having suicide demons all around me after having recently been released from the mental institution for trying to take mine and Ezekiel's life. Most importantly he spoke of God's sincere and undying love for me at a time I was searching for love; when I didn't even know the true meaning of the word.

What is Love?

Love is not a noun like many of us try to make it be

It is an action word that ought to be shown constantly

It can't be measured, touched, or even humanly defined

It can't be broken, comprehended, or limited to our time

Love is not just an emotion of falling head over heals

It's far beyond kindness and touches whomever it wills

It's not doing something for someone but your attitude and reason

It doesn't prosper with money and it never grows out of season

Love is forgiveness when the wrong thing to you was done or said

It is the sacrifice of oneself to bring life to a head

Love is blind because it sees not the color of one's skin

It's not the judge of one's outside but rather searches deep within

Love can be summed up in one word although it may seem odd

But when you're defining Love you are defining God

GOD IS LOVE

Chapter Five

Praise God through Tribulations (PROSPER)

Life was surely difficult before the prophecy and it would become nearly impossible afterwards. My situation though I thought it couldn't get much darker, did in fact get gloomier by the day. It didn't take long before blackness crept in and overshadowed every aspect of my life. It all started with Dawn deciding to relocate her family to New York, which meant I could no longer stay at her residence. But I was determined not to take my children back to Ben's house if I could help it. I decided to rent us a weekly room at a local hotel even though I wasn't sure how I was going to pay the fee. A room with two full size beds, a small refrigerator and a microwave became a home to me and my small children since Chandreka was living with me on and off. I struggled to pay the fee with my welfare check and selling my food stamps. More often than not I still came up short one way or another. People would often take advantage of the fact that I didn't have any experience with business affairs, and wouldn't even give me the price on the street for my food stamps, which was usually half the dollar amount in cash. Instead they would give me only a third of the food stamp value. When your back is against the wall some people don't sympathize with your situation, but instead try to use your situation to their advantage. This is an area where my mother hurt me immensely.

On a week that my weekly payment was due I sold my mother and her drug addicted boyfriend some stamps in order to pay my rent. She had agreed that she would go shopping and bring me the money that she owed me later. When the time came for her to make good she neglected to honor it. The reason she gave me for it was that her boyfriend had better things to do with his money. Better things no doubt meant drugs, of course she wasn't going to tell me in such a forthright way, but everybody knew her man had serious drug problems. His problem was self-inflicted. My children, her grandchildren were innocent, but that didn't matter to neither of them.

Housing was the main dilemma that was causing me so much frustration in my life at that time. My name still had not come up on the housing list, it was as if things were purposely going wrong for me.

God answers prayers even when we are too immature to acknowledge or appreciate His grace as I had been and sometimes those answers do not come in the form that we think they should come. Eventually I started hanging at another friend's house named Sharon who used to stay in the same neighborhood I did before she was called by the housing authority and given her own place. I didn't have any other choice, but to drag my recently born baby everywhere with me, but I was grateful to my daughter's paternal grandparents for taking her in every time I needed them to.

While at Sharon's house her boyfriend and she suggested I stay with them from time to time so I would not have to come up with the weekly fee of the hotel room. Staying at her house was amazing for me because there was so much history between us. Her family had somewhat adopted me and my sister into their family and because of the fact that she and a few of her siblings were older and already had children before I had mine, I got the practice and knowledge I would need to take care of my children. Her house was actually a great get-away from being cooped up in one room all the time.

Barbeques and playing cards were things I participated in to pass the time. It was during these gatherings that Sharon's boyfriend friends would all try to flirt with me, but I was not intrigued with their bold and hideous sexual comments. I was still helplessly in love with Juan, and was still hoping and praying that he and I would get back together again; that was before *he* walked in and changed my mind.

He didn't come there looking for love or looking to hook up with anybody, he was already in a committed relationship and like me he was just enjoying the company and fellowship of good friends. On one occasion Sharon and her boyfriend wanted to play cards and needed two other people to play along and that is where Rico and I first became acquainted with one another. Something was different about him. He didn't press for my attention, his presence demanded it. I was consumed by his confidence because he wasn't like all the other guys who acted as though they were dogs in heat.

Rico was calm, reserved, business oriented, well dressed… and soon to be my next baby's daddy. I respected the union he told me about from day one and I wasn't the type of girl to impose on another woman's territory, but after meeting up with this man night after night after night I started to question whether or not he actually had a girlfriend or was he just giving me an excuse not to be in a serious relationship. I was willing to wait things out and just allow things to happen naturally. In the course of trying to figure out this mysterious man he and I developed a close friendship and he demonstrated that I wasn't just one of many sexual encounters. I was someone he actually came to care for.

I was always honest and upfront with him and I informed him of my troubled life from the very beginning. He never once judged me by what I was going through but liked me for who I was.

The fact that I had two children already, was living in a hotel, and struggling to make ends meet did not stop him from liking me. In the presence of friends and strangers alike, he made me feel like the most important person in the room and was proud to have me on his arm. I can't count the times he picked me and my children up and loaded our belongings in the back of his truck to go visit our friend's home, before long he was even assisting me with paying my weekly hotel fee.

Things were going perfect between us, until reality hit me like a bolt of lightning and I had to face the fact that he would never be mine because his girlfriend would eventually make her presence known. Months had gone by and my feelings for him were not only developed but actually deepened immensely at that point. He made me forget Juan who had recently been sentenced to eighty years in prison. Rico became a consistent aid in my time of trouble until I unconsciously brought trouble to his door and he would prove to me that he did not need any help exiting my life. His birthday actually became my worst day.

I remember the tightening in my stomach when Rico's girlfriend came looking for him earlier in the day to give him his birthday present. Thinking it was him, I was excited to see his truck pull up to Sharon's apartment, but when she exited the truck my heart fell to the ground. There would be no more hope for obtaining a committed relationship with him because she was no longer this imaginary person I thought he had made up to avoid settling down with me. When she walked up to the door to knock on it Sharon and I were currently outside talking, she asked Sharon if Rico was over there. My friend responded with a blunt no, his girlfriend gave me a look of disgust and then left in his truck. Not even moments later she was on the phone asking Sharon's boyfriend who I was.

I took it that it was because Sharon's boyfriend didn't care much for this girl or that he actually thought Rico and I were a better fit that he didn't mind giving her a hostile answer by telling her who he has at his house is none of her business. Later that night the truck pulled back up and I thought that it might be Rico's girlfriend again and suddenly I thought about having to face her twice in one day. I was relieved when Rico exited the truck and I knew then that despite his relationship status he was choosing me over her; we were not going to leave each other alone anytime soon.

After spending the entire night together for his birthday, I realized I needed to go back to the hotel room to retrieve some things, Sharon offered to babysit while Rico took on the responsibility of getting me there. He and I stopped at his apartment and one thing led to another. We were in the middle of making love when we heard a deliberate and demanding pounding at the door. I wanted to stop so he could see what was going on, but he insisted that we continue and so we did, until she came bursting into his bedroom. His girlfriend said, "What the! How could you do this to me, and with this slick tramp from your friend's house, when you know I'm pregnant." She was crying and trying hard to attack me. I was guilty as charged and I felt terrible about what we had done to her. I had just come to terms with their relationship, but I definitely wasn't aware of any baby. I tried to gather my clothes, and myself while he tried to restrain her from striking me which just caused him and her to get into a physical altercation.

After what seemed like forever, things finally calmed down and he convinced her to allow him to take me back to the hotel where I could be alone and get my mind right. Once we picked up my kids and returned to the hotel, he and I discussed what had just transpired and he told me he wasn't for certain whether or not she was really pregnant; in my mind I was hoping she wasn't. After our discussion he decided that he didn't want to leave me and ended up staying with me at the hotel for several days.

It was like clockwork every morning around a certain time he would leave to go make his money and return home to me around the same time every evening, but one day he never came home and I knew in my heart he was with her. When he finally returned to me a day or so later he gave me the devastating news that she was expecting and I knew I had no other choice but to do the right thing and subtract myself from the equation but instead of subtracting myself I only added to the problem and multiplied its severity.

* * *

Although we had decided to no longer see each other in the sexual capacity, our friendship and hang out spot remained the same. Rico was still a close friend with Sharon's boyfriend and I was still close to her, I continued living there from time to time with them. It was awkward being around him and not having any more physical or emotional attachments. Everyone was so accustomed to us being hugged up around each other and they watched with anxious anticipation how we suddenly changed lanes. They also observed that I started vomiting and sleeping a lot and made gestures that I may be pregnant. The fact that he could possibly have two girls pregnant at the same time was hilarious to them but for us it was no laughing matter.

The last thing I wanted or needed was another child. I was sinking into yet a deeper hole, and I had no one to blame but myself. Once my pregnancy was confirmed he and I thought it best that I end it, but after having that first abortion I knew I could never go through that again.

It was difficult hearing Rico proudly speak of the pregnancy with this other woman, yet cold heartedly insisting on ending my baby's life. When I was adamant about my decision not to abort the baby he and I drifted further apart. I was finally called by the housing authority for an apartment and our distance became even greater.

The day before I settled into my apartment I met a young lady named Diane who was staying at the same hotel I was currently staying in. She was also down on her luck and in need of a place to reside. Out of compassion I offered to let her come stay at my new place, although I had not even moved into it yet. The apartment was only two bedrooms and I allowed the young lady to have her own room while I and my son moved into the other room. My daughter didn't want to leave her grandparents' house, but would visit me often.

Once in the apartment I became absorbed in everyday life, and trying to provide for my children. I completely blocked out the fact that I was pregnant from my mind and never sought any prenatal care. Some may say I went into denial because I never bought anything this baby would need during my pregnancy. While staying in this apartment I may have been in denial of my pregnancy but I wasn't in denial of my dysfunction.

By then, I had zero tolerance or respect for men. All I wanted to do, for the most part, was to get what I could get out of them. When young men came over to my apartment to visit me and Diane in hopes of sleeping with us I made it known that I wasn't going to devalue myself and allow them to take advantage of me as men had done before. To protect myself I had a collection of crowbars, an axe, and a chainsaw that I would keep in my bedroom that I didn't mind pulling out or using when threatened, and I made sure everyone knew about them. There were several occasions when I was forced to use those variety of weapons to defend myself from some of the men and their friends, and eventually even Diane. The first occurrence happened when I kicked a gift horse in the mouth. I abruptly told a young man who had a crush on both my roommate and me, to "get out of my house." He showed his desire for us by hanging out at my apartment all the time and supplying things with the money he received from selling drugs, and although neither Diane nor I gave him any inclination that we were interested in him, he tried to buy his way into our hearts and my home. When that didn't work he changed his method by trying to bully us. He felt that just because he had supplied my apartment with a microwave, a television and other things that that granted him total access to my place at his leisure. The moment I told him how I felt he quietly walked into the kitchen and proceeded to pull the microwave from the electrical outlet and then picked it up, and threw it out the door. Diane and I just sat there in total shock not sure what to expect next. Then he went over to the TV and did the exact same thing except this time he called us both a few choice words and said he was going to have somebody come by and beat us up. "Whatever", I screamed. "Just get your stuff and get out of my house!" And out of rage I got up and started throwing out everything else he brought into my home. With his things now gone, Diane and I plugged in our little boom box and began cleaning the mess that was left after all the chaos. While we were cleaning the apartment we started hearing screaming and cursing from people around the neighborhood as they were approaching the apartment. I looked out of the window and saw what appeared to be a small army. The guy who had promised he was going to get someone to beat us up was approaching us with his little posse behind him. The first thing Diane and I did was to ensure that all the doors and windows were locked. Then I said a small prayer asking God to protect us and to give me strength to fight these giants who were mostly a gang of young men. At that time prayer started becoming easy for me because the church where I had received the prophecy was now a church Diane and I visited often. Wouldn't you know Apostle McCoy Prophesied to me again and warned me to watch the company I was keeping.

By this time, I had become intrigued with reading my Bible in my own private time. I slowly developed my own relationship with God.

All their banging on my window should have scared me, but what got to me was my baby there crying his little eyes out, and I became furious. There was no one to defend my helpless child besides me, since neither Diane nor I had a cell phone or a land line at the time, we couldn't call the police. I don't know what gave me the guts to walk over to my window and not beg them to leave me alone, but threaten them with what was going to happen if they didn't. I remember the guy who had thrown all of his property out of my house told this known crack addict to punch me in my face. I didn't have time to move before this big man's hand came crashing through my window and made contact with my face. Everyone was startled when I didn't budge and I didn't have any marks on my face from his hand or the glass; I never felt the contact. I saw it coming but it was like something imaginary protected my face from getting hurt, but what was more surprising is that the crack head ended up hurting his hand badly, even more shocking is the fact that the boy who set everything up ended up going to jail the very next day on an unrelated charge. This was definitely a time I started feeling like there was a God and that He really does answer prayer.

After that episode Diane and I had some great falling outs, but we learned that we had to do more than just adapt to living together we had to learn to survive together. Sometimes when our food ran short for the month she and I had to walk to the grocery store just to shoplift groceries in order to keep from starving. I remember a particular Thanksgiving holiday where neither of us could go home for the traditional Thanksgiving meal. We decided to go to the grocery store and steal our version of thanksgiving dinner which sadly happened to be turkey lunch meat, nacho Doritos, a raisin cake, and juice. We would laugh and make jokes saying how tender the turkey was or how the nacho Doritos tasted like mac and cheese. Those were some of the better times she and I had as we came together as a unit and took care of one another, but on the flip side, there would be times when she would turn against me and gather the same neighborhood that had once turned on the both of us, to turn on me.

"Watch the company I keep", The words rang in my head but I didn't understand who the Apostle was referring to but God wouldn't leave me in the dark. Like every other set of roommates, she and I had our differences, but unlike most roommates I was the only one that had any source of income and was paying for everything. I didn't expect her to kiss up to me, but I expected her to have a little more gratitude for me allowing her to stay rent free in my apartment.

Instead, she decided to start gossiping about me with a particular neighborhood girl named Tasha who didn't like me because she thought I thought I was better than everybody else just because I chose to keep to myself. Tasha was always saying things like I can't stand a girl who is wearing a pink shirt when I would be standing there in a pink shirt. Although she and Diane were older than me I was obviously more mature than both of them because neither of them had their own place. At first I never knew that Tasha and Diane were in cahoots with one another until the day I found notes that they were passing back and forth between each other. The front doors on the apartments had a mail slot where the mailman could drop the mail in and that was how I discovered one of the notes that they were exchanging disgracing me.

The moment I read all the filthy things Diane had to say about me to this girl she knew didn't care for me, I completely lost my mind. I confronted her and threw her and all of her belongings out of my house. I warned her that the same person she was siding with would soon turn her back on her as well, and that she would see that in losing me she was losing a good friend. Later the two of them got together and decided that they were going to bombard my apartment.

It was like déjà vu, listening to these mean spirited people approach my home in hopes of hurting me in front of my children. Just as before I didn't have a phone, but this time my daughter was over there visiting and I was in no mood to allow her to witness or experience any harm or danger. When they approached my door just as they had before, I decided to put my kids in their room and kept screaming for them to stop banging and trying to kick in my door. When I had enough I grabbed my dad's axe and went outside. Several of the people had already experienced me threatening and actually using my crowbars and I heard them shout, "I told y'all that she was crazy! Y'all better leave her alone: they said as they ran for their lives. It was too late they had already pushed me to my breaking point and there was no turning back. I stood tall and firm with that axe in my hand, ready to combat anything or anyone that put me and my children's safety at risk. Tasha and Diane quickly backed down when they saw the determination in my eyes. They knew I was a person of few words once I had gotten to a certain point. That should have been the last negative experience that I had with my roommate but it wasn't.

The final straw occurred after I allowed her back into my home and she found a way to cross me again, I felt like she was trying to prostitute me. I'd watched friends have unwanted sex, snort drugs and participate in other dangerous behavior, all out of peer pressure, and I was adamant that I was no longer going to be a victim to anyone or anything.

Yet I was still playing the silly game of cat and mouse with guys at this point. That game consisted of me trying to take their cheese without getting caught in their rat trap. I wanted what I could get out of them, but didn't want to use my body as a way to pay it. One day when our refrigerator was completely empty she and I decided to flatter some guys into buying us dinner. We had several people we thought we could call on for this purpose but most of them wanted something in return because they had caught on to our little scheme by now. So Diane arranged for us to go meet some friends of hers and we were supposed to just hang out over at their apartment until they fed us. Like clockwork, after we had eaten we were supposed to make up an excuse that would convince them to take us back to our apartment.

As we were hanging out getting to know these dudes we were all supposed to sit in front of the television and watch music videos, but Diane and the guy she just met left the living room and went into the bedroom. I was not worried at that point. The young man I was left with was still being a gentleman, but then he started trying to kiss me. Although he was nice looking I wasn't in the mood to hook up with anybody. I tried to persuade him to stop and to allow us to get to know one another because I could tell that he was becoming more and more impatient with me. Finally, he got so irritated that he just told me that he wanted to have sex and if I wasn't going to do it then I needed to be finding my own way home. He said, "Diane already said you were down. I don't know why you are playing games. She's already in the room doing what she needs to do. You need to get with the program or get up out my house."

I could tell by the look in his eyes that he meant business, but I wasn't going to have sex with him for food or a ride home. I immediately got up and went searching for the bedroom that Diane and the other man went into. I didn't even knock I just burst into the room, and seeing them in the midst of their sexual encounter didn't persuade me from confronting her about what she told this man. I said, "Get up. What the heck did you tell this man? I am not freaking having sex with him." After a while she got up as I waited impatiently for her in the living room. I grabbed their phone and called the police, but the moment they noticed that I was on the phone they hung it up, but it was too late since the police had already heard me crying and decided to call back. The dispatcher asked if I was okay and said she was going to send an officer out to me. I thought back when they did not bring any charges against Ben when he hugged me inappropriately and thought they would certainly not do anything to these young men, so I reluctantly decided to allow them to take us home.

Once we got back to my apartment I became infuriated with the thought that Diane set me up to be someone's sexual conquest. I immediately told her that I wanted her out of my house. When she seemed to be procrastinating I nearly came unglued and punched out her bedroom window. I looked at her with so much hatred in my eyes as I thought back to all those times I was victimized sexually. For me to have just recently forgiven her for one betrayal and here she was betraying me again. I could not deal with it and I wanted her gone before I did something I was going to regret.

After a while, my pregnancy became a bit more obvious, but emotionally I still had not come to terms with it. I would feel so stupid running into Rico and his pregnant girlfriend in grocery stores and have them look down on me. I had accepted the fact that he and I were not going to be together again and I was actually sort of dating around. There was a guy that I was sort of involved with a little bit after my daughter was born. He could have put me and my children's lives in jeopardy because he was a big known drug dealer and became brutally violent. I guess the fact that Juan was out robbing people and doing all these other unlawful things, but was steady treating me like a queen gave me the desire to want to date thugs and get them to unveil their softer side to me as well. This guy was really dependable as far as making sure I had food and things like that when I needed it whenever he was around. This particular person named Maine used to travel back and forth trafficking drugs and would come by and talk to me about anything from God to politics. I knew I could never be involved with him seriously because of his lifestyle, but I was intrigued by his level of intelligence and kindness towards me, however he also would prove to me that the thug side of his life was very real and very unsafe.

Whether it be stupidity or my soft heart or fear of loneliness, I forgave Diane and allowed her to move back with me. One day Maine had taken me and her to the grocery store and filled the apartment with groceries. He told me that he had to run a few errands but would probably come by later that night to check on me. Sometime during the middle of the night he walked into my bedroom because Diane had let him in. Once he turned on the lights I noticed that his hands were bloody and I jumped out of my bed. I asked him what happened and asked if he needed medical attention. He answered no and asked if he could just use my bathroom to wash up, of course I obliged. After he came out of the bathroom he explained that he had gotten into an accident and that the scratches and marks came from him escaping out of the car. It seemed believable so I decided to end the line of questioning and allow him to get a little rest after he called a friend for assistance.

Maine slept on the very edge of my bed with one leg hanging off the bed as if he was preparing to escape. The next day when we could talk privately he and I headed for the lake that was near my apartments. While holding hands and walking toward the lake I noticed again how bad his hands were bruised and I felt so much compassion for him because although he was a known drug dealer he was a really good friend to me. Once at the lake he started getting really spiritual with me but I wasn't that surprised. I always made the relationship that I was building with God, known to everyone, and he shared the same interest in God as I did. Although I didn't necessarily live a sin free life I was actually falling in love with God and I didn't mind sharing that with the world. He began to open up to me about his need to settle down, give his life to God and change his ways. We were in the midst of conversing when the friend that he contacted to pick him up came by and got him. He told me to come by that friend's house later because he really needed to finish the conversation with me.

Later I asked that Diane accompany me to his friend's house so that we could check on him. When we arrived she informed us that he wasn't there and then asked me if I read the newspaper or watched the news. Of course we didn't own a television and were not much into buying a newspaper, so we were always a little out of the loop and just begged her to tell us what had happened to my friend; she simply handed me the front page of the newspaper.

I can't recall exactly what the headlines read but the story entailed something about him walking into a local strip club and pistol whipping an underage girl who was currently stripping there. The paper indicated that he had broken several bones on this girl including the ones in her face and he shot her several times. My mouth hit the floor to know that this man was capable of hurting someone to that extent, especially a woman. This man had surpassed anything I could have ever imagined and to think he had the audacity to come to my house afterwards, to sleep in my bed.

Maybe I was a little judgmental of this young woman whom I would never get the opportunity to meet, but I often tried hard to figure out what she and I had in common for him to be dating both of us at the same time. I mean she and I were from different worlds. She was a stripper, who still lived with her grandmother in a lovely home and seemed to have the love and support of her family, but for whatever reason she chose to indulge in the fast life of the world of drugs, crime and exotic dancing. I was just an ordinary shy, old fashioned girl living an uninteresting, very poverty- stricken life, with minimal to no support from family members, but God would reveal to me that she and I had more in common than I cared to consider. We were both seeking something more powerful than ourselves in whom to rely to fill our empty lives or maybe even alter us and our situations. Though the means may differ the choice remains the same, Good or Evil. Like the rest of the world she and I would make our choices, and like it or not would suffer their consequences.

Choose Ye This Day

Many people say that Satan is not a god but this is not true

If God is not Lord over your life, then Satan is god over you

So why do you serve a god who doesn't care about your well-being

Why glorify him when in your life hell is all that you are seeing

Yes, he gives you pleasure but that only lasts a short time

But when you need a miracle Jesus is the first name to come to mind

So why not call on Satan if he is the god of your choice

Is he that evil that he won't answer his own children's voice?

Oh how you praise him as you indulge in your everyday sins

God pleads for your repentance yet you ignore him time & time again

He sends his messengers only to watch them be criticized

He listens as you blaspheme his name as though He's not alive

He sits back patiently waiting for He knows the day will come

When you are forced to admit Jesus is God's first and only begotten son

So continue to call out to Satan but I promise you it's all in vein

For even he knows his power is limited and so is his reign

His master plan is tragic as well as his theme

His demise is written clearly and so are his schemes

To seek, kill, and destroy the human race by any means

To take as many souls to hell for all eternity

Yet heaven and prosperity await those who live in Christ

Health and abundance are only some things Christ brings to life

Blessings and miracles are normal to God's believers

Just as tragedy & sickness are normal to those who serve the deceiver

So choose ye this day whom you shall serve forever

Don't take my word, but study the Bible and gather facts together

Pray for wisdom knowledge and understanding to study it better

Study every single statement down to the last letter

But for now flip to the end of the Bible and you will get a clue

Satan is thrown into the lake of fire with the rest of his crew

And now your destination is basically up to you

But hurry time is running out It's time for you to choose

Chapter Six

Eat Only from the Tree of Life (PROSPER)

Eventually, after no contact with Rico, and after absolutely no prenatal care I ended up giving birth prematurely to another daughter I allowed my sister to name Ciera. God works in mysterious ways, because thankfully my mother was visiting me from Jacksonville, Florida when I went into labor with my daughter and she was able to watch my other children while I was in the hospital. I contemplated putting Ciera up for adoption because I was already struggling with my previous two children, and my oldest daughter wasn't even living with me at the moment, but once I laid my eyes on her I knew I couldn't abandon her. Giving birth to her while only seven months pregnant, meant she was really premature and suffered some slight medical conditions because her lungs had not developed yet, and she had to remain in the hospital a little over a month after I had been released. I contacted her dad whose girlfriend would give birth less than a week after I gave birth to our daughter. He never came to the hospital to check on me or his baby. The love and respect that I had once received from him had been traded in for disgust and disregard. If he had any doubts for one reason or another that the baby belonged to him he could have simply come by and seen her for himself and better yet he could have demanded a paternity test, which I would have happily and readily given to him. There was never any doubt that she belonged to him, because although we were cheaters, I never cheated on him. The hospital diagnosed me with depression once again and recommended that I seek therapy because all I could do was cry uncontrollably. I had been in such denial about my pregnancy that I had put it out of my mind and somehow convinced myself to believe that the pregnancy would disappear. I had so many questions running through my mind while laying up in that hospital after giving birth to her. I questioned how I was going to financially take care of yet another baby with no job, was her dad ever going to be active in her life and could I emotionally handle a new responsibility? For a month or so I had to bum rides to go visit my daughter while she remained in the hospital. Sadly, that meant I only had a month to prepare and get all of the things I needed to take care of her. One day after coming home from visiting her in the hospital, I met someone who would come into my life and take some of the burden off of me, but like everything else in this world; there was a price to pay and his price just might cost me my life.

After Ciera was released from the hospital I made it a point to try to contact her father and extend an invitation for him to have a relationship with our daughter, but he continued to show that he wasn't interested in being in her life. I even took it upon myself to take her by the friend's house where he and I had first met so they could inform him how much she resembled him, but all that did was peek an interest for him to see her and nothing further. It was incredibly sad too, because all of his friends thought his girlfriend's baby did not actually belong to him, since she was rumored to have been cheating on him the same time he and I were cheating on her... Her baby looked nothing like him. It was so humiliating to feel as though I had to almost stalk him. The old friends that were so supportive of us before I became pregnant, were now hiding and covering up for him; helping him to avoid having a relationship with or responsibility for his daughter.

Out of the blue it appeared that God had sent someone who was willing to step in and become the male role model for all of my children, well at least the two that were living with me. He and I met as I was riding with a neighbor back from visiting Ciera. We were both passengers in cars that were driving adjacent to each other and so we kept meeting up at the same red lights. He started a careless conversation, I responded and later we were hanging out with one another at my neighbor's house and from that moment on we were inseparable… at least voluntarily.

One of the things that made me fall head over heels for Nick was the fact that he was so family orientated. It was not long after we met that he took me to meet his mother and the rest of his family. He was proud to be with me and my children and he let everyone know it. He respected me and my readymade family, my relationship with God and my shortcomings.

It's not every day that a man in his early twenties comes to visit a girl who is enthralled by her Bible and can't seem to shut up about God. I was like a little old lady in a young person's body, but I was going through things my elders could never imagine.

Finally, my children and I were experiencing a somewhat normal life and I thought things couldn't get any better for us. We were in our own apartment, I had a boyfriend who was helping me to supply our needs, his family had accepted us, and I was being showered with love, but from experience I had grown accustomed to being let down and I came to the knowledge that everything that glitters can't be gold.

Just as gold is tested by fire, so is the human character tested by the furnace of humiliation. Pride is the beginning of destruction in so many relationships as it began when Lucifer decided he wanted to exalt himself higher than God, so it is in so many other relationships where someone wants to be superior to someone else. Pride is also the result of yet another destructive behavior that when used incorrectly abhors and undermines the ways of God. Pride would become the factor that Nick and I would build upon and inevitably become the sledge hammer that would break us apart.

It all started when we were visiting a nearby friend's house and she mentioned that her daughter's birthday was coming up on a particular day. All I did was simply state that my oldest daughter's father, Stacey, shared the same birthday and left it at that. Later when Nick and I got home he started in on me, saying that I was still in love with Stacey. I began to refute him and tell him how asinine that was since clearly he and I were not together and also because I had two more children with two separate men after that relationship with Stacey was dissolved. I thought that would calm him down but I was wrong. His pride and jealousy would not let things go and he convinced himself that I was being unfaithful and making a fool of him.

It didn't matter how I tried to convince him otherwise, my words were being ignored and I could tell that he was no longer his normal loving self. I don't remember exactly what words were coming out of his mouth when he balled his fist up and punched me dead in my face. I thought back to my mother and all those days and nights I heard her fighting for her life and I imagined what my children must have been going through and then I told him to leave. Those words infuriated him even more because Nick then snatched me by my hair and threw me unto the floor and began pounding my face. I knew I couldn't physically beat him while pinned to the floor underneath him enduring those direct and powerful punches to my face.

I had to think fast if I wanted to survive I began sweet talking him, begging and pleading with him to stop. I had to convince him that I was in love with him and that he was the only man for me. After a while my soothing words seemed to calm him and he allowed me to get up. Surprisingly he wanted a hug from me in order to prove that there weren't any hard feelings and I almost got sick to my stomach, but I knew I had to accommodate him if I didn't want him to start in on me again. After I hugged him I proceeded to the bathroom where I looked at myself in the mirror. I had so many knots and bruises all over my face that I reminded myself of my mother. While staring at myself in that mirror something came over me and I started tearing up and shaking my head in disgust. I got so angry at the fact that he violated me in such a way that I wanted to make him pay right then and there. Ciera was screaming her little eyes out and so I picked her up in order to try to comfort her because I didn't want him to touch her. When I went into the kitchen to prepare a bottle for her he was standing in the walkway and I had to squeeze by him. Once I made her bottle I noticed a butcher knife in the sink and so without thought I grabbed it and I placed my daughter in the sink to fend for herself. Luckily she was sitting up by herself at this point because now that I look back on it she could have really gotten hurt.

Fury had taken over and there was no turning back, he wanted a fight and now I was prepared to give him one. I walked over with the knife in my hand and I said, "I'm going to kill you today!" And then I tried to stab him. The altercation became more intense and violent. He tried to grab the knife out of my hand and I knew if I allowed him to take possession of it he would use it to kill me, so I fought with everything in me and held onto the knife by the blade. My hands were getting cut up and I was getting weaker by the second, so I started hitting him over the head with anything I could get hold of. Once his head started bleeding he pushed me off of him and ran out of the house.

Common sense should have told me to go get help and then lock my doors and stay away from him, but that's not what my stupid pride allowed me to do, instead after getting my children into a safe place, I went back outside where he was already lying and telling people that I had started in on him and that I was jealous and violent. I couldn't believe how quick he turned the story around. I didn't want people to believe him so I ran outside yelling my truths. There wasn't much reaction until I told him I never loved him and that I never wanted to see him again. The words had just come out of my mouth, when he ran and dropped kicked me straight in the mouth, breaking my jaw.

When the police and ambulance arrived Nick had run and hid somewhere. My neighbors watched my babies while I was in the hospital but then the doctors informed me that they were going to have to perform surgery and wire up my jaw put stitches in my hands as well. When I called my neighbor to check on my children she let me know that her boyfriend wasn't comfortable keeping my children there and that I had to find other arrangements. My mother had moved to Florida and I wasn't going to allow Ben the opportunity of watching them. And pride would not allow me to reach out to other people because of sheer embarrassment.

I told the hospital staff that I didn't have anyone to babysit while I had the surgery done and I needed time to make arrangements. They allowed me to sign myself out, against doctor's orders and they rescheduled the surgery for the next morning at 7 am. I might have done the stupidest thing any mother could do when I asked my boyfriend to come over and watch my children at my house while I had the surgery, but I knew he loved them like his own.

Surprisingly, he agreed. Then he came over and acted as though nothing had transpired, even going so far as to desire sex.

In his sick and twisted mind Nick actually thought he was making love to me, and the fact that I refrained from fighting him off was not because I was enjoying it; it was because I was just trying to keep him in a calm state so that I could survive and have my surgery done. Knowing I could only open my mouth so far with a broken jaw, he tried to force me to kiss him. Tears flowed down my face from the pain and agony he was causing.

The next day I got ready to go in for the surgery and I couldn't believe that I had actually spent another night with this sick man. I just knew I had to hurry home and get my children away from him. Immediately after the surgery I called the police and told them I knew the whereabouts of the person who attacked me and that I wanted to press charges against him. They were shocked when I told them how I had him come over and babysit for me, but I knew I couldn't let him get away with what he had done.

The police agreed to give me a ride home and pick him up simultaneously The plan worked as beautifully as I thought it would. He was so shocked that I tricked him that he didn't have time to react, but while he was in jail he conjured up his own plot to pay me back.

* * *

While he was incarcerated Nick tried desperately hard to contact me, but I was confident that I didn't want anything else to do with him whatsoever, therefore I ignored his letters and didn't respond to his request to come to the jail for a visit. I was surprised when my neighbors came to get me to let me know some lady was on the phone for me, and I was more surprised when I got to the phone to find out it was his daughter's mother calling for him to speak with me on a conference call. I didn't understand how she had the audacity to be calling me for him, she and I never met and we still had bad vibes between us. Especially when she found out that after she had been pistol whipped and shot several times in that strip club, her boyfriend came to my place of residence for advice and companionship.

When I had met Nick months prior and shared that incredible story, trying to testify about how God had always seemed to keep me from danger, he informed me that the stripper in the story was none other than his daughter's mom. I take it that when he told her about me she instantly took a disliking to me because I dated two of the same guys that probably meant the most to her in her young life. I had always wondered what happened to Maine after he had turned himself in, but I couldn't bring myself to write or go visit him. My curiosity would finally be satisfied the moment she spewed from her mouth that she had dropped the charges against this guy who beat her almost to death and that if I loved Nick, then I would do the same. This girl had been shot numerous times and was blessed to make it out alive, and now she was bragging about dropping the charges against someone who nearly killed her. My pride couldn't fathom allowing someone to get away with hurting me that badly, and although my injuries were minor compared to hers, I certainly wasn't going to allow her daughter's father to violate me and get away with it. I wanted him to suffer and the fact that he had bruised my pride by telling her to contact me just may have put the last nail in his coffin.

I went and got a new outfit to wear to court the next day. I wanted to look good when I came into the courtroom to testify against Nick and in a way I wanted to make him jealous, but those immature and childish motives backfired on me. I looked like a promiscuous tramp with low morals or standards when I entered the courtroom that day. The judge had no problem telling me how inappropriate my dress was and made me leave the courtroom right away. He almost dismissed me from coming into his courtroom to testify at all.

Thankfully the judge had compassion for me and gave me the chance I desired to tell my side of the story after allowing me to hear Nick's testimony. To hear him tell it I was the one that was aggressive that day and I had actually attacked him out of a jealous rage. I had to hand it to him, his lie was consistent with what he had already told my neighbors, and to be honest, if I hadn't been there to know what really had transpired, even I would have believed him. He was experienced with the court system and he knew all the right things to say. I was naive to believe that the truth would prevail. His lawyers were way too crafty for me and it didn't matter to them that I had suffered such significant injuries from him, all that mattered to them was winning and if it was at me and my children's expense, so be it.

When his lawyers asked me if I pulled out a knife and tried to use it against my boyfriend, they didn't give me a chance to explain that it was in self-defense. The moment I said 'yes but', they were instructing me not to speak out of turn and just answer yes or no to the questions that were asked. I never had a voice that day, back then domestic violence victims couldn't be heard sometimes even if they spoke from the grave.

After the judge had found him not guilty, he blew me a kiss as he walked past me. It didn't take a rocket scientist to know what he meant by it, but I didn't think he had the nerve to appear at my house just hours after being released from jail and I certainly didn't think he was crazy enough to break into my place, but once again Nick would prove me wrong.

I had taken my children in their stroller to the corner store to allow them to get some fresh air. I was busy trying to get them out of the two seater stroller and into the house where I could get them settled down and prepare dinner for them. All of a sudden I heard a noise come from my bedroom that startled me, but I didn't think that anyone was in the house. I thought maybe something had fallen off the wall. I made sure my children were secured and slowly crept to my bedroom, opened the door slowly and looked into the room but didn't see anything out of the ordinary. So I went about my daily chores. Later that evening after their baths and everything I was laying my children down for the night and out of the corner of my eye I saw something run into my bathroom I knew then we weren't alone. I blurted out some excuse to go over to my neighbor's house. Just as I was getting my children out of the house Nick suddenly appeared out of nowhere and asked me where I thought I was going.

I couldn't believe that I was face to face with him again and I thought certainly that he would want to repay me for setting him up and having him arrested. "We can do this the easy way or the hard way," he said as he picked up my little girl. Nervously I asked what he meant by that. He replied, "You see everything you tried to do against me failed and you know why? And answered in the same breath, "God doesn't like ugly. You tried to set me up after having me watch your kids while you were in the hospital." I was thinking that he couldn't have been serious, after all he was the cause of me being put in the hospital in the first place. I didn't know what I had gotten myself involved in but I knew it wasn't going to be good.

One of the hardest things about being involved in a domestically violent relationship is its roller coaster ups and downs; emotionally, physically, and psychologically. You never know how your abuser is going to react to certain things and what sets them off, because often times they themselves do not know either. When they are in a good mood and are in control they are usually the best thing since slice bread, and when they are in a lousy mood, usually due to the lack of control, they become even more out of control, irritable and violent. Although most roller coasters are located at an amusement park there was nothing amusing about this distorted relationship, so I cannot explain why I stayed on that horrific ride for seven whole years.

* * *

Maybe it was all routine, maybe it was because I couldn't find a safe way of escape, or maybe it was because my mother endorsed it by telling me that I wasn't going to find another man who would readily come into my life prepared to provide for me and my already made family. In reality it was a combination of these things, but most of all it was because I was only 19 years of age and I was madly in love with him. After all he was a good man, he made me laugh, and when we weren't fighting things between us were awesome. Still there were more violent times between us than I care to remember, and the sad part about it is the longer we stayed together the more violent I became.

I tried to take my mother's advice and humble or submit myself to him as she would call it. I treated him like the man of the house fixing his plate and serving it to him not because I was taught to do that but because it was just in me. I wanted to learn from Jesus and be blessed by becoming a servant, knowing the Bible promised to exalt me in due time. Maybe I didn't know the definition of pride and humility after all.

After all those times I dreamt of being able to come to my mother's rescue and save her from her tormentor when he was abusing her and now she was advising me to stay with my tormentor. When my mother uprooted and moved to Florida, I was left in Augusta to fend for myself and it was a little overwhelming to suddenly be alone and not really have anyone I could fully depend on. Sure I had friends that didn't mind extending a helping hand from time to time, but it wasn't anything that was consistent. Once I had put Diane out I didn't have that day to day assistance with my children that I used to have, but Nick came in and gave that back to me. It was refreshing to share the load of parenthood with someone who did it joyfully, so I decided it was in the best interest of my children to try and learn what he liked and disliked so as to not set him off. Little did I know that there was no controlling his over active jealous imagination and to try to appease him I would have to endure things like his humiliating physical exams.

He was no doctor but he would examine my vagina to see if I was having sex, he would hold me down and put passion marks all over my body in order to dissuade people from being attracted to me, and he would tear up my clothes if he thought they were too sexy. He'd then use verbal or physical violence against me if I tried to stop him from doing any of these things.

Sometimes I would just let things slide because I didn't even have the strength to fight back, but most times I would increase the level of violence by introducing weapons into our altercations as I had first done when I pulled the knife on him. The weapons that I began using against him seemed to become fiercer and more ruthless, but never seemed to satisfy my desire to make him suffer; not just for the hurt that he was presently causing but for all the pain I had endured my entire life. Our altercations began to happen more often and it took less to make them occur. It had gotten to the point where he would actually hide out at the lake near my home with a change of clothing. When I would call the police to report what had transpired and describe what he was wearing, he would literally change outside and walk right in front of them. Afterwards he would watch and wait until they left the area and come right back to my apartment.

I couldn't take living in constant torment, not knowing when he was going to possibly take things too far and accidently or purposely kill me. Although I'd tried to commit suicide before, I didn't want to leave my children and so I sought out the last person in the world I thought I would ever go to for protection, Ben. Ben purchased my first gun and then took the time out to take me out for target practice but Nick would become my target in real life. Consequently, after he continually broke into my apartment I had gotten to the point to where I realized the police couldn't keep me safe. Restraining orders could not and did not restrain him from his childish and vicious tantrums, so the next time he broke into my apartment I was waiting for him with gun in hand and my finger on the trigger.

I didn't want to kill him, or maybe I was afraid to suffer the consequences of jail and being torn away from my children. I didn't trust the justice system which always seemed to side with the assailant rather than the victim, so I didn't trust that they would see me shooting him as grounds for self-defense, so my strategy was to shoot at him just to scare him. Upon having me shoot the gun at him several times, he finally stopped breaking into my home and tried a more logical approach to getting back with me. Nick began with just courting me again and we decided to move along with our relationship, but take things nice slow this time. Until the day I went against my friends' advice and made the big mistake of allowing him to spend the night, and have sex with him. The night was perfect and he and I really enjoyed one another along with the kids. I expected it all to end well and then possibly resume more normalcy, until my daughter's grandmother came by to take me and my children to their doctor's appointment.

It all started when I told him that he had to get up and leave because I had to get my children ready for their appointment. Although he and I were working on fixing things I didn't fathom that he thought we could fix them things all in one night. I definitely didn't think I led him to believe we were a couple again, but obviously that's what he thought. In his mind, asking him to get up and leave so I could get everyone ready for their appointment was like telling him I didn't want to see or hear from him again. He didn't think twice before he started wailing on me in my face with my kid's right there in the bed with me. I didn't fight back because I didn't want things to get so violent that my children got hit in the midst of the altercation. So I laid there and took every deliberate blow until he got tired. My babies were screaming and trying to get to me and all I could think about was trying to get to my gun. When Nick finally allowed me to get up he tried to keep me from going into the restroom because he didn't want me to see the damage he had done to my face, he knew I would become hysterical and he was right, but this time he was prepared.

Once in the bathroom I tried time to wash my face in an illogical effort to regain the sight that had diminished from his violent and ruthless blows.

I couldn't believe my face, my nose was bloody and I had two black eyes staring back at me. I immediately ran back to my bedroom and went to grab the gun that I had hidden in my closet, but when I put my hand in the coat pocket that I hid it in earlier it wasn't there. I tried to fumble around in the closet to make sure that it didn't fall between the clothes and that's when I almost lost consciousness. "Looking for something," Nick said, and I just completely froze, I knew what was waiting for me the moment I turned around. The barrel of my pistol was staring me in the face and this maniac now held my life in his hands.

Nick knew my daughter's grandmother was coming and he needed to get out of there before she arrived, therefore he didn't take any time stealing my gun, and leaving through my back door. Rage did not begin to define what I was feeling. I had learned from previous experiences that he always found a way to elude the police, and even if he'd gotten captured he probably would never be convicted for it and I couldn't allow him to get away a second time.

I remembered from the first incident with the knife that one of the reasons he didn't get convicted is because they narrowed the charges against him as a simple domestic abuse and if he had broken into my house and attacked me that would enhance the charges to a felony where he would actually be required to serve time. It was a no brainer for me and I had plenty of experience breaking in windows with my fist so I had no problem hitting it with an object and then ransacking the place and accusing him of doing it.

By the time my daughter's grandmother arrived my place was in shambles. She didn't hesitate to call the police and help me make a report. We had to cancel the doctor's appointment and thought it would be better if I sought out a shelter for battered women. I don't recall the name of the center but can remember how low and worthless they made me feel. My body was sore from enduring all the punches and I could barely move but the people who ran the facility didn't seem to care. They had a list of chores listed for every victim that they were housing and they expected them done right away. There was no compassion for allowing someone the opportunity to let their body heal, instead they expected me to push through the pain and suffering to accommodate their housing rules. I knew I couldn't get the proper rest I needed if I remained in that facility so I decided to leave and return home the same day even though I didn't know whether or not Nick had been apprehended yet. I knew I wasn't going to be comfortable in my home so I was invited by my neighbors to come stay with them temporarily.

I wasn't brave enough to go home, and was very appreciative when my neighbors invited me to stay in their already overly crowded house. I thought I would be safe there, but his obsession may have been stronger than my will to survive; he wouldn't be stopped. It came to the point to where he would even steal his mother's car when she was asleep, just to see if I was in place and who was at my house.

One time in particular, I started allowing my neighbor's sister and her boyfriend to stay at my house in an effort to free up some room for me and my children at her sister's house where I was currently staying, he made an attempt to crawl through the window while they were lying in my bed. If her boyfriend hadn't come to the window and scared him off, then there is no telling what he would have done to her thinking she was me in that bed. Her sister came and informed me what he had done and suggested that I might need to find somewhere I could stay that he didn't know anything about. I had a place in mind I just wasn't certain how safe it was.

* * *

The best option that I could think of at that time might seem asinine to most, but for me it made perfect sense. I decided to go back and reside with Ben, although I knew that choice might come with certain consequences. You might think that *I was just like a dog who returned to eat its own vomit,* because I had become a victim of familiarization and fear of the unknown kept me eating this disgusting bile of dysfunction and abuse. More disgraceful was the fact that I was now feeding it to my children.

On the other hand, there were some advantages in returning home under Ben's roof. For one I was back in the same neighborhood as my daughter's grandmother, which meant I could have more quality time with her. Secondly I didn't have the financial burden of running a household on my own, last but most importantly, I would be safe from the stalker that used to be my boyfriend; at least that was the plan.

Things back at home weren't as bad as I thought they would be except for the ill feelings his former drug addicted prostitute of a girlfriend and I had towards one another. Still I tried my best to respect their relationship and stay out of their way as much as possible, but no matter what I tried to do to accommodate her and ensure her that I wasn't part of my mother's plan to sabotage their relationship and throw her out of the family home, she just could not bring herself to fully trust me. This dilemma caused a lot of friction in the house and she made it known that my presence was not welcomed there. Although she never told me herself, her dirty looks and constant silent treatment said it all. One day I decided to open up the lines of communication between us in hopes of bringing peace to her mind and in the house, but instead of peace all hell would break lose.

I didn't want any distractions when I decided to speak with Pam, so I thought the best time to talk with her would be when Ben wasn't home and my children were asleep. Now that I look back on it I should have waited until I didn't smell that awful stench coming from their bedroom, because at least then I would have known she wasn't getting high off crack and then call herself cracking down on me. Of course she didn't know that was never a safe thing to do, but she would certainly find out soon enough. Our conversation, if that is what you want to call it, didn't go well at all. She was obviously incoherent and had her defenses up. What was meant to be a casual and calm conversation that was supposed to bring peace, into the house escalated into a dreadful argument that brought on more confusion and chaos? As much as I didn't like her before, my respect for her diminished even further as I thought how my children could be affected by the second hand smoke that they were constantly inhaling when that same stench crept underneath the doors into my bedroom which was right across the hall from theirs. She decided she didn't want to remain under the same roof as me and she knew Ben wasn't about to put me out so she did the only thing she could do and that is leave on her own. I should have been happy with her leaving but the truth is that the moment she left I missed her. I missed the fact that she kept Ben occupied and gave me the opportunity to have a somewhat normal life with my babies.

It wasn't long after she left when Ben began his usual sneaky and slimy ways. It all started again with those lustful stares I used to complain to my mom about. No matter how much clothing I had on he still managed to make me feel like he was undressing me with his eyes. I tried to confine myself to my bedroom but it was nearly impossible keeping myself and three children comfortable in that one room all day. Besides I still had to come out to do things like bathe or feed them in other parts of the house, which meant I had to have some contact with him. I recall one day after I had cooked dinner I laid my children down for their naps and proceeded to clean up the kitchen. I was on the phone with Sharon trying not to have any communication with Ben but he kept walking in and out of the kitchen as if he was irritated by the fact that I was on the phone. Finally, after a while he asked if he could talk to me privately about something important. I told him to say whatever he had to say while I was still on the phone, but he insisted that I get off the phone for a brief moment and call my friend right back. I thought he was going to discuss bringing Pam back to live with us, which I would have been cool with, but instead he had the audacity to ask if he could give me oral sex.

I was washing a glass lasagna pan at the moment he approached me with this evil and vulgar suggestion. My eyes started tearing up and I became enraged and without hesitation I threw the glass pan at him. I began to confront him and ask him what the hell was wrong with him and why would he think that I would want him to perform any sexual act on me. I asked him about his supposed relationship with God and didn't he think I had suffered enough with all my mother and boyfriend had put me through but rage had already set in and I found myself once again grabbing a knife and approaching him with it. While I held him at knife point I decided I should call the police, unlike the first time when my mother made a report against him I now had evidence that he meant to violate me sexually and I didn't want him to get away with it. Once again the justice system let me down when they arrived on the scene and saw me holding a knife against him. Surprisingly they began to treat me like the assailant. They drew their guns on me and demanded I put the knife down. Once I had complied with all of their demands they separated us to get both sides of our story. I don't know what he said but they ended up telling me that I had to vacate his premises and go back to my residence because I was over eighteen his vulgar suggestion, although improper, wasn't considered a crime, but me holding a knife on him and throwing the glass lasagna pan at him certainly was.

Of course I wasn't going to risk being arrested and taken away from my children so I had the police take me home where I knew my stalker boyfriend had total access to me once again. In war sometimes enemies join forces to combat with an even bigger enemy such as the case with my boyfriend and me like the saying goes *The enemy of my enemy is now my friend*. It's crazy how I ran between these two insane men who became my best defense from each other. I ended up telling Nick what Ben had done and of course he was ready to be my knight in shining armor, working his way back into my good graces, by helping me seek out and obtain my revenge against Ben.

When Ben had purchased the gun he bought for me to protect myself from Nick he bought himself one as well. Nick and I decided that was the gun that would end his life, so we broke into his house and took the gun. In order to not make it so obvious that we simply wanted the gun we decided to take other valuable possessions as well. How sick was it for me to be exacting revenge with someone who had hurt me so many times before, but the fact that he took the law into his own hands to defend my honor demonstrated to me in some twisted way how much he loved me, but we all know nothing's fair in love and war.

Even though what we had done with Ben gave me temporary satisfaction and brought us closer together for a season, Nick would begin to use it as leverage against me. His threatening to expose what we had done caused me to put up with more of his violent outbursts than I wanted to, However, there was only so much of his violent explosions I could take. One day after slapping me in my face for something, I simply lost it. I grabbed an axe that I kept hidden under my couch and attacked him, but he managed to run in one of the bedrooms and close the door behind him. Once I tasted the blood from my lips I knew I wasn't going to be satisfied until I made him bleed as well, so I proceeded to hack down the bedroom door trying to get to him. God must have sent an angel there to stop me from murdering him, because the only thing that saved his life was his cousin yelling through my mail box slot located on my living room door. This was the last straw as far as my apartment management was concerned and they ended up evicted me out of my apartment, which meant; you guessed it, back to Ben's house!

This time when I moved back in with Ben he had relocated to an apartment because our house went into foreclosure. He had also reconciled with Pam, but I wasn't going to take any chances of her leaving me there for him to try to violate me sexually as he had tried so many times before. So I came to the conclusion that since I was using each of these men to protect me from the other that I should just move Nick in with me. That way I was safe from my stepdad trying to molest me and safe from my boyfriend beating me up. How naïve I must have been.

I had gotten two jobs in order to pay my share of the bills and attempt to save for another apartment. Nick babysat my children and sold drugs on the side, which meant I was an observer of some horrific mind boggling things that drug dealers and drug users do to satisfy their cravings. I came to terms with the fact that drug users would do just about anything to get their next high; from offering sexual favors to loaning their cars and even selling their baby's diapers and formula and drug dealers didn't care what these users gave as long as it proved to be beneficial to them. What I failed to realize was that some drug dealers didn't care who they were selling their venomous poison to, as I later learned that Nick was selling it to someone in his own family. I knew then there were no boundaries that he wouldn't cross to provide for me and my children. The love he had for children that didn't belong to him was fascinating to me and I felt as their mother I should be even more willing to sacrifice myself if it meant the betterment of my family. Nick taught me how to hotwire cars and later I would participate in a few *snatch and go* jobs of a few stores. At the end of the day I was falling more and more into his way of living and slowly but surely losing my morals. I found myself digging deeper and deeper into a bottomless hole with no way out.

* * *

For the most part my plan to use Ben and Nick against one another in an attempt to keep me safe from the other one was not as well thought out as I would have liked it to be. I couldn't stop my boyfriend from going into his jealous rants and he soon became jealous of Ben, which was crazy since he knew he was there to protect me from him. On the other hand, Ben had to work and couldn't be there all the time to protect me when Nick was attacking me. On one particular occasion Nick and I had a disagreement and he ended slapping me and spitting directly in my face. Of course Ben nor Pam was home at the time. I knew I could not beat him in a straight up head to head fight so I convinced him to allow me to handcuff him with some handcuffs that were found in a car he had previously stolen and then I started seducing him. Once the handcuffs were on I grabbed a golf club and I walked over to him very seductively pretending to be there for the sole purpose of arousing him sexually. The fear in his eyes should have been enough to compensate for him slapping me, but the fact that he had spit in my face required that he be punished. "Tonya what are you about to do with that golf club?" He asked in a trembling voice." I answered him, "Why are you suddenly afraid of me?" I replied while twirling the golf club in my hands and walking closer to him. When I had finally got within an arm's length of him I stopped and with tears beginning to roll out of my eyes I asked why won't you stop hitting me. "Oh my God Tonya baby, I'm sorry I'm going to get help it's just that you make me so jealous!" He tried to explain. I answered, "You always get away with it. I can't keep letting that happened," I replied softly while raising the golf club. 'Tonya please don't!" He shouted.

It was too late. Without a second thought the golf club landed across the same arm he used to slap me. Tears began to roll down his face as he said, "Okay Tonya you got me back, now please untie me and let's call it even." I shouted, "It's not even. It could never be even! Do you know how many times you have hit me, scarred up my face, and beat me in front of my children?" I asked with raging anger. I hit him again and again in different places of his body with the golf club that was now bent and if it wasn't for the fact that I thought he was going to lose consciousness I would have continued beating him until it broke. It honestly felt good to strike back after all those times he beat me to a pulp, but I knew there was no way I could remove his handcuffs until Ben got home. Hours after Ben had returned home Nick was still handcuffed to my bed. I began to nurse his wounds (which I was secretly proud of) and sweet talk him into forgiving me until I was able to lose him with no sudden consequences. We eventually made up had and actually gotten back on good terms when one day the police arrived at our house without warning.

Nick managed to run out the back door and elude them, but it was set in his mind that I was still in the state of revenge for all the times he had hit me and set him up to be arrested. There was nothing I could do or say to convince him otherwise so without warning he escaped to Miami. Time or distance didn't seem to weaken this sick bond we had with one another, and although he claimed he didn't trust me, he could not refrain from contacting me. I should have been happy that I was rid of him and all of his unnecessary drama, but instead I was furious that he up and left me with no thought of who was going to babysit for me, keep me safe from Ben and love me, even if it was a sickening and dysfunctional kind of love. I wasn't going to allow him to get by with hurting me again, and although it wasn't me that initiated the call to the police out of revenge, revenge against him became my obsession and I wasn't going to stop until I obtained it. I knew he was wanted for breaking into my apartment, stealing my gun and beating me up in front of my children months prior to his running to Miami. I had often threatened him with turning him whenever he began to misbehave, but I had never acted out on it, and now that he had moved out of the state he felt like I no longer had the upper hand, I would take pride in proving him wrong. I convinced him that I was going to send him money in order to get the exact address where he resided. A few moments after giving me the address the police were surrounding the house and apprehended him for the crimes he committed against me.

I knew in my heart that I was still in love with him and at the end of the day I could not bring myself to go to court to testify against him, so I wasn't surprised when I learned that he received a rather light sentence for his numerous charges. A year in a minimum security prison and a couple years of parole meant that I would be forced to live with Ben without any real means of protection except the two guns that I was secretly keeping in my bedroom. The hatred that I had for him constantly trying to violate me was nothing compared to the hatred I felt for him trying to set up my boyfriend to be arrested. I questioned his motives and wondered if he wanted me to be there without Nick so he could start trying to violate me again. I exerted my revenge on my boyfriend and now it was time that revenge taught Ben that he had to pay for his sins as well.

I got the idea from a movie where these three women who had been constantly mistreated by their boss decided to abstract revenge against him. In one scene in particular they were feeding him rat poison in his coffee. I made up a story of seeing a mouse in the house and insisted that he buy some type of poison to kill it. I knew he would purchase it because he did everything my sister and I asked of him. Once the poison was in the house I made it my business to put it in every meal I cooked for him, hoping that one day he would meet the demise I had set out for him. Thank God that He didn't allow any serious effects from weeks of steady poisoning. I knew that eventually the hate fear and anxiety would cause me to become more paranoid and evil. I started having dreams of just placing both guns to his head and shooting him. It was no doubt time for me to vacate the premises. I knew I could no longer safely nor sanely reside with Ben, so when my mother and sister who had already moved to Jacksonville Florida, extended an offer to me to relocate there, I couldn't refuse. A new territory should mean a new beginning… right?

* * *

Jacksonville, Florida, and all of its sunshine was quite a beautiful sight to behold for me and my two youngest children. My two daughters had visited my mother on several occasions for months at a time, but for me and my son it was a new and exciting experience. Once I arrived there I moved in with Ruth, her live in boyfriend and new baby into their small, one-bedroom apartment. I settled down as best as I could with three children in their small home. Things started turning in my favor rather quickly because it didn't take me long to secure a job, enroll my children in daycare and go back to school myself. Even though it was a lot on me, the feeling of independence enabled me to keep pushing and striving toward goals that seemed to be blocked by others who constantly threw hurdles in my path. Back in Georgia when I tried to go back to school Nick stalked me, often peering through the windows of my classroom or sometimes just lying in wait in the bushes thinking he would catch me interacting with another man. If I was even able to get out of the house in the first place to without having an altercation about what I was wearing, for the most part I knew I would not make it through the day without some sort of disturbance from him. So I decided it was easier to just quit school altogether. Now that the threat of physical or sexual harm no longer lingered in my midst I had the unique opportunity to conquer all my goals and life was finally working out for me. I was making my own money and becoming someone I thought I could be proud of, plus I had the opportunity to meet new people who demonstrated a real love and concern for me by assisting me in my transition. One of these people I would later find myself in a short term relationship with, but the impact he left on my life would last a lifetime.

Sometimes we try to force people to fit into the puzzle of our lives in places they were not intended to fit, and the results often leave us as puzzled as the puzzle we were trying to fix. I think that may best explain the relationship Ike and I had developed. As a friend there was nothing he would not do for me and he became a major part of my very new strong group of supporters, but no matter how much he did for me or how well he treated me I knew he and I were not meant to be in a long monogamous relationship, because from the very beginning he confided in me that he lived with the mother of his child. Ike explained he was only there to help raise their daughter and that I shouldn't have any concerns of his possible infidelity with her. When she started accepted phone calls from me and didn't have any problems or concerns with him staying nights at my house whenever he wanted to, I began to think it may be possible that he was telling the truth and I chose to let down my guard and fully trust him. After all I was no prize possession with my baggage of children from different dads, my mediocre job, and sleeping on my younger sister's couch, yet he remained by my side through some very difficult and trying times, but little did he know that he was in for a long rough ride.

Tribulations were something I had grown accustomed to; a very intricate part of my life. After all isn't life full of trials and errors, and aren't those the ingredients needed to make one bigger, stronger, and more close to God? Yet when you are in the midst of a trial you feel the opposite of all that. It appeared that I was constantly at the end of one trial only to begin the phase of another; that probably best describes the year Ike and I spent together. From losing my residence with my sister and having to move into the YWCA, to another attempted suicide, he steadily proved himself to be as loyal and loving as ever. So one could only imagine why I felt so compelled to leave him and get back with Nick the moment he had gotten released from jail.

I never stopped loving Nick. I accepted the fact that my current relationship with Ike, was on the road to nowhere and I wasn't going to be anything more than his part time lover. Although my prior relationship had its faults, I knew I could depend on Nick to give me one hundred percent of him. Sometimes a hundred percent may equal out to a little of his good side and a whole lot of his bad side.

When it got closer to Nick's release date I made plans to go visit him, just to see if our relationship had a chance of survival. By the time he had gotten out, Ike had helped me to obtain an apartment through the Jacksonville Florida housing program, and I had extended my good fortune with a close friend of mine named Carol, whom I had met at the YWCA. She volunteered to babysit my children while I went to clarify my relationships. In Augusta, I had a party of people waiting to extend their hospitality to me, but I knew I was going to spend the majority of my time with Nick and I knew once we laid our eyes on each other, we would reconcile because that had become our routine.

I thought things were great between Nick and I, the love and passion was there just as I had expected it to be. His family seemed to have gotten over all the drama that he and I had caused and allowed us to genuinely reconcile without interference from them. The three-day trip should have been perfect, but things took a sudden turn when I answered his mother's landline at the same time he did and overheard him talking to a young girl on the phone. "My mother isn't home you can come over now she whispered to him after hearing him say hello. Of course I was distraught and I rudely interrupted before he had a chance to respond. "What the hell?" I asked. "He isn't going anywhere!" I shouted into the phone, and then without warning he came launching from the back room trying to wrestle the phone from my hand. After minutes of tussling over the phone I found the strength to throw him into his mother's glass coffee table that ended up getting shattered. Get the F out of my mama's house he said. Fine I responded I have a boyfriend back at home waiting on me anyway. Just let me make a phone call, I convinced him. While I was explaining to my friend over the phone that I needed a ride and was in the middle of asking him to come pick me up, abruptly Nick butted in the conversation by picking up on another phone and blurted out, "Yeah this is her boyfriend "she and I just got into an argument so she is going to need a ride." Surprisingly my friend answered and said "Sure, just tell me where she is and I will be on my way." I began to tell him the address and before all the information could come out of my mouth, Nick was standing in front of me once again trying to wrestle the phone out of my hand, once he succeeded, he demanded I leave his mother's house right away. Fine I said, "Fine, you act like I don't know anybody here, I will leave so you can sneak and go see your underage little girlfriend. Why are you worried about who picks me up if you got you a little girl that you have to sneak around and see anyway?" "F her," he said. "And F you. I'm about to take a shower and leave and when I get back you better not be in my mom's house." Once he had gotten in the shower I felt like it was the perfect time to call my friend back and have him pick me up after all. I take it that he decided not to get involved with the altercation Nick and I were having because he would not answer any more of my calls. So I decided to utilize that time to check on my children. I reached out to Carol and she let me know my kids were doing well and then she said, "Guess who just pulled up to the house with his friends?" I knew it was Ike. That was the type of person he was, always checking on me and ensuring that my kids and I had everything we needed. She informed him that she was on the phone with me and of course he wanted to hear my voice. I must have forgotten where I was because I had gotten comfortable in the conversation and let my guard down. Ike knew of Nick and his violent ways but he didn't know I was visiting him in an attempt to reconcile things with him. He was under the impression that I was visiting Chandreka which was only partially true. During the conversation Nick had gotten out of the shower and was now eavesdropping. When Ike and I were nearing the end of the conversation and were telling each other that we loved one another Nick went into a rampage. He came running out of the room and slapped me extremely hard across the face knocking me to the ground. I can hear Ike yelling frantically in the receiver, but it was to no avail, Nick just simply disconnected the call. I was silently praying and hoping that the call was the only thing he disconnected.

Can you be in love with two individuals at the same time, my answer would have to be yes, although you may tend to love one more than the other. The fact remains that you can be fond of two individuals at the same time. Some may refer to this as the infamous love triangle, I was clearly in the midst of one. After that phone call you would think that Nick and I would finally go our separate ways. Maybe that would have been a possibility if we had a so called normal relationship. The pathetic truth is that Nick and I made up in our usual nauseous way, still I couldn't get my mind off of Ike and how much I betrayed and hurt him. I thought I wanted things between us to be over because I was tired of becoming second fiddle to his baby mother and whomever else he was dating but I didn't reason that love had a mind of its own and could cause such a tremendous amount of confusion in people's lives.

* * *

My visit was only supposed to be for a few days and it was nearing its conclusion, so my plan was to try to keep peace with Nick until I left and then go home and try to salvage whatever relationship was left between me and Ike. On the day I was due back in Jacksonville I purchased a one-way ticket from the local Greyhound station and to my surprise Nick purchased one too. When I asked him what he was doing he said he was going back to Florida to live with me that the girl who was on the phone with him earlier trying to get him to sneak over didn't mean anything to him and that he didn't want to be without me anymore. I had mixed feelings about this because on the one hand it felt good knowing he cared enough to stop everything that was going on in his life to make me his priority, but on the other hand I knew he would ruin any chance of me working things out with Ike.

The long Greyhound ride back to Jacksonville gave us a chance to converse without any interruptions. It reminded me how much he always made me laugh and how much he catered to my every need. In those ten hours I started looking at him differently and began imagining that there may be some hope for our already distressed relationship. By the time we arrived to my apartment I was really missing my children and they astonished me when they revealed how much they missed him. Even after all of our altercations they still referred to him as daddy and clung to him almost immediately. He volunteered to cook something for my family to eat and while he was cooking, Carol and I began catching up on all the things I missed out on while I was gone. Carol and I were sitting on the stairs that just happened to be facing the front door, my screen door was open allowing the fresh air to blow in, but air wasn't the only thing that blew in that day. Out of nowhere Ike appeared at my front door and he was astonished to see me since I had not contacted him since the incident when he overheard Nick assault me. The look on his face was shock but little did he know the real surprise was cooking in the kitchen.

In the midst of him welcoming me back from my trip Nick, who was still in the kitchen, overheard Ike and I talking came into the room to see what was going on. There they stood face to face with one another, the two men in my life who each held a significant part of my heart and my heartache. If I thought that for a moment either of them was about to back down from the other, I was wrong. Ike tried to get confrontational with Nick, which was very shocking because I had never seen him act violently towards anyone before. But I managed to convince him not to cause any disturbances in front of my children, and I managed to convince Nick to go back into the kitchen and continue preparing our supper. Once Nick left the room I knew the friction between the two men was too much to enable them to stay under the confines of one roof so I had to think of something quickly to get Ike to agree to leave my place without causing a huge scene. Since I knew his sister resided in the same apartment complex as I did I agreed to meet him over there within the hour. I tried my best to hurry through dinner because I did not want Ike to return to my apartment and start some sort of conflict. I knew I had to find a way out of that apartment and make it to his sister's house, but I ended up sending Carol to meet up with Ike right after dinner to send the message that I would not be able to make it out of the house that night because I didn't want to make Nick angry and risk him fighting me and that I would try calling him the next day. When Carol returned I could tell by the look on her face that his response to my message was not going to be anything endearing. Ike's message was that he was on his way back to my house if I didn't show up over to his sister's house in the next few minutes and that I should not be afraid of Nick or his threats because he was willing to come and physically remove Nick from my home. Eventually I came up with an excuse to get me out of the house where I could secretly meet up with Ike and try my best to persuade him to leave the situation alone and allow me to handle it on my own terms, but the truth of the matter is I wanted time to decide who or what I really wanted.

Once I arrived at his sister's house I was instantly introduced to another side of Ike, a dark and violent side. Not that he was getting physically violent with me or anything like that, but the gun in his hand let me know that he was adamant about not allowing me to return home to my abuser, an abuser I loved. There I stood confused in my mind about these two men but not confused about the fact that Nick would be looking for me if I didn't return to my apartment in a timely manner. I knew this wasn't a time for me to decide who or what I wanted, I just needed to get back home at this point. Ike asked me why I had even contacted Nick in the first place when my visit was supposed to be for the purpose of seeing my oldest daughter. Then he asked how in the world I could bring this violent man back home after he had heard him assault me. I don't know if I could explain the fact that having all of Nick meant having Nick's good and bad side as well and it felt better than the part-time relationship he was giving to me. Plus abuse was all I knew. I reminded Ike that if I wasn't back at a certain time Nick would come looking for me and then want to fight me. I kept trying to make my way out of his sister's bedroom door where he had taken me to speak to me privately, but he kept blocking me from leaving. I would have bombarded my way out of her room, but he had never been this physical or confrontational with me. Since his back was to the door I wasn't certain if his family knew that he was holding a small caliber gun in his hand the whole time he was blocking me and telling me that I wasn't going anywhere. After what seemed like an eternity Carol came over to inform us that Nick had left the house in a rage and was looking for me. I tried to get Ike to let me leave and that's when he cocked his gun and said "not without me. As we were walking out the door he asked his friends to accompany us and without hesitation they agreed. While we were walking back towards my apartment I could see Nick coming from a distance and my heart suddenly dropped. Ike noticed my fear and it appeared to enrage him even more. "Does this dude have you that scared" he asked me and before I could even answer I heard the gunshot.

When I woke up I was back in my apartment lying down on the couch and paramedics were putting ammonia sticks underneath my nostrils in an effort to bring me back to consciousness. Apparently I had passed out outside when I heard the gunshot thinking Ike had shot Nick and someone had to carry me back home. After the paramedics were certain that I was alright they left me in the care of Ike and some neighbors. I didn't know where Nick was at the time and to be honest I mentally could not digest everything that had just taken place. Before I could even regain my thoughts, the police were knocking at my door and they had Nick with them. I didn't open the door right away. I had to allow Ike time to escape

The police asked me a series of questions but I decided not to cooperate with them because I didn't want to see Ike arrested for trying to defend my honor. Nick knew I was withholding information and he was heartbroken because he felt foolish after the police had escorted him back to my place in hopes that I would give a statement incriminating Ike. Although I was grateful that he was alive I was in no way about to incriminate someone who was trying to protect me. The police informed Nick that without my cooperation there wasn't anything else that they could do to assist him except help him leave my residence if he still felt unsafe there. It was sad to see him leave but my mind was made up and there was no turning back for me. I guess in some strange sort of way the love triangle was finally over and I was ready to live with my decision. The only question was for how long.

* * *

Nick was now back in Georgia, but things between my current boyfriend and I didn't go as well as expected either. Although he was showing me more attention and revealing more of his genuine feelings for me, he still insisted on living with his daughter's mom and I could not get passed that. He promised he was only going to reside with her long enough for his daughter to start elementary school which would have been coming up within a couple of years or so but I wasn't sure if I wanted to wait that long or if I even believed him, but against my better judgement I decided to stay in another unhealthy relationship

One day while I was cleaning my apartment my phone rang and to my astonishment it was the Georgia Parole office asking to confirm a transition for Nick to relocate from Georgia to my residence in Florida, I pretended the phone was getting a bad connection and I disconnected the line. I immediately called Nick and told him about the call from the parole board and before I could get all of the words off of my tongue he intercepted and asked me what I said to them. Then he shocked me to the core when he begged me to please allow the transition to go through and give our love one final try. I told him I needed some time to think about it and I would let him know shortly. Every day I went through the why and why nots of each relationship and I just couldn't seem to make an informed decision. Finally, Carol who had just recently gotten her own place suggested I allow her to use her three way in order to call the psychic hotline. Thinking it couldn't hurt I went along with what I thought was an outrageous suggestion.

I waited patiently for the stupid music and recording to go off before being connected to a live person. The lady gave me a list of potential life circumstances that I could choose from that she could go into deeper details about. Out of all the things she named, I undoubtedly wanted to discuss my love life and I reluctantly relayed this to the psychic. She then paused for a moment and then said' I see a man". I laughed to myself because I thought that was basic information that anybody could guess, but when she said "wait I see two men, one who lives in the same town as you and the other who lives a different state, she had my full undivided attention. "Which of these gentlemen would you like to know about first" she asked and I replied the one in town with me? Surprisingly she was on point with everything she said as she described our so called relationship to a T. She began by telling me how he loved me but how he suffered with commitment problems and that he enjoyed dating multiple women at the same time. She confirmed what I always knew to be true in my heart, that even though he loved me, she didn't see a future for us together. Then she began to tell me about Nick who was currently living back in Georgia but before she began to go in depth about our relationship she threw me for a loop and asked if my hair was blond? If I was amazed about the knowledge she had of me and Ike, then I was completely astonished that she knew my hair color since I'm not a natural blond and had just recently dyed my hair. Yes, I told her in anticipation of whatever other words was going to flow from her lips. She responded, this man loves you and you and he are what the world considers to be soul mates. She said he flirted with other women, but his love and devotion were to me. At this point I began to feel a bit more comfortable with her and I decided I would see if she could give me any insight about a weird dream that I had a couple of nights before. In the dream I had given birth to two babies and when the second baby came out I was showing him to Ike, but when the second baby came out with teeth already in his mouth and it made Ike scream, which made me wake up screaming. Her interpretation of the dream was that I would have two babies either twins or babies very closed together with Nick and that Ike would be hurt by it, but the younger baby would be born stronger and more mature than the first baby. She said that the babies would not only be born close together, but that they would be the same sex. She said Nick and I would be together for seven years as a trial period and if we made it passed those seven years we would remain together till death parted us. I soon found myself drifting away from Ike and starting to pursue the idea of salvaging the relationship between Nick and me. After weeks of communicating with him, I thought I would throw caution to the wind by finally agreeing that he could make the transfer of his parole to Florida and we could give our love another try.

 I didn't want the same thing to happen to Nick that had happened before so I called Ike and informed him of my decision to get back with Nick. Ike wasn't ready to give up so fast either because he loved me or he just didn't want to lose me to the man he had come to despise. However, my decision was made and I knew it was time for me to move on and to prove it I agreed to give Nick the baby he had been yearning for since the day we met, which met I had to have the implant that was supposed to prevent pregnancy for at least five years surgically removed. Maybe having his child might very well be the bond that we needed to fix our relationship.

As soon as we found out I was pregnant things started really looking up for us, but things began taking a downward spiral when I started having complications with the pregnancy and had to be put on complete bedrest in the first part of my third trimester, but it was to no avail. After many complications the hospital allowed me to take the contraction monitoring equipment home and taught Nick how to use it and take my vital signs. The fact that he became the sole breadwinner in the house and my part time nurse caused us a lot of distress, so I thought it was a good idea for him to begin socializing and hanging out with some friends after work. That simple gesture would turn out to be a grave mistake.

I was always respectful, well-mannered, and friendly, but I was not much of a socializer, Nick was the complete opposite. He was forever trying to convince me to come out of my shell, learn to trust people and allow people to get close to me, but when you have been violated time after time, trust becomes more difficult to give. Still for the sake of argument, I agreed to meet these mysterious people he came home and bragged about nearly every day, after our baby came. My reservations about us meeting this new couple weren't just a result of my prior bad experiences, it was also because I began noticing that shortly after he started hanging with these people he began to display subtle changes for the worst. His already abusive and jealous behavior seemed to escalate. He started becoming flirtatious with other women and he started hanging out at all times of the night. Pornography in the form of magazines and videos were constantly being found all around the house and sex became a list of demands I could not or would not meet. Although we were supposed to be at one of the happiest times in our lives, our relationship steadily declined and something told me that these people had something to do with it.

Although I had the contraction machine at the house connected to me, I still almost gave birth to my baby at home when my water suddenly broke after an altercation between us. Although I cannot recall what the argument was about, I do recall the urgency of suddenly going into labor without warning. I was grateful to make it to the hospital in the nick of time and gave birth to my baby right away without the assistance from my doctor. A resident of the hospital who just happened to be there visiting someone ended up delivering my son while wearing his ordinary clothing that day.

I'd never had any of my other children's dads in the labor room with me, so I was comforted knowing that he and I would share this experience and it most certainly brought us closer together. Now we finally had something in common; a sort of monument of our love that we made together. He was a beautiful baby, the only child I made on purpose. Yes, Nathaniel brought much needed joy back into our home.

Nick and I had agreed to get my tubes tied after our son was born. I was all for it after watching him drool over his son I felt like we had everything we needed to complete our family. I mean I now had a set of boys as well as girls and four children seemed like more than enough to support for such a young couple. I didn't recall the dream, or prophecy, that the psychic and I had discussed almost a year earlier, but two days later when the doctors came into my room to begin my tubal procedure, I suddenly felt the need to change my mind. I don't know what it was and I most certainly wasn't planning for another baby after just giving birth but, getting my tubes tied was not an option. I had a lot of resistance coming from the hospital staff and Nick, who all felt like I should have the procedure done since I was a young black woman with little education, on government assistance, and now with four children from four different men. I had a lot of factors as to why I should have my tubes tied, nevertheless, with all those opposing opinions, I was adamant about my choice, and nothing or no one could change my mind.

The new baby brought some much needed changes into our lives; joy and laughter became residents of our home. After eight weeks or so of recovery I was ready to go back to work and help out financially. I got a job working the opposite hours of Nick and things seemed to be going rather well, except for the fact he was still constantly begging me to meet these mysterious people whose house he loved to visit every single evening after work. No matter how long I tried to put it off or what excuses I tried to use to avoid meeting them he was determined that we hang out together. He often accused me of being unfriendly or preventing him from having a social life. I had made him a promise and he expected me to honor it. Maybe I should have followed my intuition or told him about the near death experience I'd had when I entrusted people who took advantage of my youth, inexperience, and kindness. I'd been naïve about the dangers of the world, and I had the emotional scars to prove it. I knew I could not continue keeping secrets and it was high time I opened up and was honest with him if I expected him to understand where I was coming from. I thought that by sharing some of the most horrible and scariest events that happened in the short time that I had lived in Jacksonville I could somehow persuade him to be more cautious about who he allowed to enter into our space, but more important whose space we would enter into.

* * *

The first occurrence happened with Carol while staying at the YWCA when another resident invited us to go over to her older uncle's house one day while I was off from work and my children were in daycare. She claimed that her much older uncle had a house where we could hang out and do things like watch music videos and make phone calls which was appealing to Carol and myself since we both had people out of town we both wanted to make long distance calls to. On the surface he seemed to be a very nice older gentleman who was enjoying his retirement years. He was a man of very few words, and for the most part stayed out of our way each time we made the visit to his house. After going to his house on several occasions my roommate had wanted to go use his phone even though his niece wasn't there to accompany us. Carol needed to talk to her daughter and her dad who was living in another state about something important and I agreed to accompany her.

Once we made it to his house we weren't certain whether or not he would allow us in without having his niece present, however to my surprise he did. The phone call that was only supposed to take a minute went longer than anticipated, but he didn't seem to mind. Since I had paid some teenagers to watch my children once they got out of daycare, I wasn't in that much of a hurry to get back. We made a day of watching his television and running up his phone bill. When it was nearing our curfew we called out to him to let him know that we were leaving. We never noticed anything strange until we walked to his front door and that's when it hit us. Every other time that we came over, there were keys that hung in the keyhole of the inside of his front door and this time they were not there, which meant we couldn't get out of the house. When we asked him to open the door and told him we had to get going, his reply was not until I get what I want. In my mind I'm saying that he was probably only playing, maybe trying to teach us a lesson since we obviously knew his niece and could easily identify him if he did anything inappropriate to us. He said, "I am not opening that door until you ladies pay me for all those long distance calls you made on my phone." Surprised that he even knew about the calls so quickly, I said sure when I get paid, I will bring you your money. "Oh," he replied sarcastically, "You and your little friend are definitely going to pay me, yawl done ran my phone bill up, ate my food up, drank up my alcohol, and disrespected my house for weeks and yawl going to pay me, pay me tonight or yawl not going anywhere." "I have children back at the Y, and it's getting close to the time for our curfew,'" I nervously tried to plead with him. His response was cold and wicked as he stated he didn't care what dilemmas I had all he knew was that neither of us was leaving his house until he got paid. "How can we pay you, when we just told you that we don't have any freaking money?" Carol shouted at him? "Who said yawl got to pay me with money?' He asked. "What are you talking about then? Cause we're not about to have sex with you," I added. "I don't want to have sex with you ladies, there is no telling what y'all have. I want to watch y'all have sex with each other," he said calmly, with a slick look on his face. "Hell no! Are you crazy? I'm not gay," I shouted. "Now open the door or we are going to call the police." "On what phone, he asked while grabbing it from the wall socket. We were in trouble and time was ticking as we needed to meet our curfew. I especially needed to relieve the teenagers of their babysitting duties before their parents called the authorities on me and possibly reported me for abandonment.

I became frustrated and impatient with him and his sick shenanigans. I didn't know what caused his drastic personality change, but I knew I wasn't going to allow him to violate me by forcing me to do something I was not comfortable with, and I knew I had a very limited time to make it back home to my children. No matter how hard my roommate and I pleaded with him to let us go, our words fell on deaf ears. Eventually his coldness brought my roommate to tears as she too had been a victim of sexual assault. Although I was quite fearful about what the outcome of the night would hold for us, my fear evolved into rage. I knew he wasn't going to let us out of there of his own free will, and if we wanted freedom we were going to have to free ourselves. Thinking back to when I had used the lure of sex to entrap Nick when I had beat him with a golf club for hitting me, I suggested to my friend that she and I do the same thing. I told her that we would pretend that we were going to accommodate his sick desire to see us have sex with one another and eventually we would attack him for the keys that he had in his pocket.

Once we had devised the plan we immediately put it into action. My roommate lured him over into his couch and started to dance seductively in front of him. I suggested we have a drink but in reality I was trying to make my way into the kitchen so I could find something to strike him over the head with. As I was pouring the drinks I observed a cast iron frying pan located on top of his stove. I waited impatiently as I tried to get her attention to let her know I was prepared to attack. I was just about to pick up the frying pan while she was still seducing him with her dancing, but he turned around to see what was taking me so long with the drinks. My friend was able to turn his neck back towards her as I explained that I was coming. As soon as his head was turned and he showed signs of being captivated by her again I rushed and grabbed the pan and proceeded to hit him over the head with it. Amazingly he stood up to fight back right after being struck by me with all my strength and that in itself startled me. I was grateful that Carol joined in the fight because I was clearly no match for him. We had broken several lamps over his head and almost knocked him out before he was beginning to show any signs of giving up. After minutes of tussling and fighting we were able to retrieve the keys and we knocked him out long enough to run and get help from one of his neighbors down the street. We contacted the police and informed them what had happened but when they confronted him he claimed that we were trying to rob him. After realizing they could not sort out the stories the police decided to just take Carol and me home.

I was hoping that my very dramatic but true story would compel Nick to change his mind about being so trusting, but it didn't. Instead of looking at things from a new perspective he insisted that the incident that transpired happened because my friend and I didn't know the guy, or even his niece who introduced us in the first place, that well. He said the girl may have never actually been related to the man in the first place and just helped him lure his victims over into his territory where the man could victimize them. At the end of the day he could have been absolutely right, but that was my point exactly, not being so trusting. If this story didn't convince him maybe my next one would.

This time it was with a guy named Marcus that I had known briefly, who I knew had an interest in me. I didn't return the same feelings toward him because I thought he may have been an undercover homosexual. Even though I don't condone the homosexual lifestyle I was not judgmental towards him or anyone else for that matter. I simply had absolutely no desire to get involved with him beyond the boundaries of friendship and thought I made that clear to him. To spend time with me he would volunteer to take me to and from work. I thought his kindness was contributed in part to his liking me and the fact he wanted to help a young mother who was struggling to make an honest living for her family. One day he let me know that he felt like I was using and abusing our friendship just to get what I wanted out of him. He stated he was more like a taxicab than anything else and he was tired of being my sucker. I tried to convince him that he was wrong but he wasn't hearing me. When he asked why I never hung out with him not particularly in a romantic setting but in a friendly atmosphere, I couldn't defend myself because I knew he was right. I felt rather guilty about it because he was picking me up from work at some of the most inconvenient times for any person to get out of their bed. I knew I had to do something if I wanted him to continue getting rides from him because I had come to depend on him. Honestly I was just using him, but I didn't like how guilty that made me feel. So I decided to go against my better judgment and offer to accompany him to a movie or something under the condition of him allowing me to bring Carol. That was fine with him being that he had a friend that could double date with her, but when I remembered that I was babysitting my nephew I explained that he would have to accompany us as well and we agreed to watch a movie at his place. The night began badly and ended awfully. It all started with their movie choice. Malcolm X and his comment of the blue eyed devil in one of its lines made them laugh and rant about all Caucasian people, but it really upset me and my Caucasian friend. I couldn't blame her one bit when she locked herself in his bathroom to sob overwhelmingly. I tried desperately to get her to come out of that bathroom and to insure her I didn't appreciate their ignorance nor did I want to tolerate it any more than she did. No matter what I said to her she refused to come out and before long I had to use the restroom. It was obvious that she wasn't going to open the door so Marcus suggested that I use his upstairs bathroom. Grateful that I could finally relieve myself I asked him to show me where it was located and he directed me upstairs into his bedroom. Not thinking anything of it I immediately went into the restroom to use it. As soon as I exited the bathroom he grabbed me and threw me onto his bed and forced himself on top of me. He started saying weird things and asking asinine questions like did he look like he had a wrapper on his head. When I asked him what he was talking about, his response was, "Do you consider me to be a sucker? I am not a sucker," he blatantly repeated in my ear. "Okay, okay you are not a sucker and I never said you were, so please let me get up. I need to check on my friend," I pleaded with him." "No, you are not getting up," he said. "And why did you even bring that cracker to my house?" Shocked at his sudden rudeness and prejudice I yelled, "What did you just say?" I asked in frustration. "Man just get up off of me and let me and my friend go," I begged. but he continuously refused. With no other option available to me I started screaming from the top of my lungs for Carol to come help me. Before long she was standing at the door asking him to get off of me so that she and I could go home. "Get out of my room B!" He told her. Matter of fact get out of my house." "Not until you let her go," she said. Suddenly he jumped off of me and ran over to attempt to push her out of the doorway and that's when I jumped up to try and push my way through the door as well, but he would not allow me to leave the room with my friend and he wouldn't allow her to enter his room, which made me believe he was going to try to rape me or something. I became very frightened and furious. I looked around the room to find something to hit him with. I noticed a hammer nearby and I grabbed it to hit him with it. As soon as he saw the hammer in my hand he tried to wrestle it from me, and the three of us started rumbling all over his bedroom. I finally jumped on his back and placed him into a choke hold, while my friend wrestled the hammer out of his hand. Surprisingly enough my nephew and his friend slept soundly during the whole altercation, which brought a little comfort to me in this insane situation. Once Carol and I had broken me out of his bedroom we ran downstairs to call the police. The hysterical phone call to the police woke up his friend who was shocked by all the chaos. After hearing everything that had transpired his friend convinced us to allow him to drive us home and persuaded us to leave with him before the police arrived and I obliged because from my experiences, I really didn't want to involve the police either. Reluctantly we chose to ride back home to the YWCA with them and although the ride was quiet my temper was raging and I wanted revenge. The moment we arrived back at the Y I told my friend to take my nephew inside and I would be in there shortly. I was pretending to gather all of our belongings. After I saw that they were back inside the facility safely, I grabbed my nephew's diaper bag, which was full of large ready-to-feed infant formula, and swung it into their car's windshield, cracking it badly, then I ran into the facility before they could do anything, but once I made it inside I remembered this person knows where I work.

* * *

I was in tears by the time I finished reminiscing and sharing these hideous stories with Nick and I was hoping that revealing some of these horrific encounters would explain why I was not a really sociable person, and why I just chose to meet people on my own terms and in my own time. Unfortunately, Nick needed to be a socialite and his weakness for quickly trusting people would be the demise that would forever affect my family and its spiritual foundation.

The stress of raising my children was starting to weigh heavily on me. Nick helped me out in a lot of areas but there were even more areas in which he brought about more stress and confusion than I could tolerate. The new associations that he developed became a thorn in my side. What was meant to be a moment of leisure for him became a ritual and our family began feeling its effects. I wasn't much in the mood for meeting up with people who were able to cause so much confusion in so little time, but I needed an outlet, so work became a time of relief for me; an escape from the home that was becoming my prison, with Nick serving as warden. Unfortunately, this was also the time that I was separated from my newborn baby whom I was breast feeding. Since he was my only planned baby, I was more emotionally attached to him which made me a bit more sensitive than usual. Nick blamed my increased sensitivity on the fact that I shut myself off from the world, even at work, I just performed my duties and I chose not to converse with many people. The only person who seemed to have the key to unlock my shell while I was a work was a young lady who began ministering the Word of God to me. Listening to the comforting words of the Bible brought peace to my troubled soul. After all it was God who had brought me out of countless tribulations. I felt I had experienced His genuine love and mercy on so many levels, but at this point in my life my tank was on empty and it needed to be refueled quickly.

My coworker eventually convinced me to attend her church and I thought it was just the thing to revitalize me spiritually. Although Nick had observed me reading my Bible and praying many times, he and I had never attended church together. I also knew that his family was a very spiritual and faith based people who attended church ritually, but I didn't know just how close to God he was or how close to God he desired to be. I was excited about asking Nick to attend church with me. He was even more agreeable to going to church once he knew the young lady was married and her husband was going to accompany us to church as well. When they picked us up we noticed that she was wearing a very long dress without any makeup on and it occurred to me that this may be one of those "holiness" churches that I grew up in and almost grew to hate, but I didn't want to judge the book by its cover and decided to hold off on my opinion until I had experienced their service for myself.

My intuitions about the church proved to be right. I walked into a very small church filled with women who were dressed in long skirts or dresses, no makeup, barely any jewelry and old fashioned hairstyles; the same religious traditions Ben's organization believed in, and tried to shove down my throat. I immediately wanted to turn around and march right out of there and if they were going to try to convince me again that God was more concerned about my outer appearance than my heart, then I didn't want any part of them or their beliefs. I would have packed up my family and stormed right out of there if we'd had our own transportation, but since we rode with someone else we were stuck. I thought I was coming to be revitalized, but from prior experience I knew this so called holiness group usually preached judgment, hell and brimstone and barely spoke of God's love. From my perspective they believed God's love and faithfulness was based on following a bunch of men's laws and traditions; not God's unmerited grace. My spirit was down and in the dumps when I entered the church; God only knew what state my spirit was going to be in when I made my exit.

The devotional part of the service was very anointed. Although they didn't have much in the way of musical instruments, their drummer and keyboardist were extremely talented and kept their entire church on their feet praising God. When Pastor Griffin finally had his opportunity to preach I was astonished by his sincerity, love, gentleness, boldness and anointing. He was an old fashioned man and it seemed fitting that his church compliment him in that area as well, but what made him different from some of his wide eyed staring me down congregation, was the fact that he wasn't a judgmental person at all. Their stares probably came from the fact that I was dressed totally opposite of what they obviously believed was appropriate for a woman. My makeup and pants said to them that I was a women of the world and that I had not come into full submission to God, however during the close of the service God used this preacher to not only speak into my life and what he had to say would leave me and my judgers speechless.

In his closing Pastor Griffin asked us to form a prayer request line. I didn't hesitate to get in line because I knew I needed God and I wasn't embarrassed to demonstrate it. Just like Apostle McCoy, this man seemed to know a lot about my life and seemed to have the ability to see into my future. I didn't understand the gifts of the spirit at that time and the fact that he was able to speak in what I now know as tongues was a complete mystery to me. I wasn't as impressed with the tongues as I was with the fact that he knew so much about me without ever having met me, and I hadn't revealed much of myself to my coworker either. The words he spoke about my present situation paled in comparison to the effect he brought when he spoke about what God was showing him for my future. "You are not going to be a bench warmer," he told me, as he was putting oil on my head and hands. God is going to use you mightily. God is going to begin to use your vocal chords and speak through you, and He is going to open up your eyes in the spiritual realm. Do not depend on Nick," he said. And that's when I really started paying attention because I had never revealed my boyfriend's name to anyone. His prophecy rang in my ear for weeks and the more we came back to visit the church the more God seem to speak through this man of God about his desire to use me. I did not comprehend any of the prophecies, or the dreams and visions I began having. If only I had waited for the revelation of God to give me the wisdom, I could have saved me and my family from so much pain and torment. I remember a particular vision of me dancing with a man in a tuxedo. I looked so beautiful and happy, dressed in a Cinderella gown as a man twirled me around in his arms. I strained my eyes to see the face of the prince that had me so mesmerized and was startled to see that it was the cartoon image of the beast from the show Beauty and the Beast. Why was I dancing with this creature and what in the world was he trying to lure me into?

* * *

"This girl is into church just like you," Nick would often tell me, she teaches Bible study at her house all the time and she could probably help us to understand the Bible better, and all that stuff that Pastor Griffin has been telling you. I think that hanging out with a couple that attends church would be good for us. Besides her boyfriend works with me and they live in our neighborhood, so can you please give them a chance, so I don't I look stupid going over there without you all the time. They are probably thinking you are not a real Christian and that you are just like some of those religious people at that church that judge people without even meeting them," he said convincingly. He promised me that these friends were not judgmental, and that they also believed as we did, that God did not judge people from the outside, but searched their hearts. He knew I didn't understand the prophecies and that I was not comfortable talking to anyone about them, because people started exhibiting jealousy towards me; at least I felt that way about it. I don't think they understood why a big God would choose to use a little nobody like me, and to be honest I had asked God the same question for many years, but, Nick was absolutely right, I was no better than some of those from the church who I felt looked down on me. I wanted to change that immediately. The perfect time to start was now and with these people. I was willing to attend one of her Bible studies, but I would learn more from her than I ever bargained for.

The first time we hung out with his friends Shawn, and Louise, they came over to our apartment to play an innocent game of cards. They both seemed genuinely nice, soft spoken and down to earth people who loved God but weren't the "religious" type. They had four children, each from separate relationships, but seemed to mesh their already-made families well. More importantly than anything, they brought fun and excitement back into mine and Nick's relationship. While we were playing cards Louise inquired about my religious beliefs, stating that Nick had spoken to her about how much I loved God. During the conversation I became more and more intrigued with her knowledge of the Bible, and I was assured just like Nick told me that she was the perfect person to ask about the recent prophecies that had been poured into my spirit by Pastor Griffin and his Junior Pastor Henry week after week in the church services. I began telling her about the preachers telling me that I wasn't going to be a benchwarmer, that God was going to open up my eyes into the spiritual realm, and begin utilizing my vocal chords to speak through me. I also told her about the time he said I was pregnant in the spiritual realm, and that I was going to give birth in the spirit, which was the most confusing of the prophecies, since I had just recently found out, that I was pregnant in the physical realm as well after not having my tubes tied. Both of these pregnancies would prove to be overwhelming and I wasn't certain if I was excited about either one of them. I was having dreams of giving birth to my baby then losing it. The only question left to ask was which one of these babies I would lose, the physical, the spiritual, or both.

* * *

Nick was excited that I was finally opening up to someone and agreed to accompany me to the prayer meeting that was set up by Louise with a group of her friends to ask God to give me wisdom concerning all the prophesies. Once we arrived, Louise briefly introduced me to the few women she had invited to pray with us, and Nick and Shawn left the room and went upstairs. soon the ladies gathered around in a circle and held hands as Louise began to pray. Everything seemed ordinary at first, but without warning I fell down as my knees suddenly collapsed. Then the women started speaking in what sounded to me like gibberish all the while touching me all over my body. I didn't understand what they were doing so I just laid there frightened on the floor, and watched them move all around me as they began singing and praying over me. I noticed every time they reached a particular part of their song where they needed to say Jesus, they started going back into the gibberish and once again I couldn't comprehend what they were saying. After what seemed to be a long time for me, Nick came downstairs to see what all the ruckus was about. When he noticed me looking almost lifeless on the floor he inquired what the hell they were doing to me, but he never got a chance to hear their response because Shawn immediately came and convinced him to leave us alone and allow us to continue the prayer meeting. I wish to God he would have not listened to Shawn and rescued me because the moment he went back up the stairs things became even stranger.

As soon as I was able to stand on my own two feet I started acting erratic and I began participating in their weird singing and gibberish. Again Nick came to investigate and this time he didn't like what he observed, so he ran over to grab me and carry me out of their home, but again I collapsed to the floor. The women asked him to leave me alone, but he insisted that something was strange and he didn't like the way he saw them touching me while praying things neither of us could comprehend. Nick who had always picked me up and carried me around even with my pregnancy weight, tried several times to pick me off of the floor, but could not lift me. It was as if someone had stuffed me with a ton of bricks. Eventually Shawn came and convinced him that nothing was out of the ordinary and again he left me alone.

After a while the other ladies left the house and Louise and I were left alone to sit on her couch to converse more about the spiritual realm. I was always infatuated with the Bible and its many miracles and mysteries. I was always one to believe that today God was the same God of the Bible days, and could perform the same mind boggling miracles. I became infatuated and maybe even jealous about her unbelievable stories of her personal interactions with God and I desired what I thought she had, which was a personal relationship where God would actually converse with me as He did her and the people in the Bible. Little did I know that there are many gods that people pray to and she and I were definitely not praying to the same one.

While we were conversing, out of nowhere a light, like from a flashlight being pointed to the ceiling, appeared on her ceiling. The light began to expand and brighten in radiance on the ceiling until what appeared to be a scene from a projector appeared. I could not believe it, but I was actually staring at a scene with a ladder and what looked like angels ascending and descending from it. A man dressed in a purple robe appeared on the ladder and the man seemed to be staring from the ceiling back down at us. I was absolutely mesmerized by the magnificence of what I was seeing, but suddenly the room was blindingly lit and there was an overwhelmingly eerie presence in the room. Louise grabbed me by the hand and told me to just repeat thank you, I receive it. So I held up my free hand and began doing as she had instructed me to do. While I was chanting the words "thank you" repeatedly, something caused my eyes to close tightly and I could not open them up. While my eyes were closed I could hear strange communications and evil laughter as if ghost or some evil entity was in the room. I wanted to wake up from what I felt was like an evil trance, but I was startled and completely frozen in fear and disbelief. After a while the light and the evil voices left and she and I were left alone in the room once again. She informed me that my prayer session was over and that I could get Nick and go home. On the way out, Nick quietly stated that we were never coming over there again. I noticed that she was standing in the background with a grin on her face, because she knew I had to come back and nothing or no one could stop me.

**

I started going about my daily life as usual, but I wasn't my usual self. I tried praying and reading my Bible as I always did, but I began to be slapped in the face by unseen forces every time. When I prayed or said the name of Jesus my voice would become deep like a man and I would nearly choke on my own saliva. My personality was changing and sometimes I even felt like I had multiple personalities, because I would go from being belligerent and spiteful to charming and considerate in minutes. I could not figure out why, nor could I control it. I turned into some sex maniac and nothing Nick did could satisfy my sick urges. Also the fights with him that I used to try so desperately hard to avoid, were now appetizing to say the least. Everyone could tell that there was something strangely different about me but no one could explain my drastic changes, nor could they explain why my eyes would suddenly close without any effort on my part, and why for the life of me, I could not open them. Also I started waking up at all hours of the night needing to see Louise. A while back I was absolutely adamant about not going to meet Nick friends, and now I was constantly demanding Nick take me over there. Each time I went to her house the phenomenon seemed to increase in its weirdness, I started doing things like reenacting Jesus on the cross, washing her feet, and allowing her to rub on my boyfriend's bare chest and other body parts while reciting her gibberish.

One day while Nick was upstairs being entertained by Shawn, another vision appeared on her ceiling. This time the vision was blurred and I had a difficult time straining my eyes to see it. Somehow it seemed liked someone was adjusting the clarity of the scene because without warning it became crystal clear. The scene was a man having sex with a woman. I wasn't sure why I was seeing this vision, but eventually the scene seemed to put a spotlight on the man's face and I screamed like a baby when I realized the man in the vision having sex with another woman was none other than Nick.

I felt like I had to go to church to get some clarity about everything that was going in my life. My family and I were starting to experience our television and other appliances shut on and off by themselves. We were also seeing and being tormented by evil spirits that roamed our apartment. It even came to the point that the evil shadowy like figures were having sexual intercourse with me. I didn't know what to do; if I prayed, I would get choked, if I read my Bible I would get slapped, if I went to bed I would get raped. It was humiliating to lie next to my husband and watch a demon enter my house from the second floor window and have sex with me like I belonged to him. I would keep screaming "THE blood of Jesus until it got up and left me, but it always came back. How could I ever explain this to anyone, and who would ever believe me. I decided the best thing to do was go to church, but not before I had another prayer meeting with the lady who was causing all this evil havoc in my life. After the prayer meeting with the young ladies I was slain on the floor. I could see evil images of demons in my mind as I heard them laughing and chanting weird things. Suddenly I had the sudden urge to write a poem that I wanted to recite in church because by this time I had starting doing my spoken word in the church from time to time. I would often deliver a poem as a testimony during devotional services. The assistant Pastor would tell me that my poems (that are included in this book) even though they were written about situations that had occurred in my life were not for my own testimony but would be used to minister to others. God had gifted me with writing just as Apostle McCoy prophesied and now Satan desired to pervert it.

While we were driving to the church my eyes went into the normal routine of shutting on me. I recall rubbing my legs and feet and reciting some gibberish my intellect could not comprehend before I entered the building. Everything seemed to be normal; God was on my heart and I was ready to worship Him. When they started the devotional service singing and praising God I joined in as I normally would, except this time my worship was more intense because somehow, out of the blue I started doing sign language along with the verbal singing. I never knew how to do or interpret sign language before, but I suddenly became a pro at it. On top of that I started mimicking everything I saw certain people in the congregation do, but nothing compared to the evil poem I delivered in the deep manly voice that would arise from time to time when I was praying. The assistant Pastor grabbed the microphone away from me and told me that I had demons inside of me because someone had placed a spell of witchcraft on me. He told the entire church to pray as he tried to lay his hand on me and pray. I ran away from him screaming in the manly voice in full terror. Once several people had grabbed me I started cursing them but in my mind I wanted to be free from these evil spirits who were using my body and forcing me to do things I did not want to do. I didn't want anything to do with the devil, his witches or his demons, but somehow or another there I stood fully possessed.

I noticed one of the girls who had attended the prayer meeting with me at the Louise's house sitting in the back of the church by herself sneaking out while they were praying for me.

As they were praying my chest expanded and I could feel something in my throat trying to escape. When I opened my mouth a wind of cold air came flowing out and then my chest would rise again, but nothing else came up. Instead I was being choked from within and I thought if they kept praying the demon or demons were going to kill me right there. After a while, having my boyfriend crying over me and the whole congregation praying for me, the demons seemed to calm down. I think the church felt as though I had been delivered from them, but I knew when I left that church those demons left still inside of me.

Nick was frightened to go home with me and I couldn't blame him after everything we had just experienced. We now understood all the hauntings that we were experiencing in our apartment and no one in the family felt safe returning there, so we decided to go to my mother's house. I called my aunt Rita who had become like a spiritual mother to me, to pray for me. My Aunt informed me that God showed her that I had several demons that were imparted in me by these witches who pretended to be my friend, and that I needed to be delivered from them. Once she started pleading the blood of Jesus I began screaming until I couldn't take anymore and ended up hanging the phone up in her face. Even after hanging up the phone I knew when we had finished our conversation that I was still possessed. It was crazy because I almost feel as if I was fighting with myself because part of me wanted to be delivered but there was something inside of me that didn't want any part of God, nor did it want to be free from the body it was trying to take over. I didn't know what to do, but I knew I needed help. I knew my heart was aching because I had unknowingly worshipped evil. I stared into the mirror of my mother's bathroom while crying hysterically and told God how sorry I was to have given my worship to anything other than Him. I begged for His forgiveness and confessed my undying love for him. When Nick, who was nervous enough being alone with me came back from going to the store for the one hundredth time to avoid me, he became more and more fearful of me, especially now that my eyes were swollen and red from crying.

I don't know what was going on in his mind, but he didn't know that I had spent the last few minutes crying and praying to my Creator to forgive me for hurting Him. Telling Him I wanted to be free of the demons that were causing me to make a mockery of the God I so loved very much. I told Nick that I needed help and I wanted to find another church to go to, one that I was more familiar with, one I had experienced and witnessed of the power of God.

It dawned on me to call Apostle McCoy, who had first spoken the heart changing prophecy into my life after my suicide attempt. It just so happened that he had recently started building more churches in different states, and Jacksonville happened to be one of them. I didn't know exactly where his new church was located so I called the church hoping to get some information about the times of their services and the address of the church. When the secretary of the church answered the phone I could hardly speak from all the sobbing I was doing. Somehow I managed to ask her if Apostle McCoy was going to be there that night, and that I needed to see him (I didn't want to go into details). The lady told me that the Apostle was not going to be in Jacksonville that night but I should come to church anyway. She said that I was coming for God and not any particular man she told me God would take care of everything I was going through and to try not to cry. After I had gotten off the phone with her, I told Nick that I still didn't feel like myself and that I wanted to go to Apostle McCoy's church later that evening. He agreed to do anything I needed to make certain I was better. The only thing we could do was wait, pray and hope.

We arrived to the church while they were still in the devotion stage, I didn't know who was going to be preaching that night because I was only familiar with Apostle McCoy. Once my family and I were seated, I made an unusual eye contact with a certain man whom I later learned was named Evangelist Green, who was sitting on the pool pit with two other men on each side of him and we could not seem to take our eyes off of each other. After the devotional portion of the service was over, the man got up to preach, but he still kept his eyes focused in on me. In the midst of the service he suddenly paused from his sermon and announced that God was leading him to take the service into another direction. Soon after he began preaching about false gods, witchcraft, and the fact that the Creator was not going to share His glory with any false gods or demonic deities, and that God was ready to demonstrate that He was the one and only true God. I listened intently to his words that seemed to penetrate through my heart and I knew I wanted to be reconciled with my Creator. But I wasn't sure if God would forgive me for unknowingly participating in the rituals the witches had me partake in after putting their demonic spells on me. I had allowed these evil people whom I should have never entrusted, to literally bring hell and torment into our lives. My children were being tortured by shadowy figures in our home I now believe were demons that followed me home the night the woman conjured up the whole prayer meeting.

Once the preacher summed up his sermon he walked over to me and as he took me by the hand he led me into the middle of the aisle. The first thing he said to me let me know without a doubt that God really does exist and that His love for me is genuine. "God saw your tears and He heard your cries," he told me, causing me to break down in tears. No one knew that I had spent a majority of my time in my mom's bathroom crying out to God, but God.

The preacher said to me, "God saw what they had done to you and how they tricked you, and your Father has come to deliver you. There are several evil spirits that they conjured up and imparted in you, but your Father has come to deliver you from each and every one of them. God has created you with a special anointing and you are one of His chosen vessels from your mother's womb. You felt as if God had left you but God has promised to never leave nor forsake you. He was with you every minute of this evil ordeal, and what the devil meant for bad, God is going to turn around and use for your good. God allowed you to go through this ordeal for a reason so that now you will be able to recognize the devices of Satan when he tries to steer you away from your Creator. You will be wiser about the wiles of the enemy," he said. He then he asked me to lift my hands and warned everybody in the room that he was about to call demons out of me and that everyone should begin praying.

I began feeling the trembling in my chest just as I had in the previous church, but this time I was able to open my mouth as if I had to vomit and each time I did, I released a vapor of cold air that left my body. After I was delivered I immediately started crying and worshipping God for His deliverance and forgiveness. This time I felt like my usual self and I knew that my life would never be the same again. The preacher let me know that part of my deliverance required that I not go back and participate in the same known sins I had before, and that I cut all ties with the evil witches and warlocks that had deceived me and imparted the demons into me and my home in the first place. He also let me know that if I entertained the known sins and or went back and affiliated with these evil people that the demons had the right to come back and bring seven more demons worse than them.

I cannot remember the exact number of spirits that I was delivered from that day however, being delivered from the demons that were dwelling on the inside of me was only half the battle. My family and I knew there were numerous demons awaiting us at home. Once we left the church fear began to set in as I realized just how traumatic my experience had been, not only for me, but for my children as well. I could not fathom taking my children back into that environment until those evil spirits had left my home, so we decided to return to my mother's house who was now single for a while. During the stay with my mother she suggested we have some people who we knew had a real relationship with God come and pray through our home. I decided I didn't want to continue fornicating with Nick, so he and I came to the conclusion that it was time to get married and try our best to live right before God.

I must admit that I was afraid to go into my apartment while the pray warriors were praying the evil spirits out of it, but I knew I had to fight for my home and my family, so I reluctantly participated in casting them out. My house felt at peace and I was confident my battle with these evil forces intruding my house and terrorizing my children was over until I went to bed and the rapes started up again. Out of desperation I ended up calling Pastor Griffin, and for as long as I live I will never forget him commanding this foul spirit to leave my house and to never enter it again and he sent his angel to guard my house. I don't claim to know what took place in the spiritual realm but I know none of the demons ever came back. Unbeknownst to me my husband, Nick, with all of his hesitations and suspicions while we were at the prayer meeting that night, began to assume some of the same evil signs I had just been delivered from. The vision, as I call it came to fruition when my husband began an extramarital affair right after we were married. Although the affair was very detrimental to our marriage, the witchcraft that they placed on him, made him literally hate the baby that I was now pregnant with. Our relationship seemed to diminish overnight and although things with us were never perfect, he was obviously a different person. He and I had just recently enjoyed becoming parents to our first child together only a few months prior to me finding out I was pregnant again. He was very considerate and caring with me and our first son together, but he had an unexplainable hate for the baby I was now carrying in my womb. I recall while I was possessed, Louise rubbing his chest and praying over my husband in the midnight hours while he was asleep. Me and my house, had gotten prayed for, but nobody prayed over my husband or my kids. The demons had obviously transferred into him. Just when I thought the battle between me and the unseen world of evil was over.

Although the timing for this new baby may not have been what we deemed as perfect, I accepted the fact that I was going to have yet another child with my now husband. Actually this was the only baby that I would give birth to where I was married to their dad, but he made me feel as if I was a single mother because he didn't share the same excitement as I did with this pregnancy. He would say things to me like he hoped the baby I was carrying died, and that he hated both me and our unborn child. I don't know whether or not the stress of my pregnancy caused my husband to stray, but I kept in mind that vision that had appeared on the ceiling of what I now know to have been a witch's home. The demons who were in her house and acted out that awful scene were now using my husband's body to act out that infidelity in the flesh. During the time of his extramarital affair he began pulling away from our family, but I used that time to draw closer in relationship to God. I made sure I kept my family in church regardless of the fact that my husband and I were having marital problems, but having Nick literally curse me out for attending church was new to me. All of a sudden he became disinterested in the things of God and seemed to be infatuated with his new woman

I initially came to the knowledge of the affair by calling his place of employment looking for him one night and essentially ended up being told by his manager that he had not worked there for several weeks, even though he was leaving my house every night and not returning until the morning as he always had on the graveyard shift. I became infuriated with the fact that he had been able to commit adultery right under my nose. While he was obviously spending time with his adulterous lover I literally packed everything that belonged to him and drove it to the nearest school dumpster where I left if for trash. Afterwards I drove me and my children to church where I desperately tried to put Nick's affair out of my mind, but that was to no avail because it seemed that every testimony given was about a new wedding or an overly zealous and happy marriage. With each testimony I found myself becoming more and more upset until I finally ended up in the spirit of covetousness and jealousy. I prayed silently to myself and asked God to take those feelings away from me. God answered through the Pastor, "Put your cares aside and worship God he kept insisting." "Worship God?" Worship was the last thing that I wanted to do at that time. I really didn't feel like I had anything to worship Him for. Yet God continued petitioning me to worship Him and so I hesitantly did, and it was a good thing because the devil had plans that I didn't know about.

I stood up with tears in my eyes as I tried to take my focus off of me and what I was going through in my marriage and place it on God. Before long I fell into an intense worship. I was in the process of worshipping when some young girls notified me that my husband was outside wanting me to come out and talk to him. I asked some of the church members to look after my children and I went outside to have a much needed conversation with my husband but I intended on using more body language than words.

While I was outside Nick admitted to the affair and blamed his infidelities on me and my lack of love and affection towards him. I could only concentrate on the fact that he had been unfaithful to me while I was carrying his child, and that he could have put me and our unborn child at risk for sexually transmitted diseases. I forgot about God, let alone worshipping Him. I allowed my anger to overtake me and unfortunately took everything into my own hands. A fight emerged, I was the aggressor, and Nick and his car inevitably was the target and victim of my rage.

After the altercation was over and Nick managed to escape in our car to avoid any responsibilities for what he had done, I went back into the church to try to continue my worship to God. I had not been in the church ten minutes when in the midst of my worship, I was tapped on the shoulder by a police officer who was there to arrest me for assaulting my husband. The officer who came to arrest me also happened to be a minister, and although he could clearly see that I was pregnant and emotionally torn, he had to obey the laws of the land and arrest me for the scars my husband received during our altercation. The officer used the time it took to transport me to the police station to minister to me while I was hysterically crying in the back of his squad car. His empathy for me didn't allow him to put me into handcuffs so the drive felt like I was more in a conference with a counselor than taking a ride to jail.

God continued to demonstrate to me that He was with me during this entire frightening ordeal. After I had been booked and sent to my cell, my first mission was to seek counseling or prayer from some strong faith filled Christians, so I immediately started making phone calls in hopes of someone accepting my collect calls. Although several people from the same church in which the fight broke out between Nick and I did accept my phone calls and prayed for me, my emotions seem to over shadow my faith and I could not find any peace. I felt like I was in torment, not knowing what was going to happen to me or my children who were now living with my cheating husband in our home. The two calls that stick out to me the most are one from the Pastor Griffin who said the quickest prayer. I can remember this call because even though it was short in words, his prayer was precise, and filled with faith and power. I cannot recall his exact words but I will never forget how he ended our conversation after the prayer. "Believe and God will do it, my sister, just believe and it's done." 'Yes sir,' I managed to say through my sobbing. But after we hung up the phone my doubt caused me to call another church member, Pastor Henry's wife, whose call also remains vivid in my memory. The assistant Pastor's wife was a dear friend of mine and she and I began confiding in one another. She was always someone to whom I could turn for advice; especially where marriage was concerned. Surprisingly, when she and I spoke she said she could no longer give me advice about my marriage, and that I should not consult everyone about something so intimate. She told me to start praying to God and He would answer me. I didn't know exactly what she meant by God would answer me. Was He going to speak to me in some loud audible voice like I have seen demonstrated in so many Biblical movies, or was He going to respond to me in a soft subtle whisper as the bible sometimes describes, either way I needed to hear from Him and only Him.

I remember the day I began speaking in what the Bible calls "tongues". I was in the privacy of my cell and I was reading a Bible and praying. My prayer was that God would give me direction and guidance concerning my marriage and life as a whole. I was tired of seeking advice from everyone else and only ending up more and more confused from people's advice or perspectives on things. I needed to hear from God and so I began to cry out to Him.

All of a sudden my tongue began to do what I can only describe as a dance in my mouth; I could no longer control its movements. Suddenly I started speaking in what I perceive to be some sort of foreign language, although I could not tell you the exact language I spoke, I was able to somehow translate every word I spoke back to myself in plain English. The Bible defines this as two of the gifts of the Holy Spirit; known as tongues, and the interpretation of tongues. God himself spoke to me and through me, just like Pastor Johnnie Griffin prophesied. Through the gifts, God revealed that the baby that I was now carrying was going to be a boy and that I should name this child "Prosper", as a sign that God was going to Prosper me in my life. God said that He was going to Prosper in my finances, ministry, marriage and spiritual life. He told me that He had chosen me from my mother's womb and that He had plans to use me for His kingdom. God also told me that there was witchcraft associated with Nick's affair and that he would deliver my husband and that He even had desires to use him as well.

I was let out of jail the very next day and I thought long and hard about the experience I had with God while I was in there. I thought that God would begin turning things around for my marriage the moment I was released, but that could not have been further from the truth. Nick's hatred for me and my unborn child never ceased and neither did his affair, still I kept attending church, but my faith was slowly waning. One day one of the women who had previously testified about how wonderful her new marriage was, approached me and asked if she could have a private word with me. After I agreed she asked me if I knew anything about spiritual warfare or how it's conducted. She told me that I had been wrongly fighting against Nick when all along my target should have been the devil and his evil cohorts.

She definitely had my attention because I was certainly guilty of physically attacking him and the encounter at the church proved that fighting was all I knew, but now it was time to fight in another realm.

My mind was in a continuous state of confusion and I started to even doubt that God ever spoke to me or through me at all that day in jail. I wondered if I was going crazy or maybe I still had some determined demons inside of me that I hadn't been delivered from. The more questions that arose, the more I prayed, and the more God used the gift of tongues and interpretation to confirm his Word. I recall one particular time when I was praying upstairs in my bedroom after reading the Bible about an individual named Gideon whom God had spoken to and revealed specific things about future events that God wanted to use Gideon for. Gideon in return, asked God to give him a sign that those events would transpire and that God truly was going to use him. So as always I felt the God of the Bible was the same God that I loved, served and was praying to, so I thought it only fair that I could ask God for a sign in my situation as well.

Inevitably I asked God to give me a sign that everything he spoke to me that day was going to transpire. I asked God if it was really Him who was speaking through me, to give me a sign and allow my husband to come over to our house that same night. This was rather a peculiar sign since my husband had moved in with his lover. I could barely stand the sight of him and his short visits with our baby, which were starting to occur less and less were becoming aggravating, but something told me to open my eyes right then and there while I was still on my knees kneeling and praying to God. I was shocked to see Nick sitting there on our bed. Granted, God is a God of miracles and the Bible is full of countless numbers of miracles that testify to his omnipotent ways, but to have this miracle unfold before my eyes was astonishing. I did not know how he entered our house because I'd had the locks changed, nor could I explain why it was that I didn't hear him enter. The miracle was surprising in itself that day, but it did not prevent the two of us from arguing, like we always seemed to do since his affair, but God didn't promise me things were going to change that particular day, nope He just gave me a sign that they would.

* * *

The circumstances with my husband seemed to seesaw out of control seeing that I was finally taking the lady's advice from church and learning how to conduct spiritual warfare. I started learning how to pray with more power and authority and I tried hard to stop allowing these evil forces to control my emotions, and to operate in faith. "With love and kindness have I drawn thee," says God through His Word. So I knew love and kindness was going to be the only way I would get my husband back.

I kept standing in the gap for my husband. Every chance I had I was in the prayer line at my church. I knew if I wanted my marriage to work, then I had to keep my hope and faith alive. One day while I was getting prayer in the prayer line at church for my husband and our marriage God spoke to me and told me it was over. "It is finished", were His exact words, and He kept on repeating this phrase to me over and over until it was embedded into my spirit. I left church that day thinking that was the day my anxiety would cease, and Nick would finally come to his senses and come back home to our family. Instead the devil proved to me once again that he wasn't going to let go of the hold that he had on my marriage that easily, because after this ensuring word from God, I would have an encounter with Nick the very same day. On the surface nothing had changed, he was still the same bitter, rude, uncaring, unloving, demon possessed, person who abhorred me and our unborn child. After he had rudely poured out his detestation about me and everything affiliated with me, he spat in my face and proceeded to go make a life with his lover. Although I used to try to fight him to convince him to stay with me, I was ecstatic to see him leave.

I felt maybe this is what God meant when he said that it was over, maybe my marriage was over and I had to learn to accept that fate. Immediately after he left, my mother came over and invited me and one of my friends named Denise to go to church with her, even though I had just gotten out of church. After another intense episode with my husband, I was more eager than ever to accompany her. After all, my faith had just been drained and if I didn't get help soon my whole life would soon follow.

While heading to my mother's church she kept telling me that I should not be so easy to allow the devil, through this woman whom my husband was cheating with, to steal my marriage. She reminded me that this pregnancy would produce my fifth child and that I would need assistance in raising all these children. She also reminded me about my faith in God and about the ever present lesson of spiritual warfare, God was trying to teach me about and prepare me for.

Mother told me that I shouldn't take what the devil was doing to my family lying down. I shouldn't give up on God or my husband, because the fact that my husband was still coming around us proved that he still had love for me and that if there was even a microscopic chance that my marriage could be saved then I should try to save it. After all God just needs a mustard seed of faith she would often say.

While at her church I decided to do as I had learned during my course in the lessons of spiritual warfare. I placed my cares and concerns to the side and gave God my full undivided attention and worship Him. With tears flowing from my eyes and uncertainty in my heart I gave alms to my Creator.

In the midst of my worship my mother's Pastor stated that sometimes we forget who we belong to and who our worship belongs to and sometimes we worship our problems more than the problem solver. Then as if he were speaking directly to me he said he said Don't be concerned about that unfaithful husband, God can turn him from that woman and send him right into these doors. If I thought that my husband appearing out of nowhere in my bedroom that time I asked God for a sign was a miracle then I was about to become even more astonished, because at that very moment Nick walked into my mother's church. He wasn't even what society likes to describe as dressed appropriately for church because he was in nothing more than a pair of shorts, a tank top, some sandals.

I didn't know what to think or how to react when Nick was walking over to sit with me, because my spirit man and my emotions definitely seemed to be at war with one another. Part of me wanted to embrace my husband and what God had just spoken through the pastor, but another part of me despised this man who seemed to be turning my life into a chaotic combustion of hurt and despair, He took our son from my arms and held him on his lap, he even tried holding my hands, but I couldn't bring myself to join hands with his. I had been praying for God to reconcile our marriage and God was trying to do just that, but my heart wasn't ready to forgive and I didn't know if it ever would be.

Although I had attended two church services already that day, I still ended up back at my church for their Sunday night services. We were in the midst of the pastor's sermon when Deja vu seemed to occur again. Once again without warning Nick walked through the door still wearing the same ensemble he had on earlier, but this time he didn't approach me. Instead he walked directly towards Pastor Griffin and whispered something in his ear. The next thing I know Pastor Griffin passed the microphone to my husband and he went and sat down. Nick then addressed the congregation. He not only confessed, but he openly apologized to me and God for his infidelities. He begged for my forgiveness and declared his love and desire to be reunited with his family. He could barely fight off his tears as he begged me to allow him back into my heart and my home. I didn't know if I had the power to forgive but I couldn't deny my love for this man and I couldn't deny God and His word "It is finished".

Jesus Can Forgive Me, Why Can't You

I'm a born again Christian I just got saved today

Jesus said come here my child and I will wipe your sins away

I won't remember them, nor will I throw them up in your face

You can rest assure with me your sins have been totally erased

I won't nag you or complain or either bring up your past

I am a forgive and forget merciful God you need not ask

For forgiveness more than once at a time

Because once I hear sincere repentance I get a clear mind

And forget everything you have done against my will

I have always been full of love and mercy and I am that way still

I got off of my knees with a pleasant smile on my face

It felt less burdening knowing my guilt had been replaced

With forgiveness, and mercy and yes even great love

I wanted to experience this with everyone I could think of

That I've done something wrong in one way or another

I thought I should try first with my Christian sisters and brothers

I just knew way down deep in my heart

That once they heard my repentance I'd get a fresh start

But that wasn't the case because they were still rather mad

So now I'm confused because I thought they would be glad

That I gave my life to Jesus and wanted to make my wrongs, right

I heard of Christian tribulations but never brotherly fights

They were so unforgiven and although I tried and tried

Sincere forgiveness was time after time to me denied

Now this is something I never could understand

How the loving laws of Jesus could be changed by any man

We want to follow Jesus and walk in all of His ways

But do you recall Jesus turning sincere repentance away

Jesus said I'm the same with me there is nothing knew

Well if Jesus can forgive, my friend why can't you

Now that Nick and I were making efforts to mend our broken marriage, we would soon discover that the penance for sin was something that we, in and of ourselves could never make amends for. We suffered the consequences of our sins, and sometimes those closest to us suffered as well. I was learning the true meaning of forgiveness. I realized that saying that you forgive someone and actually forgiving them were two entirely different things. It proved to be difficult, to say the least, trying to be intimate with my husband after knowing he had been with someone else. I became obsessed with finding out why he became unfaithful to me in the first place. I could not allow him to think for a minute that he had gotten away with his infidelity or that I would put up with it again. So I made him pay, and pay again, and then pay some more, until I was satisfied that he had paid the penalty for hurting me and our family. The only problem was that I couldn't bring myself to be satisfied no matter how much I was making him suffer. I even went as far as to physically attack him every time he went to sleep, accusing him of dreaming about the girl he had been unfaithful to me with. Everything he did reminded me of his cheating ways and our life became one big round in the ring. His affair cost us more than we could afford to pay but never the less we would pay and pay big time.

For example, when Nick was gone off into his so called perfect adulterated world, he left me to be the sole provider for our family. I did my best as a high risk pregnant woman to work as long and hard as I possibly could to make ends meet, but I would often come up short. To keep a roof over our heads sometimes I would be forced to pawn things and write checks I knew I couldn't cover. One time in particular I had to pawn some things that Nick had acquired when he was selling drugs. Sometimes you feel like you are forced to do things, in spite of your better judgment. This was definitely one of those times, and sometimes a one-time bad decision can cost a lifetime of pain.

You would think with all that I had been through, my life would finally turn over a new leaf, yet with everything I had gone through, the worst was yet to come. Out of nowhere there was a knock on our door and to my dismay it was a police officer. The first thought that came to our minds was that they were there for him and it had something to do with his selling drugs. He decided I should open the door while he found some place to hide. "Tonya?" They questioned me when I opened the door. "Yes," I responded to them in fear. Then they told me that they were there to arrest me for dealing in stolen property. When Nick heard all of this he came from out of hiding. I gave him a look that showed my unhappiness for what we both knew was his fault. I was deceived into thinking that this was something that they were just going to sweep under the rug, instead I was about to get beat like a rug.

I was stuck between a rock and a hard place in both my mind and my physical state as well. The detectives tried to convince me that they knew that I was an innocent victim in this whole ordeal. They told me that they noticed the look Nick and I gave each other when they were putting the handcuffs on me while telling me the reason for my arrest. They told me that they believed in my innocence and that they knew my husband was the guilty party, and that he had to be a moron for allowing his pregnant wife to serve time for a crime she did not commit. Maybe they were right, but I was not there to serve time for my husband, just like I had made the decision to pawn those items to keep a roof over my children's head, I made the difficult choice of sitting there, keeping quiet and serving time for my children. My thought at that time was that the police didn't care about neither the wellbeing of myself let alone that of my children. Their sole purpose was to solve crimes and punish those they thought committed those crimes. I knew if I told them that it was Nick who had acquired those stolen items from people he sold drugs to that they would arrest him as well, and my babies would be sent to live in a foster home. I couldn't bear the thought of them taking my children away from me so I did what I thought was best for my children and kept my mouth shut so that they could at least be with one of their parents.

Although I didn't open up to the police, my public defense attorney, or cell mates, I kept an open communication with my Creator by reading my Bible and praying often. It was just months since I had been arrested for having that altercation in front of my church with my husband, but in that short time, both my relationship with God and the knowledge of His word had been strengthened tremendously. I had learned a lot about spiritual warfare, and the gifts of the Holy Spirit had become increasingly evident in my life. One day while lying down reading my Bible, a vision suddenly came to me. In this vision I saw the outside of a big beautiful house, when I made my way into the house I walked into many different rooms, but I still could not tell you whose house I was in or the relevance of me being there. Suddenly I saw hands that bore scars on them appear out of heaven and as I was mesmerized by them. I suddenly felt myself falling, but those same hands caught me before I ever hit the ground.

I was awakened from my vision by the guards who were notifying the inmates that it was time to be counted and fed. As I was coming back inside my room with my tray of food, I unexpectedly took a hard fall. As I had fallen the glory of the Lord fell upon me as well, though I was unconscious to this world, I was conscious to God. I knew the vision that God had shown me surely came to pass that day for in that day my baby and I should have been injured from the fall. In my heart I knew that God had caught me with those same scarred hands he had revealed to me in my vision.

When I finally came to from this traumatic experience I was in the infirmary. The guards were not sympathetic to me at all. They were downright evil because they treated me worse than an animal on the street by threatening to pepper spray me in my face because I was praying to God in my spiritual language. I asked God to reveal to them that I was indeed His child and to please set me free from the bondage that Satan had enslaved me to. One of the guards who was also a child of God had become very fond of me came into the infirmary to check in on me. When she noticed the guards were threatening to pepper spray me she spoke up for me and threatened to inform their supervisor of their cruel behavior to a helpless pregnant woman. She informed them how hard and terrible my fall was and that I needed to be checked to ensure that the fall didn't cause me to go into premature labor. It was a good thing that she came through the door of the infirmary that day because sure enough when they hooked the contraction machine to me, it revealed that I was indeed having full fledged contractions, but once I was able to calm down and rest, the contractions seemed to subside.

Till this day I don't know whether or not the guard was responsible or my mother, but some kind of way a lawyer who didn't work for the public defense attorney agreed to meet with me and take my case pro bono. Three days later I was released in the middle of the night on my own recognizance and it was recommended that my case be sent into a diversion program, which meant I would only have to do probation and community service to stay out of jail.

Being that I was in the middle of a high risk pregnancy with threats of possibly going into premature labor my probation and community service was only set for a minimal time. Because of my high risk pregnancy, the community service that they gave me to do was to attend AA meetings every week and clear the facility's ashtray afterwards. Thank God that he had shown me favor with both my probation officer and the director of the AA meetings, because both had sympathy for my situation and both of them recommended that I get an early termination from the deferment program, to which the judge readily agreed.

Now that that horrible chapter was behind me, my husband and I could finally concentrate on the joys of becoming parents to our unborn child. Ever since the day he came into the church and confessed his sins openly so that I would consider giving our marriage another opportunity, he had greatly changed his uncaring and selfish attitude toward our unborn child. He was once again the caring dad he used to be when we were pregnant with our first child. Everything that God spoke to me about saving our marriage and using my husband for his glory was beginning to manifest. Nick was not only more considerate of my needs while I was pregnant, he became more supportive of my relationship with God and even managed to develop a personal relationship with God for himself. God's Words were coming into fruition but that didn't mean the devil paused for God's cause.

God was surely proving his loving faithfulness and devotion to us because miracle after miracle kept happening in our lives. No matter what dilemma came our way God was always faithful to deliver us from every test, trial and tribulation. The gifts of the spirit were manifesting in my life and God used them to remind me to name my unborn child "Prosper", as a sign that He was going to prosper me in every area of my life. God said that the child I was having was going to be a boy and my baby was going to be a personal sign that God was going to *Prosper* me in everything He called me to do. Eventually I began having dreams of giving birth to this child, but in my dreams I was never giving birth to my baby in the hospital. I informed my husband everything God had revealed to me about our special child, but I don't know whether or not he believed me. What I do know is that he was totally against naming our child Prosper and thought I was crazy to give my baby such a bizarre name. Nick and I finally agreed that when we went for the ultrasound to find out the sex of the baby if it was indeed a boy we would use that as a sign that God really did speak to me and would go forth with naming our son Prosper, but if it was a girl then I would resign myself to being mistaken about God speaking to me, and I would never mention it again. When we arrived to get the ultrasound I was very confident in what God had told me and when the ultrasound technician asked if we wanted to know the sex of our baby I told her that God told me that it was a boy and she said I was most certainly right, but then she surprised me when she said that he was actually holding his hands together as if he was praying. If ever God confirmed His word to me, it was right then. So I knew I had to learn to trust God in everything He spoke to me. Nick was not as ready to give in as I hoped he would have been. Even though he agreed to name our son Prosper if it was a boy, he reneged on his promise and began to ridicule me once again.

The church that we were once attending split when the Assistant Pastor decided to leave the church and start a church of his own. Nick and I were in conflict about which church we wanted to continue supporting so we decided to visit both churches for a while until we could make up our minds. At the new Assistant Pastor's church my husband began leading devotional services and became what is commonly called an Armor Bearer to the Pastor. That means he assisted the pastor with whatever the pastor needed, often calling for him to travel with the pastor whenever and wherever he had to perform a sermon. This was a good transition for my husband because it led him not to be as physically aggressive with me as he had always been in the past. Pastor Henry also got Nick a job where he worked so that he could be able to better support our family. My husband's new job paid very well but it was also demanding as far as hours were concerned, and because of my high risk pregnancy, his new job became our only source of income.

I did not go to the same hospital that I had gone to less than a year before when I had my last baby. So when I started experiencing premature labor the same opportunity available to bring home the contraction machine and have the nurse's staff monitor me from the hospital was not available to me. This time the only option I had to preserve my pregnancy and not risk the chance of losing my baby, was to be admitted into the hospital. This was not easy on my family because my husband didn't have anyone to help him look after our other children and I had over nine weeks to go before my pregnancy would be considered full term. Although I should have been appreciative for all the rest and relaxation the hospital permitted me to have, it was stressful, thinking that Nick had to keep missing work and maybe end up losing his job because I was in the hospital. Against my doctor's advice, I made the decision to sacrifice my peace and relaxation and decided that I would go back home. I knew I would not be able to move around much and that I would be confined to my bed a lot, but at least I would be there to supervise my children.

My husband and I thought it best if he pulled our mattress down to the living room where I could rest but at least go in the kitchen to prepare meals for our children to eat. Everything seemed to be fine for a while but then again I never felt a contraction before so I could not know that I was experiencing premature labor. On October 10th, 1996 at approximately 3 a.m. I would no longer have to wonder how long I was going to be able to hold my miracle baby inside of me, because when I went to the restroom I noticed that my baby's head was trying to make its way from between my legs. I immediately called out for my husband and showed him that the baby was coming. Nick was as astonished as I was so he ran to our friend, Denise's house who came over and held my hand while my husband made the call to the ambulance for me to be transported to the hospital. Once the Emergency Medical Technicians arrived they thought they had time enough to place me on the gurney and transport me to the hospital. That was, until they saw my baby's head trying to come out, then they knew he had to be delivered right then and there on my bed. After just minutes of pushing I was holding God's gift, his sign to me in my arms. As I took one look at my 4 lbs. 7 1/2 oz. little bundle of joy, I remembered God's Word pertaining to my new baby. His being a boy, being born in a place other than a hospital and seeing him, in my belly praying to God while they did my sonogram were all the signs I needed to know that God was true to His Word. Reading and studying my Bible had taught me that faith without works was dead, so if I wanted God to bring this prophecy to fruition I would have to demonstrate my faith by my works. So without a second thought I looked over at Nick who had just cut my baby's umbilical cord. and while looking down at my baby in my arms I said with the biggest smile, "His name is Prosper."

Chapter Seven

Rest and Reap (PROSPER)

Although Prosper wasn't born in the hospital, he ended up being hospitalized for a month after he was born due to him being premature. I was ecstatic the day we finally got to bring him home, I vowed not to spoil him because I knew it would be difficult raising four children, which included two babies that were less than eleven months apart, at my tender age of twenty-two. That was one vow that I wouldn't keep for long, and one that God probably would have never honored in the first place. After all, Prosper, was the promised child, my symbol of how God planned to prosper me in every area of my life, but what does a promise child look like or how is he supposed to act. Yes, Prosper, was a beautiful baby. He had all of his vital organs and body parts, he cried when he needed to be fed and changed like any other baby. To me there was nothing particularly special about him that would stand out when looking at him. Which could be the reason I almost forgot what God had told me Prosper represented in my life; representation of God's Word, his solemn promise. I may have temporarily forgotten God's Word, but the devil sure didn't; he was more than ready to attack it and him.

Prosper's miraculous birth not only brought forth a bundle of joy for me, but it also simultaneously brought forth God's word with confirmation of everything He had said would happen as a sign that this baby was truly heaven sent. The signs seemed to slowly fade from my memory as I began the everyday task of being a wife and mother. My husband and I were arguing and fighting all the time, because we could barely make ends meet. The toils of life began to suppress my faith and the miraculous baby that I had just given birth to became more of a burden than a blessing.

One day after Nick and I had gotten into another one of our many physical altercations. He had gone to jail for actually knocking me unconscious outside in a field, during a very heated argument. When I came to I didn't have much recollection of what happened to me. I was appalled to find myself in the middle of a ditch covered in mud with my husband trying to help me out of it. When I asked him what had happened to me he said that I had fainted, but the pain in my face let me know that there was more to the story. As he got me up and we started making our way back to the apartment, flashes of our argument came to mind, and then it dawned on me that he had punched me in the face and literally knocked me out. Once we made it back to the safety of our house he was no longer safe. I went into all-out rage and grabbed a four by four piece of plywood that we kept in the case of intruders invading our home and began beating him with it until he managed to escape. He called the police on me! It was a good thing that witnesses spoke up for me that day and corroborated my version of the story and although my husband had some bruised ribs he was the one arrested that day. It was after this incident, while I was all beaten up, dazed, and emotionally frustrated that the devil would strike.

It was time for me to feed Prosper. I picked up my innocent little baby and held him close to my bosom to prepare to try to breastfeed him. That's when I noticed that he would stop breathing for long intervals, then suddenly revive and begin to breathe again, but his breathing remained weak and inconsistent. I immediately called for an ambulance to come transport my baby to the nearest hospital. Once we made it there he was rushed into an examination room in which I watched them force a breathing tube down his throat. I couldn't stand the sight of the procedure and felt so faint that I had to be escorted back into the waiting room. The next thing I knew, the hospital was informing me that he was going to have to be airlifted to another hospital. With tears flowing down from my eyes I said a silent prayer for the baby I had taken for granted, and that God would send my husband to help me through this emotional trauma. Although we weren't getting along; I knew no one but him could share the pain I was experiencing with the threat of losing our son.

God quickly answered my prayers that day. Before I knew it Nick was racing to the waiting room. All of my anger disappeared the moment I laid eyes on him and I found myself rushing into the same arms that had been pulling me out of a ditch the day before. Yesterday was a faded memory in a cycle of abuse that Nick and I shared, but that day our infant son was fighting for his precious life; and like it or not, he and I needed to bond together. Once we arrived at the hospital where they had transported Prosper, I was relieved to find out that they had been able to stabilize his breathing and we were able to see him. It wasn't long after we were standing over his incubator staring, praying and crying over him together, that he stopped breathing again. I felt like Nick and I needed someone with more spiritual authority and more faith so I began to reach out to Pastor Henry and his wife for prayer. It was during that call that God used that man of God to remind us how unique Prosper was. The Pastor reminded me why I had even named my baby Prosper. I had not been thinking of the significance of his name and the prophecy that came along with it. The Pastor had to remind me how real God is, how true His word is, and how much the devil despised both. "Sister, you are going to have to protect that gift God has given you," he said. "The devil wants that baby because that baby represents God's Word over your life. I already told you God has great plans for your life and the devil doesn't want them to come to fruition. You must begin to war in the Spirit. You and your husband need to come together, stop fighting each other and start fighting the devil," he said to me over the phone. "How do I fight him and why can't he just leave me and my baby alone?" I asked him. He said, "The devil is after that Word, and you have to fight him with the Word of God. That's how Jesus defeated the devil when he was tempted him in the wilderness. You are going to have to get in the Word, learn the promises of God, and get faith enough to stand on

His promises. When the devil comes at you, you need to throw the Word of God back at him."

Unfortunately, when we went home from the hospital that day Prosper didn't get to go home with us. It would be another three weeks or so before my baby would be reunited with us. The fact that we only had one car at the time, and with my husband working an incredible amount of overtime to support our family, meant we couldn't see Prosper as much as we would have liked. Thankfully my mother worked at the hospital where Prosper was, and could hold him and give him that much needed affection that I was not able to. So I made a schedule of studying my bible and on the days I could go to the hospital I read Bible verses over my son. One verse in particular became my favorite verse. I continuously spoke it over my son, even after he was released from the hospital. I spoke this scripture over my promised child so often, especially at times he experienced some type of tribulation in his life, that he and his older siblings grew up learning it and reciting it for themselves. **Isaiah 54:17, No Weapon that is formed against you shall prosper** became a vital scripture in our lives. Little did I know just how essential it would become.

* * *

For a while, things seemed to be going favorably for my family, and the prosperity that God spoke to me while I was in jail began to flourish in our lives. My husband and I were very active in the church and we were teaching our children about the goodness and love for the Lord as well. Our fights were replaced by prayer as we learned to be obedient to God and learned to lean on Him for guidance, provision, and protection. Although Nick still battled with small habits, he was surely becoming a new creature, as God was patiently working with him; slowly but surely changing his heart. Patience is something that I didn't have. Instead of encouraging him about the changes God had made in his life, I beat him down about the areas he still struggled.

His occasional beer or two after work was one of them. Little did I know, I had become a self-righteous, judgmental person and I was allowing the devil to use me to push my husband away from God, away from the church, and ultimately away from our family. Nothing my husband did was good enough for me and before long the old him resurfaced; with a vengeance. His time for trying to be a better person was over as far as he was concerned. He returned to being a sinner, with no holds barred. The cursing, fighting, drinking, and partying were nearly impossible for me to deal with, but I remained confident that if I prayed for him long enough the devil, who was fighting him, would flee from our home. Every day I was praying, pleading the blood of Jesus over my husband and every day I would criticize him and remind him how much of a failure he was to God and his family. Of course his reaction would be one of hurt, frustration and anger due to the one person who was supposed to help him in life was constantly tearing him down. These combined negative feelings would often lead to an explosive rage and he became combative with me. All my prayers for God to change him never entered my thoughts as I took it upon myself to react to his combative manner in an even more aggressive manner. I often grabbed meat cleavers, cast iron frying pans, irons, extension cords or whatever I could get my hands on to defend myself.. After the altercations I would find myself praying once again against the enemy that was tearing apart my marriage. Little did I understand that enemy was none other than me.

    I recall a day when I was forced to come to terms with what I was allowing the devil to do through me. As Nick and I were sitting next to one another in Pastor Griffin's church listening to a sermon about how God can change any situation and that if people don't want to change it is not due to the power of God, but their reluctance to let things go. I sat there in agreement with what the Pastor was preaching, because I assumed he was referring to my husband and that God was giving my husband the opportunity to see how right I had been all along to tell him he wasn't saved for real. Pride took over as I yelled out my **amen**, and **preach it preacher**, but the moment he walked over and stood next to me without addressing me directly he said, "When you become saved you should not be impatient, judgmental, or merciless to your fellow brother or sisters. God didn't save you to be prideful or self-righteous. The Holy Spirit doesn't make you go around chasing people with meat cleavers because they are not living up to your standards. We are supposed to be mature Christians with compassion and love those who are babes in Christ. Instead we beat them down forgetting about how God had to show mercy for us, and continues to show His mercy; no one is perfect except God." Then he came over and took Nick by the hand and began to prophesy to him. "The devil has been beating you down, telling you that you are not saved and that you don't have a real relationship with God, he told him." Nick started shedding tears and I started shedding my pride as I began slouching down in the pew as far as I could. I couldn't fathom the thought that I was allowing the devil to use me. I should have run to the alter to beg God for His forgiveness or perhaps I should have apologized to my husband and tried to console him, but my pride wouldn't allow me to and eventually my pride gradually turned to anger. When we got home from church I still hadn't let up on my husband and I was certain that he told my Pastor everything. I was embarrassed about the skeletons in my closet being put on full display in front of the congregation. I didn't want to go back to church from that moment on and I began to slowly backslide; into the world

Over time I had learned to be self-sufficient and I often worked at least two jobs, in order to be the primary breadwinner in my home, which meant Nick was often the one left taking care of our children. Eventually, my not being home to attend to the needs of our family caused him to seek the attention of another woman again. Although I never met this woman I knew he was communicating with her because her number showed up constantly on our caller id. Like most woman who suspect their man of being unfaithful, I went into detective mode and began investigating where this woman lived. When I realized it was the same low income apartments his last lover lived, I got extremely angry. At the time I discovered all of this information he was at work, but I wasn't going to wait for him to come home before I confronted him. I called his job and made up an emergency about the kids so that I could go pick him up from work and confront him. At that time my oldest daughter was there visiting so I felt comfortable leaving all my children alone sleep.

When he made it into my car he looked in the back seat to see if my child was as sick as I had just claimed over the phone. I responded by telling him that I had lied and then I asked him about the name that kept showing up on my caller id. He asked me what in the world was I talking about and he said he was tired of me not trusting him. I said fine I know where the girl stays, let's go over to her house and you can prove to me once and for all that you are not cheating. He yelled, "Fine Tonya! We will go over there and you'll look stupid when she says she doesn't know me, then I want a divorce!" When I pulled up to the light to make a right turn he shocked me by jumping out of the car and running away from me. The first thing that came to my mind was that he must have been guilty. I forgave him for one affair that he had while I was pregnant with our last child and I wasn't about to subject myself to that pain again. I sat at the light for a brief moment, wondering how he could betray me yet again. I watched him run across the street and try to make his way into an Auto car place. There's no other way to explain it, except I lost it. Without giving it a second thought I chased him with my car and tried to run over him. If it hadn't been for some concrete barriers that stopped me in my tracks, he would be dead. I was determined to make him pay for hurting me again. So although the concrete blocks stopped my car from reaching him, my pursuit did not stop. I got out of my car and ran in the store where he was hiding behind the counter. I tried to get to him, but the people in the store threatened to call the police on me so my rage and I went home and waited.

When I arrived back at my house my children were still soundly asleep. I wanted him to pay for hurting me again, and since he couldn't be there to feel the effects of my pain I decided to take it out on his belongings. While I was in the middle of destroying the things that I had purchased for him, the police came banging at my door. I tried to turn off my lights and pretend not to be home, but their banging eventually woke up my children, who started screaming and crying. With the threat of them kicking the door down to take my children, I hesitantly opened the door. They said that they were just there to observe him getting his belongings, but once they realized I had stabbed and cut up his belongings they decided to arrest me. One of the officers asked me to turn around in order for them to place the handcuffs on me and I told him no. The officer told me that he wasn't going to ask me again, but I wouldn't comply to his demands. He tried to force me to the ground. I resisted and before I knew it I was entangled in a tussling match with both officers. After wrestling with them, vomiting and being hogged tied, I passed out from all the adrenaline rushing to my head. When I woke up I was in the hospital, handcuffed to the bedrail with the officers in the room observing me. My stomach had been pumped because I told the officers that I had taken a bunch of pills when I came to the knowledge that my husband was having an affair.

Being arrested was embarrassing enough, but being identified as someone with a psychological disorder and having to wear an orange uniform that bluntly displayed it, was downright humiliating. The fact that I had told the arresting officers that I had taken an undisclosed amount of pain pills in an order to commit suicide, gave the impression that I was not only in danger of hurting others, but myself as well. It made me a prime candidate for ridicule from the other inmates and some of the jail officials. I found myself charged with a violent felony, which threatened to destroy my life. The only thing that gave me some gratification was that I wasn't pregnant this time. This time I was incarcerated and I didn't have any innocent baby inside of me being punished for my mistakes and bad behavior.

I had to make a home for myself behind the confinement of locked bars with lack of freedom or privacy in the midst of strangers who had their own demons and dilemmas with which to deal. I observed the desperate plea for love from some of the hardest criminals I would probably ever encounter. I had the opportunity to befriend drug addicts, prostitutes, abused woman, and many others who had fallen prey to a society that chooses to treat them as an outcast rather than delve into their lives to determine the source of their pain, and figure out why they were acting out in a manner that was unhealthy and dangerous. It appeared to me that society wanted to simply lop off the offending branch from the tree. It was a lot cheaper and faster that digging up the root.

Unfortunately, I had been a victim in this kind of charade since I was an adolescent. It almost became ordinary for me to be cut-off from society and my family in an attempt to rid me of my abusive behavior, but each time those attempts clearly failed. I continued riding on a never ending roller coaster of agony, rage and regrets with no chance of getting off. Although I could compare my life to the ups, downs, twists and turns of a roller coaster, my life was no amusement park; especially now that I was facing an extended amount of time away from my babies. Just like a roller coaster, my life seemed to be spiraling out of control, with the effects surfacing into different parts of my body and soul. These were the times I might have been acting out through violence in the physical realm, but crying out to God for help in the Spiritual realm.

We all have heard that loud ticking in the back of our minds; however, the sound of our eternal clocks is often shut out by preoccupation with our everyday lives. Family, friends, careers, extracurricular activities, and life's problems have taken precedence over our eternal instincts. I can admit to being one who was absorbed and influenced by the so called cares of this current world. A materialistic, driven world that we pass through as just a vapor of time, often challenging us to war against God as life wars against us.

So there I was a young wife and mother driven by my own selfish motives and tarnished by life's unfairness, abuse, and problems. My need to justify myself by righting the wrongs in my life had overshadowed my God given common sense and morals. Becoming enraged by life and its tormentors, I soon found myself a danger to myself and those who channeled their hurt on me or my babies. Being jailed was more than just a moment to take a serious time out and analyze my course of actions; this was a time that God would actually have my full undivided attention, and plead with me to get my life right with Him. This was a time for me to ponder over and get control of what really mattered, my eternal well-being.

I can say that I have had more than my fair share of spiritual encounters with God, having seen angels and demons, and experiencing visions. But nothing had prepared me for what I was about to encounter.

After leaving a church service I attended while in jail angry and confused, the sermon's message had pierced straight into my heart and mind, leading me to wonder "what would happen to me if I was to die right then". I never contemplated the thought although I had attempted to take my life on several occasions. I never really thought about the consequence of dying. Once again I was enjoying Jimmy Swaggers book "Questions and Answers about the Bible" when all of a sudden I felt as though I was dreaming because suddenly I appeared in my bedroom with my husband and kids watching them as they slept in our bed. I just stood there at the foot of the bed looking down on them and then suddenly I woke up back in my jail cell. I had to have been dreaming I convinced myself, but during a phone call later that evening I asked my husband if our boys had slept with him in our bed the previous night. To my surprise he answered yes and asked how did I know? I told him I had a dream about it and then I changed the topic. This was just the beginning of my outer body experiences. The next night while continuing with my reading I felt myself fall into a deep sleep when all of a sudden I felt like I was floating over Jacksonville. I saw Ezekiel in school at his computer desk then I saw my baby boys in their day care as I was looking down trying to get a closer look at them I suddenly starting drifting towards the earth. But it was unexplainable as my body actually went through the earth into this very dark mysterious tunnel. I remember trying to stop myself from falling. I was kicking crying and pleading with God for His mercy. I kept shouting, "No I am not dead what's happening?" I was magnetically captured by a dark evil force that pulled me down effortlessly into a waiting pit. Thank God before I ever reached the bottom of that terrifying pit I felt my spirit re-enter my body. I was so shaken that I went around the jail crying and trying to get people to persuade me that I was back in jail and that it was all just one big nightmare. I looked for answers from people, but no flesh could possibly explain what I had just experienced in the spirit.

 The only one I could consult about this matter was the one who allowed me to experience it in the first place, God. While praying I asked God to reveal to me what the experience meant for me, sometimes God would respond in a soft calm voice like my conscience, other times He would speak to me in tongues and interpretation of tongues. Other times he would answer me in the form of a Bible verse that would speak to me during my quiet reading time, but strangely God started speaking to me in my own writings through my poetry and songs and this is what He said to me concerning my experience...

Court

This is a story for inmates and it was written in a concrete cell

Nevertheless, it's a story of a lifetime (how to escape eternal jail)

Let me take you back to the beginning if you would please go with me

To the sin you committed freely, but now has you bound so securely

Accusations were made against you; police took the report

After gathering all the information, they haul you off to court

You stand there silently while the evidence is being seen

You can't speak unless directed to although this may sound mean

Evidence is shown against you although you may try to explain

You may have a co-defendant but they'll never take all the blame

You stand nervously feeling a bit paralyzed inside

Knowing your love ones can't help you so of course you begin to cry

Flashbacks of memories flow rapidly through your mind

You wish you went to church if only you'd taken out the time

How many times did you put God off just for the enjoyment of today?

You hardly taken out the time before but now you long to pray

Help me Lord you cry from deep within your heart

Instead of hearing that still small voice you endure the devils bark

Your honor the defense has done this and that calling each sin by name

You hold your head down slowly because of the embarrassment and shame

Your accuser is reading off your life your final moments of fame

But as he goes down the list only the bad things he does name

You plead with the judge hoping to get his mercy and his grace

He feels your sincerity and so decides to dismiss your case

You leave there feeling happy like you just conquered the world

But before you know it you are standing in front of the gates of pearls

An overwhelming feeling comes as you wonder how you got there

An angel shouts from behind you Your Honor the defendant is here

Come forth you hear a voice shout but your feet won't even budge

You stand there shaken wide mouth as look upon your judge

Yes, it finally does occur to you that you no longer dwell on this Earth

You begin to tremble all over as The Book of Life is searched

Your Honor the defendant has done this and that another voice does appear

You feel the terror of evil as the voice approaches near

It's that old serpent Satan for the Bible says he's our accuser

His voice becomes real stern as he says I say let's burn this looser

An evil laugh comes about him as you hear the words they're all dumb

I use them and abuse them and in the end I still won

He's done a lot for me says Satan this ole slave of mine

It was easy to possess him with temptations of any kind

Sex was often a weakness although drugs were not far behind

Cursing and gossiping was the ultimate and stealing was next in line

Jesus looked at me sympathetically His eyes were a flaming red

He pointed towards the earth and said this is what they do with their dead

I looked down curiously and saw them zip me up in a big black bag

I tried to shout to them "I'm alive" as my big toe was being tagged

Jesus I said but the judge he decided to dismiss my case

That was an earthly deed now let's judge your eternal fate

He started crying bitterly as He said you give the wrong people all the credit

It was I who touched his heart for you but like everything else you'd forget it

Restitution is what you pay back when you've wronged a man

How can you pay me for these showing me the scars in His Hands?

They beat me said the Lord then gave unto me a crown of thorns

But I endured the agony and pain for everyone that has been born

No excuses He said no excuses can you give unto me

For I paid the price for you when I died at Calvary

I have given you blessings and my protection was always there

When you called upon me speedily, did I not answer your prayers?

So what can you give unto me in exchange for your soul

Nothing He shouted as he pointed to a deep black hole

My body started drifting off as I was carried away by angels

I gasped and gasped for breath because I felt like I was being strangled

Pillars of smoke filled the air as hell's flames grew about me

People screaming in agonizing terror Lord let us warn our families

Hush said an angel you know it's too late for that

They can study the Word of God it has all the facts

In just a prayer life with God he will reveal himself unto them

He'll show them the way to salvation and help clean up their sins

Unfortunately for you it's a little bit too late

Unfaithfulness and sin have decided your eternal fate

Desperately I began to cry, wondering where I went wrong

I grew up in church and knew almost every gospel song

Crying bitterly and all of a sudden my scenery has changed

I wake up locked in a concrete cell and if that isn't strange

A guard yells out for me "inmate Tonya prepare for court"

Now my priorities are different as the facts I did sort

Which was more important my fleshly life or eternal court

"Tonya five minutes to court" I heard the guard say

Do I brush my teeth or comb my hair? No I got on my knees and prayed…

The message that God was giving me through this unforgettable experience and through my poetry went hand and hand with my real life situation because my court appearance was less than a week away and all I could think about was how it was going to turn out for me. The thought of spending the rest of my life in prison away from my children dominated my brain and my time. Not once did I fathom the thought of spending an eternity away from them and God in the everlasting confinement of hell. The message from God was an awakening for me to get my grip on reality and put things in their proper perspective so my court appearance in the next few days took a backseat to me getting things right with my Eternal Judge.

Once the day arrived for me to finally have my case heard in front of a judge I felt very confident because I had been praying before my Heavenly Judge nonstop, asking for His favor, but either way my spirit was at peace with whatever decision the court made concerning my temporal fate on earth. The day before my court appearance I spent several hours on the phone with my husband rehearsing our story so that my charges could be dropped and I could return home to our family. It's funny when I think of all the times he would dictate to me the things I needed to do to get his charges dropped when he was my assailant and now his memory seemed to fail him when it came to informing me the procedure in which to get my charges dropped.

The night before my court appearance I had the Christian guard who had taken a liking to me before remove me from my cell during the middle of the night and pray with me. I was confident that God had heard and answered that prayer and I displayed that confidence in the courtroom. When the judge asked me what had happened to cause me to try to run Nick over, I simply repeated the story Nick and I had come up with the night prior, "I had taken a large amount of sleeping pills then I accidently lost control of the vehicle." The judge seemed to believe my story but of course needed to confirm with my husband who shocked the entire courtroom when he denied everything I just said and said that I had deliberately tried to run him over. Then he began revealing scars that had occurred from previous altercations that he and I had. My faith most certainly started to dwindle as I began to wonder if my going home was even feasible. I looked on at Nick revealing the nasty scar from me cutting him with a box cutter. The judge asked if I had in fact cut my husband to which I honestly answered yes, and that he was probably disrespecting and violating me like he had been doing almost since we met and that I was tired of being his victim. I explained how he had broken my jaw, fractured my collarbone and even fought me while I was pregnant with our sons. I told the judge that I was fine with whatever decision he had made concerning my punishment but, that I was ready to return to my cell because I couldn't stand watching Nick play the victim after knowing everything he had put me through. Surprisingly Nick interrupted and tried to explain to the judge that he didn't want me to get punished any more than I already had been and he was ready for me to come back home to our family. I think his whole unstable behavior began to aggravate the judge who began to show signs of being tired of our whole ordeal. He simply said that we deserved one another and that the next time either my husband or I came before him in a domestic violence dispute he would charge both of us as habitual offenders and take our children from us. God clearly worked in my behalf and although I was angry with my husband for revealing the truth to the judge I later came to realize that it was all in God's doing as God's power is only revealed in truth. I was ecstatic that this case was now behind me and I was going to be released from jail that day. I knew in my heart I was going home to another one.

***

Once I settled back into my everyday life with my family I thought I should share with Nick about all of the out of body experiences I had while I was incarcerated. In an attempt to get him to be serious about God, I went into great detail about my spirit leaving my body and nearly going to hell. I don't think my husband believed me, but one day while watching a program on the Trinity Broadcast Network about near death experiences, several people including a famous Pastor Kenneth Hagin were all sharing their awesome stories. To my astonishment other people had experienced some of the same encounters that I had experienced, and God was enabling Nick to see that my experience wasn't an indication of me losing my mind but was shockingly factual.

For years Nick and I would go through seasons of good and bad times together, but when the bad seasons seem to outweigh the good ones we decided that we may need to relocate and get a new start in another location, so we jumped at his sister's offer to live with her and her famous engineer boyfriend. I should have known that although the climate changed, my husband was incapable of changing his behavior and in some instances it actually became worse. The deal was that he and I would babysit their three children while they were on the road touring or working with a variety of artist in the mainstream music industry, in exchange for free room and board while we both worked to save money to eventually move out on our own. Now this was an offer that should have put me and my husband in a really good position to prosper, but as usual my husband managed to mess it up by not working and eventually losing focus on our goals. He began having an affair with one of his sister's friends and began to act like a teenage groupie instead of a married father. There I was holding down two jobs and helping to take care of six children with no hope of ever getting out on my own because of Nick's infidelities and abusive ways. After a few months of his hideous ways I decided I had had enough and threatened to move out with our children back to Jacksonville with our old assistant Pastor. After seeing that I was adamant about leaving him, my husband decided we should both relocate to his mother's house and with that things got worst.

* * *

Nick's family treated me like I was their own flesh and blood, but my husband did everything in his power to destroy that bond. Now that I was separated from my family and isolated from most of my friends, my husband began to display even more of his domineering and cheating ways. He went so far as to have a sexual relationship with a fifteen-year-old girl ten years his senior, who lived across the street from his mother. During his illicit affair he became unbearable for me to live with. Thankfully, Rico moved me and my children into a hotel until I could get the funds to relocate to Jacksonville. While I was at the hotel I would allow my children to speak with their dad which gave him a way to determine my whereabouts; of course he soon came searching for me.

 I could hear him questioning one of the housekeepers about whether they saw someone of my description. I was beside myself when she led him directly to my room. Once my children heard his voice on the other side of the hotel door and began crying and trying to open the door to see him. I couldn't deny them their dad and so I ended up opening up the door for him. After a long conversation he asked if we would ride with him so that he could buy us all something to eat. While on that simple mission we got into a horrible car accident when his brakes suddenly failed while we were going down a hill, causing us to plunge right into a huge tree. Thankfully none of my children were hurt in the accident and I was the only one that ended up with a fractured foot. My husband was hysterical with fear and seemed to regret everything he had put his family through and wanted to make amends. His tears seemed so genuine I thought that maybe this accident triggered something in his heart to do right by me, boy was I wrong.

 After leaving the hospital Nick's generosity and sympathy were overpowered by his jealous ways. Now that I was inambulatory, I would have to be more dependent on other people to help me do everyday chores. My husband had a fit when I needed his younger brother to drive me to my son's school to remove him out of school after the school nurse called that he was extremely sick. He questioned me all the time about who came to the house while he was at work and wanted me to isolate myself whenever one of his male friends or family members came over. One day while we were taking a nap together, one of his male cousins came over to visit his mother. I could hear him ask her where Nick and I were and my husband's little brother let him know that we were taking a nap. Then the cousin continued asking why

I acted so stuck up and left the room every time he came over. Again my husband's little brother answered and told him that Nick made me leave the room, and that he would often accuse them of lusting after me and would try to fight me once he or any other male left the house. This statement enraged his cousin who absolutely thought it was asinine to believe that he would betray Nick's trust and he wanted to confront my husband with these foolish accusations. I knew that there was going to be hell to pay if he woke my husband up with this nonsense, but I didn't think I was going to be the one to pay it.

Nick woke up to his cousin cursing and accusing him of being insanely jealous and immature. I thought when he woke up and jumped out of the bed that he would confront his cousin for making a scene, but instead he tried to rationalize with his cousin and began accusing me for their quarrel. The person who had just laid down next to me holding me close in his arms while we slept heartbeat to heartbeat was now humiliating me to all of his family. I just laid there in the bed completely shell shocked and thrown for a loop. I laid there quietly with tears flowing down my face listening to insult after insult from the person I made vows to before God. Although he had previously showered me with vulgar words to my face, it pierced my heart more listening to him say these words to his family. I made up in my mind right then and there that I was finished with him and all of his negative baggage. My heart hardened towards him in that very moment and somehow I knew that he and I would never be the same again and his place as my husband, lover and friend had officially been removed. I knew I had to find a way to leave his mother's residence. But I knew I would need help doing it so I called the only person I knew to call, Ben.

Before I asked my step dad to assist me in leaving my abusive husband, I explained to him how much he had hurt me in the past by continuously trying to molest me. I actually poured out my heart to him and asked if it were possible for him to treat me like a step daughter and to actually be there for me without lusting after me. I told him that I felt like he needed to apologize for his past behavior and that he could make amends by doing something right. I think he was shocked to hear me be so forthcoming and he actually did apologize. Ben had to work early in the morning so I thought it would be a good idea for him to bring his truck to me and allow me to take him to work so that I could pack up and leave once Nick left for work. With all the bickering and cursing that he had done the night before, I decided to sleep on the couch. I thought that by me sneaking out early in the morning he would never know that I had left to take Ben to work. It wasn't until I was returning home from dropping Ben off that Nick woke up searching for me.

As I was pulling up into his mother's driveway he came outside. He was enraged and demanded that I get out of the truck. I knew if I stepped out of that truck that he was going to hurt me so I blew on the horn as hard as I could, in order to get his mother's attention thinking she could somehow control her son. When his mother came to the door she saw how irate he was acting and convinced him to calm down and allow me to leave if that was what I desired to do. Against my better judgement I got out of the truck and as soon as I entered the house he started in on me and began slapping me across the head, accusing me of sleeping with Ben. Punch after punch went to my head as I tried to gather my things. Although his mother demanded that he stop he completely ignored her orders. As I was walking through the kitchen I noticed a big knife sitting in the sink drainer and I just grabbed it and turned around to attack him with it. "Stop!" I yelled at the top of my lungs. "Stop freaking hitting me. I am so tired of you!" I told him as he tried to run for cover. He immediately ran to go get his mother who was now in her bedroom getting ready for work. He told her that I was crazy and that I had threatened to kill him. His mother came out and acted as though I was the assailant and yelled at me to leave her house. Stunned by her sudden change I became even more angry as the feeling of betrayal and rejection began to set in. Everything he had taken me through, everything I had lost and given up for him flashed through my mind. I felt like I had given him my life and now I wanted to take his. I must have blacked out momentarily because when I came to I was still holding the knife in my hands and his mother was standing in front of me slapping my face while trying to pull the knife out of my hand. I looked at her with silent rage in my eyes and warned her not to put her hands on me again. I ended up leaving there with only my oldest son, Zeke and I returned to Florida where I could begin to get my life back on track and get to work on bringing the rest of my babies back home with me.

Rico ended up driving me back to Florida where I would move in with my mother and her new husband Jeff, the same man that tried to go out with me when I was locked up. Although I had temporarily given Ciera to her Godmother, Rico and I managed to salvage our friendship. After years of noticing that our daughter had some emotional problems that caused her to act out I thought it would be best for her to be with someone older and more mature who could give her the attention she needed. I loved my daughter tremendously but I knew she wouldn't be safe with me and I didn't want to expose her to the physical abuse I had grown up with so when I found myself becoming impatient and abusive towards her I made the difficult decision to release her from my life and all its negative influences. I was waiting for God to change her but God needed to change me and once he did he gave my daughter back to me.

Chandreka was still living with her grandmother, while Nate and Prosper were living with their dad, so Ezekiel and I were alone to settle in with my mom and her new husband. Knowing that he was attracted to me and desired to date me while I was locked up, and the dilemma that the sick attraction from Ben and her drug addicted boyfriend caused, I knew this wasn't going to be an easy transition. I started working almost right away, got my son into school and tried to be out of their house and away as much as possible. I thought that would keep down any confusion that tried to rear its ugly head, but instead it only aggravated it. He accused me of being a whore because I went out on dates. He told my mother how he wanted me out of his house and off his couch, both belonged to my mother. My mother told me all of the horrible things Jeff would say about me and Ezekiel and then begged me to not confront him about it, claiming it would only stir things up. I decided to respect her request until one day after walking my son to school I walked in to hear him on the phone talking offensively about me. I just couldn't stand there and listen to his vile lies and my mother wasn't there to stop me from telling him off. I kicked the bedroom door and told him to come out and say whatever he had to say to my face. I called him a coward but he refused to open the door and face me like a man even though he didn't have a problem bullying my mother around. When my mother came home I told her what I had done and she got upset with me because she knew she would be the one to suffer the consequences, but I didn't care. I was tired of pretending that I didn't know Jeff was putting his hands on my mom. I was tired of him trying to control her house even though he wasn't working and contributing anything and I was tired of him insulting me.

My mother went into their bedroom. I pushed my way into the bedroom before he could possibly attack her. I began yelling at him and told him whatever he had to say that he didn't need to say it to her, he could say it to me. I wasn't prepared for him to say that my mother didn't want me there in the first place and that if it hadn't been for him she would never have agreed to let me and my son come live with them. I stopped yelling at him and just stared at my mother, waiting for her to deny this accusation, but she didn't because she couldn't. Her betrayal and rejection was harsh and crushing for me. Although I stopped my contribution to the argument he kept it going, getting agitated to the point of physically threatening her. My mother was forced to call the police and once they arrived he was apprehended.

While he was in jail my mother and I were getting along fine that was before I found her letter to him in the mailbox; what she had to say would almost destroy our relationship.

I knew it was wrong to open that letter to him but I had to know what she was saying to him and if he had been threatening her so I opened it without her knowledge. In the letter she went into full detail of how she wanted to save her marriage and how I was in the way, and that she planned on putting my son and me out of her home before he was released from jail. I was stunned and I wondered when was she planning on telling me that I had to find somewhere else to live? Where was I going to move with the little income that I did have. I stared at the pictures of my children on her wall and decided she wasn't worthy of those pictures nor was she worthy to be my mother or their grandmother. I called my sister and told her what the letter had said and she said take down her children's pictures as well. When my mother came home she found me packing up my things, I confronted her with the letter and told her she deserved everything he was going to do to her. With that I moved out of her house and into a rooming house.

The rooming house had a lot of rules. One of the most important rules was that no children were allowed overnight. I snuck my son in for a while, but one of the residents made a complaint to the landlord, who warned me I was going to be evicted if I allowed my son to stay. Since I was back in church I asked one of my church members if they would take him in temporarily while I got back on my feet and glory be to God, she agreed. While at the rooming house I got a job at a local hospital and had to catch the bus to and from work. Getting there was never a problem but because my shift ran past the time when the bus ended its route I always had to find a ride home. Therefore, I was extremely thankful when I met someone at a local club while attending a friend's birthday party. He wasn't someone I was ordinarily attracted to but slowly but surely he began to sway me into believing that there was more to a man than his looks. He let me know that chivalry is not dead as he showered me with countless dates, flowers and gifts. Even the number of children that I had or my current near homeless situation did not detract him from wanting to make an honest woman out of me and be a father figure to my children. At first I ignored his attempts because I was beginning to enjoy my single life. I liked being able to date several men at once and seeing them whenever I wanted to. I was finally in control of my life and I wasn't sure if I was ready to give up that control, my heart or my soul to anyone anytime soon. To my surprise little did I know that Nick wanted to reconcile our marriage as well.

When he called my phone one day out of the blue and told me he was in town for me to see my children I was filled with excitement. I had no other choice but to sneak him and my children into the small room that I was renting for the first night that they were here. Nick tried his best to be intimate with me and although I allowed myself to be cordial I knew intimacy would never be a factor with us again. Nick and I had always had an on and off again relationship that expanded into our marriage and although it was customary to get back together after a break up I knew reconciliation with him was out of the question. The communication, trust, and respect for him was long gone so it was no wonder that the next day when I went to the bank to pull out funds, I noticed that some funds had been taken and I thought he was the culprit. I tried to confront him right there in the parking lot of the bank. Thankfully a Pastor and his wife noticed the chaos and came over to talk some sense into me. Later that night I discovered that the funds were never missing and that my deposit just had not hit my account at the time I was at the bank. I apologized to Nick for the misunderstanding, but it was very clear to me that my feelings for him were fading. They had completely diminished once I found out about the young teenager who lived across the street from his mother was now pregnant by him. It was sealed in my heart that he and I would never be together ever again and though I was sad to see my young babies leave with him I knew I couldn't support them in that little rooming house, after all I was barely supporting myself.

* * *

Of all the guys I was currently dating at that time, there was only one I thought would be a real positive influence on my children, Calvin showed me the deepest desire to help me better myself in order to get them back. So I stopped dating drug dealers, and men who were basically just looking for a good time. Despite the fact that Calvin was not that good looking he became my knight in shining armor. Although I could never bring myself to love him, I learned to respect his love for me and his desire to ensure my happiness. Eventually he and I got a small two-bedroom house together, and one by one my children were returned to me. The neighborhood we moved into was considered to be middle class and we were surrounded by wholesome people, including a loving Pastor and his wife who happened to move right next door to us. This was extremely beneficial as my children made friends with their children and had positive reinforcements and activities to keep them occupied. It was different attending a church that was led by a Caucasian Pastor, the over dramatic yelling and falling out all over the place was not included in their service, yet my children learned more than they would ever learn from any other of the past or future churches that they would attend. The church as well as the neighborhood held mostly Caucasian people but no one took notice of race or color. It was nothing less than unconditional and we in turn fell in love with our new church and especially its first family, the Osbornes.

Our house was crowded with five children living there especially with his son often visiting, but we were so happy being together that we barely took notice of it. For the first time in a long time it was good to see my children happy. This man was showing us how a man was supposed to love and provide for his family. He never once called my children step children, instead he accepted them as if they were his very own. He did everything in his power for and with them and he continued to spoil me as well. I began to think that I could eventually fall in love with this man… until alcohol revealed the other side of him.

As we began settling down, absorbing the new foundation of our combined family, I started taking notice of Calvin's jealous, dishonest, and very controlling ways. Alcohol became a constant trigger in his personality change and once he had consumed more than he could handle there were always bad repercussions. Like most individuals who get intoxicated his behavior changed dramatically; he became even more hostile and rude. At first my children and I learned to blow it off and not take his outlandish stunts seriously, but being ignored by us only seemed to increase his desire to act foolishly. He expected to win our love and respect by spoiling us with money and materialistic things, then throw everything he did for us up in our faces. He would actually go into hours of ranting and raving reminding us that he was the so called big money maker of the family and therefore expected everyone to honor him as such. His bragging was done to belittle us and make us feel inadequate without him. He also began to show me that he was a man of double standards and even though it was okay for him to go hang out with the fellas, he would have a fit if I tried to hang out with my friends. I must admit the only time Calvin became abusive was when he was drunk, but when his verbal abuse began to escalate into physical abuse I knew I could no longer ignore it.

After several warnings to him about the past abuse that I had experienced with Nick and my violent reaction to it, he either didn't take my warnings seriously or just flat out didn't believe me. I begged him time and time again to stop grabbing, pulling, pushing, and shoving me around, but he wouldn't. I didn't know what to do about the situation because he and I both knew I couldn't financially support my children on my own. After constantly being bullied by Calvin, who had recently become my fiancé I was at my wits end with all of his antics. One day he pushed me to the point of no return and he learned first-hand that he should have heeded my countless warnings.

It happened after we had entertained some guests at our home. When everything was done and everyone was leaving, some of the girls stated they were going out and I had plans to go along with them. In front of everyone else he openly agreed, but once they had left he informed me that he had lied and that I couldn't go anywhere. Reminding him that I was an adult, capable of making my own decisions and the fact that he had gone out the past two weekends didn't seem to persuade him. So I decided to stop arguing with him and show him that I meant business. The whole time I was trying to get dressed he harassed me. I kept trying to avoid the conflict that I clearly saw coming. After grabbing me and shoving me onto the back of the couch and literally throwing me over it I wound up on the floor. As I was picking myself up I knew I'd had enough and that I needed to leave before I ended up doing something I was going to regret. I begged him to apologize but he refused and he kept insulting me and trying to bully me around. Going out was no longer an option, it was time for me to gather my children and leave the house. I hurried and put my children in the van as quickly as I could. I tried to hurry out of the driveway away from the house and away from him. As if he wasn't already drunk enough, he decided he also wanted to walk to the local convenience store to purchase more alcohol. As he was walking past us he kept mouthing off and belittling me and my children. It was one thing for me to listen to his hurtful criticism, but it was an entirely different ball game when he began to bully my children.

I could have easily just ignored him, I was already in my van safe and sound, away from any danger but I knew if I didn't show him that I wasn't going to keep accepting his bullying ways he was only going to get worse so I decided that I had to show him that there was a penalty for hurting me and my babies. Something told me to just take my van and hit him because that was the only way I could shut up all his screaming and yelling. Without a second thought I hit him with my van and watched him fall to the ground, but my anger wasn't satisfied and so I turned my van around and ran over him. I was about to run over him again when Ezekiel suddenly jumped out of the car and shouted, "Ma stop you are going to kill him." Still my anger wasn't satisfied and I walked over to him, watching him squirm in an attempt to get away from me, and told him that this is what he gets for constantly putting his hands on me. He started yelling for someone to help him and before I knew it the dark empty street was flooded with people. "Help me," he shouted at the top of his lungs. She is trying to kill me. I heard someone say to call the police and I just knew I was about to spend the rest of my life locked behind bars away from the same children I was trying to protect.

    I chose not to leave the scene of the crime because I knew in my heart that would only make matter worse. I remained there, uncertain what the police were going to do to me. Once the officers arrived on the scene, people began shouting to them that I had run over my boyfriend with my van. One of the officers immediately came over to question me while his partner went to question Calvin. The officer asked if I had struck my boyfriend with the vehicle and I answered him with an honest yes. Calvin, who was lying on the pavement unable to move his lower limbs shouted that I hadn't been the one who had struck him. He told the officers that he was involved with a hit and run. I took the story from there, realizing that his blood might be on my van. I told the officers that I wasn't paying attention on the poorly lit street and that I was trying to attend to my children, but before I realized it, my van had struck him. I mean who was I to argue with him once he began trying to fight for my freedom. I didn't know why he was trying to save me but I thank God that he was. Now the only people who had to corroborate that story were my children.

    The officers separated my children one by one and asked them individually to recall the events that had transpired and Lo and behold each of them corroborated the story to perfection and the police had no other choice but to release me with only a traffic ticket. After he had taken up for me I should have had some level of regret or remorse, but as much as I wanted to, I didn't. I went and spoke to Pastor Eric about the situation since He was supposed to be officiating our wedding, but when I laid out all the facts about the circumstances and shared the fact that I wasn't remorseful, Pastor Eric was not taken aback by any of it. He said as our neighbor he had witnessed the drinking, the verbal and the physical abuse that Calvin had subjected my family to. He did offer us counseling if I so desired, to try to work things out with Calvin. He even went as far as building a wheelchair ramp in front of our home when it came time for him to be released from the hospital.

The mood of the entire household changed drastically while Calvin was in the hospital. All the anger, fighting and drunken rages suddenly came to a halt and there was a new found peace in our home. It was days before my children and I would go visit him. I had traumatized them with the image of him lying motionlessly in the street after seeing me hit him with my van several times, they needed to see that he was alive and well. As I was approaching the room I could hear how happy they were to see him, and how happy he was to see them. He asked where I was and they told him I was coming. I heard him tell my children that he loved me and them very much and he was sorry for all the hurtful things he had said and done to them. I walked into the room and immediately had to walk out the moment I noticed his leg in a full cast and up lifted in some sort of medical equipment that hung over his bed. Sadly, I didn't leave the room because the thought of seeing him in pain was too much too bare, I left the room because I couldn't stop laughing. As evil as it may sound, after all the bullying and him terrorizing us on countless nights it was funny to see the tables turned.

For the life of me I couldn't find a way to be merciful to Calvin, his foul mouth and demeaning ways didn't help matters either. I didn't help him to the restroom, give him sponge baths or do anything particularly special for him although I was the cause of his broken femur bone and hip. The tables may have seemed to be turned in my favor for a while, but one day as I was about to attend my dental assistant class he started in on me and my children as usual. I thought I would just ignore him or just use my own words to retaliate against him. It almost scared me half to death when he jumped from his wheelchair and hopped over to the couch where I had been sitting. Although his lower body was in agony, clearly the upper portion of his body was healthy as he demonstrated by tackling me and hitting me over and over again.

Although his punches were irritating they weren't hard enough to cause any serious injury and only made me angry. I warned him that if he had struck me one more time I was going to kick him in his broken leg. He didn't believe me because he struck me again, but I followed through with my threat. After being kicked, he was in excruciating pain, but I wanted him to pay even more so I proceeded to take his wheelchair to school with me so he would be forced to crawl around the apartment all day.

Months went by and with counseling things seemed to get better, so a year later Pastor Eric ended up marrying us in a beautiful ceremony that I put together myself. I had mixed feelings about going through with the marriage, but I didn't believe I was financially capable of supporting my five children, as none of their fathers were paying their court ordered child support. Even some of his closest friends, family members, and ex-wife warned me to think about my decision more carefully. I felt just like I did with Nick, if he surrendered to God fully and gave up the excessive drinking and partying then things between us could change for the better.

My relationship with God is just that, a relationship. Even though God promises that He never leaves us I often strayed away from him due to sin and the cares of the world. My backslidden periods out of communication with God never lasted for a long time because of my genuine love for him.

I always felt that if I had a man who had the same kind of desired relationship with God that I did then my life would begin to prosper just as God had said, but foolishly I never consulted God about who to marry or allow to father my children and I paid the penalty, but so did they.

Because I felt like God could use anyone, if that person was willing to be used by Him, I lived my life hoping and praying one of these men would get on board with me and devote his life to our Creator. Once again I delved into rebuilding my relationship with God, in hopes of restoring sanity to my life, but insanely I kept bringing ungodly people to tear it down. Calvin and I started attending church regularly and even began visiting some of the previous churches where I had been a member in the past. While at church I noticed he didn't take church seriously and would often clown around during the service in order to make my children laugh, but that was not as annoying as him copying every move I made during my praise and worship. It almost reminded me of the time when I was possessed with those demons and the demons inside of me were causing me to mock people. My children took notice of his bizarre behavior as well and began to lose even more respect for him. One day when I asked him to pray with me as we both knelt on opposite sides of our bed, I was praying out loud for the both of us, but I felt in my spirit that he really wasn't into the prayer. Then I heard the soft quiet whisper of God tell me that this man doesn't have a real relationship with Me and he doesn't desire Me. Open your eyes God whispered to me while I was praying and when I opened my eyes my husband was staring at me with his hand holding up his face like he was bored with the whole idea of prayer.

Since prayer is such an intimate thing I felt violated and dirty with the way he was looking at me while I was deeply engaged in conversation with my Creator. I told him what God had spoken into my spirit and of course He told me he didn't believe me. We were supposed to be praying before we went to church with my children, but instead we were having a full-fledged argument. When we arrived at the church I didn't mention what had taken place to anyone and I even went as far as to conceal that he and I had just had a huge disagreement. Like usual, he did his silly antics of singing louder than anyone trying to make my children laugh. When Pastor Greg had gotten up to preach, he began speaking on people moving without hearing from God and the consequences that come with it. During the sermon he said some people are married to people that God never ordained them to be married to. He said God knows everyone's heart and some men are holding on to their wives by pretending to want a relationship with God but their hearts are far from God and that God was going to expose them. My kids looked at me with amazement and said mama that's for you, God really does talk to you.

I heard the Word of God and I didn't have the faith to act upon it, but the longer I lingered on in this unhealthy marriage, the more God began to reveal more and more of this man's dark habits and behavior that were trying to destroy my life. I think it goes without saying that once violence is introduced into a relationship, if counseling or spiritual help is not sought, the violence is likely to worsen over time. Just as was the case with Calvin who had been physically violent with me but had never laid a finger on my children, but that would change as well. After punching Ezekiel who was no more than about 12 years of age while at Calvin's family reunion, I knew in my mind I had to find the strength to leave him. Regrettably I didn't call the police that day because I had currently just experienced a bad injury that had caused me not to be able to work and he was our sole provider, plus his family begged me to give him another chance seeing how he was intoxicated at the time. I had always been the type of person who reveals a lot of emotions and thoughts during my sleep. Every night since he had punched my son nightmares began to haunt me, I couldn't get the image out of my mind. I knew I had to make him repay for what he did to my child and I wasn't going to stop until I did.

One day after terrible nightmares of him punching my son in his face was tormenting my mind I just decided out of the blue that would be the day I retaliated. I told him I just wanted to fight him straight up with no weapons and nothing or no one holding us back. He thought I was being foolish until I threw the first punch. We proceeded to rumble through our rather large laundry room. I managed to tackle him to the ground and once he was lying there on the floor I grabbed an older model television set and threw it directly on his chest. He tried to drive himself to the hospital in his company's van; I stopped him by crashing into it several times with my own van. As a firm believer in an eye for an eye, I felt it was appropriate that one injury against my child deserved a bigger injury against him.

After a while there was really nothing holding us together besides his money, and soon enough he began to fail me in that area as well. He began gambling and losing money at the dog tracks, throwing parties and barbeques to try to impress his friends, and our bills began to suffer. His irresponsibility caused us to get evicted from home after home. The stability that I had grown accustomed to was swept from underneath me like a rug. My stability suffered more when my past came back to haunt me like a ghost in the dark. It all happened when the police brought my mother to our house for a place of refuge from Jeff. As many times as I had been involved in domestic violence cases I never witnessed police remove the suspect from the scene to where the crime occurred to an entirely new location that had nothing to do with it. Still the police stood in my yard blocking me from going to work because Jeff informed them that I had a warrant for my arrest; clearly something my mom shared with him. I didn't make it to work that day or for several weeks after an array of charges stemming from my time with Nick were brought against me. All the axing down doors, writing checks to support my children, and not reporting income to the government agencies had risen from the graves I had buried them in. It would take five years of probation and restitution to finally lay them all to rest for good. While on probation I would injure myself and be forced not to work for several years. When the five years had expired I had managed to rebuild my life by graduating from dental assistants' school, obtaining a CDL and forklift license and not getting in anymore trouble, but I wasn't able to repay the funds that I owed. My probation officer advised me to get my affairs in order as she warned me that I might go to jail, but in prayer God reminded me No weapon formed against me shall Prosper. Needless to say God intervened and gave me favor and mercy when the judge decided to throw the entire case out.

I was never in love with this man and was only with him for the purpose of financial gain it, but it surprised me when I had learned that he was being unfaithful to me. His unfaithfulness didn't even bother me since I was engaged in my own extra marital affairs. When I found out that he was paying this woman's bills I saw no reason to stay with him any longer. My plan was to find a job in spite of my injury and begin saving money to eventually get my own place. The plan didn't even get a chance to hatch because when I confronted him about his infidelities, and then admitted that I was only with him for money, he went berserk. He knew I didn't have any form of finances and that I couldn't afford to take my children and leave right away therefore he taunted us with threats of putting us out on the street. He acted as though we were supposed to bow down and worship him because financially he held our lively hoods in his hands. My children started trying to defend me and when he lashed out at my daughter I knew I was done. If I had to take my children to a shelter, I knew it would be better than having to stay with him another day. "Jesus," I prayed. Make a way for me and my children because I have absolutely nothing else to rely on but faith.

I had informed my mother, who had recently separated from Jeff, of my decision to leave Calvin and move my children and me into a shelter. To my astonishment she offered to let us come stay with her until I got back on my feet. I thought of how things between us had played out the last time with only one of my children. I wasn't sure if moving in with four would be such a great idea.

Now wasn't the time for me to be prideful. I knew in my heart from experience that living in shelters was something I really didn't want to subject my children to if I could possibly prevent it. Therefore, I gladly took my mother up on her offer. My mother was inviting us to move in with her into her two-bedroom apartment but I knew it was more of a sign that God was moving me into my own little wilderness.

A wilderness is a place of testing and trusting. It is a place where we develop our relationship with God, because the wilderness is where he mostly shows His attributes as the **I AM**; everything that we need in our lives. It is a place where God teaches us to depend on Him and His word alone. It is a place where God tests our hearts to see who will fully trust Him and allow Him to lead us into our promised land. Unlike a school test where you study and learn the information before being given the test, with God we are allowed to study and learn while being tested. On the contrary, just like a school if we fail the test we are not promoted to our next level and are required to take the same test again and again until we pass it, so the wilderness can be likened to a classroom. Like everyone else I spent a majority of my time in classrooms learning the basic subjects required to get through life, but God's testing teaches us wisdom. Wisdom was clearly something I had been lacking as I kept trying to do the work out of my own strength, knowledge and manipulations. I didn't comprehend resting in God's promises and having faith in His finished work. Unfortunately for me, just like the children of Israel who stayed in the wilderness forty years waiting to enter the promised land that could have been entered in a few days, I as well, would spend forty long years in the wilderness waiting for the promise God was trying to accomplish in my life. The same promise I spent forty years blindly and ignorantly sabotaging. The scary part is some people in that wilderness died before seeing God's Promised Land including their leader Moses. I prayed I didn't die in my wilderness.

Things at my mother's house were not so bad after all, except for her thinking that every little thing we did was going to run up her bill and her obsession with her idea of cleanliness. So in an effort to keep my children from overwhelming her I would find places to take them to occupy their time and energy until it was near their bedtime and sometimes I would go as far as getting us a hotel room every weekend my mother's was off from work so that she could have her apartment to herself. I was able to pay for these things by working a very physical job in a warehouse, even though my doctor had not released me to work after the injury I had sustained only months prior. Regardless of my efforts, my children seemed to irritate my mother who had never really raised her own children in the first place. Every single thing that they did was blown out of proportion and disturbed her immensely.

One day when I found out that she had beaten my children with an extension cord like she had done with me in the past and then made them take a bath with salt in it so that their wounds would burn, I knew that my time with her was up. I began trying to search for apartments that were income based and I came across an apartment complex located in an area I wasn't familiar with. I told the gentleman over the phone how many children I had and it just so happened that he could accommodate my needs. Once I looked at the place with all of its single struggling mothers and children, I knew it was something that my children weren't going to adapt to very easily, but I knew if I wanted to give my children any source of stability I was going to have to start somewhere, besides who ever said the wilderness was supposed to be beautiful. The transition of moving from a middle class neighborhood to a low, impoverished one was going to be a challenge in itself. The reason I stayed in so many relationships that were unhealthy for me is because I was trying to provide the best I could for my children and these drug infested, high crime rate, roach and mice ridden, filthy apartments, were a constant reminder of how I failed them miserably.

    I did the best I could to make our new home as comfortable as possible. I decked it out with furniture and nice décor and bought my children all the latest electronics and toys in an effort to keep them occupied and protected inside our home. The fact that I spoiled them with so much was my way of trying to make up for all the hell I had taken them through with my roller coaster of abusive relationships. The materialistic stuff seemed to satisfy their needs temporarily while in the confinements of the apartment, but then they were forced to deal with reality by having to go outside to walk to and from school. Everyday my children were forced to walk passed drug dealers, they began to get bullied, but God was with us just like always,

    Eventually the bullying stopped and the toys and electronics that I had purchased for my children were used inadvertently as a ploy to make friends. Suddenly our house was the house to go to for football or to make rap music, and soon my children were becoming popular. Most of the drug dealers had a crush on me, but respected me as a no nonsense, hardworking, single mother who didn't fear them or judge them, but rather embraced them with respect and tried to convince them through verbal communication that it was possible to turn their lives around. It was at this point that my promised child Prosper had begun to first show his entrepreneurial skills. I take it that he observed the drug dealers and how easily they made their money and even though he didn't want to be affiliated with its illegality he learned supply and demand and figured a way to make money legally. At the tender age of eight or nine, He requested that I purchase some water and Gatorade for him, borrowed my cooler from home and began selling his products to everyone in the neighborhood including the drug dealers. The fact that Prosper saw me struggling to make ends meet and he knew that although I tried I couldn't fulfill every desire he had, so he took it upon himself to not only not complain but to do everything in his power to change his situation; was admirable. Even the drug dealers began to look at him with respect and started finding little chores in which to pay him for such things as helping with their mother's trash or groceries.

Meanwhile I was beginning to start dating again. I wasn't looking for a long term commitment and I made that clearly known to all the individuals I came in contact with. My heart had been bruised and I wasn't going to allow it to suffer through anymore pain… We didn't know each other but we were both there to support a mutual friend's birthday. George was certainly different than anyone I ever dated before. He had never been married, didn't have any children and was a very meek and humble individual. The only negative that I could see was his overly contented attitude and his lack of ambition to better himself or his situations, but I felt like that could be changed with a little assistance from me.

First I had to loosen the grasp his grandmother had on him and try to convince him that after 32 years of living alone with her it was high time for him to expand his horizons. This was not an easy task, but I was able to convince him that it was time to leave both his dead end job and his loving grandmother.

After he moved into my apartment things were really well between us. George showed absolutely no signs of being abusive, a womanizer or irresponsible. Although he did not have any children of his own he took a liking to mine rather quickly, and developed a unique relationship with them. To me George seemed like he was sent from the very throne of heaven. He was kind, romantic, affectionate, loving, fun, well dressed, considerate, family oriented and basically everything I could desire from a potential husband, but I had to find out if God would agree.

The fact that I wasn't attending church regularly didn't stop me from having my personal relationship with God. Of course I knew fornication was wrong and I didn't want to live a life of having premarital sex and continue to miss out on God's blessings so I made it a point to let him know that in order to be with me we had to make things right with God by making our union legal. He didn't have any difficulty with my request and he went out to purchase my engagement ring as evidence. When he purposed I gladly accepted.

* * *

Once people heard of, or witnessed my gift of God speaking directly to me while in prayer, they usually were envious of me. I never understood why because although I love my communion with my Heavenly Father it carries with it a lot of responsibility. God is an honest, spiritual being who loves the sinner, but hates the sin. And even though my intimate times of prayer and worship are often followed by God's affection toward me and his direction for my life, he makes sure to include warnings and chastisements. Though his chastisements are done in and through love, just like Adam and Eve I would find myself hiding from God. When my life wasn't quite aligning with God as I thought it should be, I would shy away from prayer for a season, but when you are in love with someone you can't stay away from them no matter how much you try.

Whenever I prayed, God told me that George wasn't for me and that he was committing abominations against Him. I didn't understand what abominations were so I studied to see what God possibly meant by this term. Abominations are things that causes disgust and the Bible clearly states several things which God calls abominations: things such as a proud look, a lying tongue, hands that shed innocent blood, a man or woman who has sex with a person of the same sex, and many more things that God calls detestable, that I didn't feel described George at all, so ignorantly I chose to ignore God's warnings until his warnings became my worst reality.

I remember the day God revealed the abomination he constantly warned me that George was committing. I had traded cars with him for a day since my car was in better shape than his because he needed to go farther than I needed to travel. I had Zeke and Nate in the car with me and as I was approaching a hill some movies slid from under the seat onto the accelerator. From just quickly glancing at them I knew that they were porn movies and I threw them back under the seat without my children ever noticing. When we had arrived to our destination and had all gotten out of the car God told me to go back and look at the movies once again, so I told my sons to go on ahead and I returned to the car. Slowly I reached up under the seat to retrieve the movies and I couldn't believe my eyes! I dropped the movies and screamed from the top of my lungs causing my children to hurry back to the car. Just like I had thought it was porn, but not ordinary porn it was homosexual porn of men performing sexual acts with other men. I suddenly understood why God says abominations make Him sick because I felt nauseated and sick to my stomach.

 I never hide anything from my children and I wasn't about to start now. As embarrassing and hurtful as it was I didn't have anyone with whom to talk about such a sensitive matter so I poured my broken heart into them. They witnessed me call this man and confront him about my findings. Shockingly George never lost his cool and responded with his usual low key tone. "The movies don't belong to me," he said. "But I can't go into detail right now. I am in the barber chair. I promise to talk to you as soon as I get my hair cut." "No, tell me now who do they belong to," I insisted. "Oh my God why didn't I listen to God when he told me that you were committing abominations?" I told him. His only response was, "Tonya, the movies belong to my cousin. I promise they are not mine, and I will talk to you as soon as I get home." Then he hung up the phone. There were several close friends I had confided in to tell them that the Lord was telling me I couldn't marry this man because of the abominations. I reached out to them to tell them that God had revealed everything to me. Some were saying that I should give him a chance to explain, that it may be true that the movies didn't belong to him, because he didn't appear to be homosexual. Since I had spent several hours talking to people who supported him and thought that he was a good man I wasn't as upset by the time he got home. I just wanted proof that what he was telling me was true. He said that his mother was a witness to these facts. I wanted him to prove it.

 I didn't care how humiliating it was for him, if he wanted to continue in our relationship he was going to have to put his pride aside and let his parents know that he was riding around with homosexual movies. I hoped they would verify that they belonged to his cousin, whom I never met. When we brought up this so called cousin of his, his mother didn't seem to have any memory of him. He had to jar her memory and still she referred to the person as having been a family friend and not a blood cousin like he suggested however, she swore up and down that her son was not gay and that she believed his story. I chose to keep my mouth shut about the situation that time but I made sure that I kept my eyes open.

I tried desperately to put the whole ordeal behind us, however God kept whispering "he is committing abominations" into my ear every time I prayed. One day I took Nate and Prosper with me to attend to some chores when I suddenly realized that I had some paperwork to turn into my rent office before they closed. I had just hung up the phone with George and asked him what he wanted me to purchase for dinner. I didn't even get a chance to purchase the items before I realized that it was almost time for the office to close for the day and I didn't have time to inform George that I was rushing to get back home. When I arrived in front of my apartment I didn't set my alarm on my car since I was only going to grab the paperwork and drive straight to the rental office. He didn't hear me as I came through the front door and then began to enter my bedroom. When I opened my bedroom door he was startled by my presence and immediately tried to retrieve a movie from the DVD player. Before I knew what was happening he and I were wrestling over the movie. When I realized that I couldn't get it out of his hands, I resorted to reverse psychology and convinced him to be open and honest about what he was trying to conceal. After breaking the DVD in half he placed both pieces into my hands. I didn't have to mend them back together to know that they were homosexual porn of men. I didn't hide my fury nor was I trying to protect his little secret. I felt a hurt my heart had never experienced before and I cried out to God in relentless agony and pain. I had to get out of that apartment if I didn't want to hurt him and spend the rest of my life in prison, but where would I go on a Wednesday evening on my birthday. The house of the Lord was the very first place to come to mind so I jumped into the car wearing a simple T-shirt and jeans. Come-as-you-are has always been my practice so I went with a broken heart and a broken porno DVD still in my pocket. Little did I know that he had plans of going as well.

He jumped into the passenger side of my car and pleaded with me that

He wasn't gay and that he only watched the movie to see what the hype was all about. He tried to convince me that he needed prayer and God's help just as much as I did. The ride to church would have been exceedingly quiet if it had not been for me crying hysterically. When we arrived at the church I didn't sit next to him. I was disgusted with him and wanted to be as far away from him as I possibly could. I imagined the fact that I could have gotten an incurable disease from his hidden affections and actions with men. I couldn't even tell you what the sermon was about because all I could do was cry. I noticed that I was interrupting the service and decided I needed to go to the bathroom and try my best to gather my emotions. As I was in the midst of crying out to God the Pastor's wife came into the restroom and tried to console me. I opened up and let her know what had me in such turmoil and she suggested that I talk to the new assistant Pastor about the situation after church was over.

When the service was over my fiancé and I were called into the Pastoral office to have a moment of counseling. Although I had been a member of this church for years I didn't know this new assistant pastor but I felt comfortable taking Pastor Griffin's wife advice so I wasn't shocked when she told me that I had God living on the inside of me and that God could deliver anyone from anything. She reminded me of all the hell the other men had taken me through and suggested fasting and prayer. I questioned them about why God would keep telling me and showing me this man was not for me. I didn't want to question their knowledge or wisdom concerning the things of God and I knew I was supposed to honor those who have rule over me so I humbled myself and heeded their advice over God's word.

I returned home and made it clear the changes that had to take place if we were going to make it. He agreed to the changes and to continual counseling along with giving his life over to God. I felt like we needed a new start as well where everyone didn't know his dirty little secret and I could save my children and myself from harsh harassment and ridicule. Plus, we needed to relocate from the negative area which seemed to be an arena of bad influences that we were constantly fighting against. For example, Ezekiel was beginning to get influenced by the drug dealers and began both using and selling drugs and acting up in school. Then Ciera who was just a preteen began sneaking off and having sex with random boys inside of abandoned buildings and I was finding myself getting into a legal altercation with the management of the premises because of my complaints to the housing authority concerning the unsanitary and unsafe conditions.

I began praying and seeking God for a way out and just like every other time I prayed God would answered me. This time God told me that He was going to bless me with a house and I informed my children what God had promised. We don't understand the ways or the mind of God and I surely didn't know how he was going to bless me with a house but I knew that faith without works is dead. So I began doing my part and began to get my credit in order. I added George to every application since I was taking the preachers advice on praying to God about our relationship, but my applications with George were continually denied. No matter what I did, or how long I fasted or prayed God kept telling me that this man was not my husband and that he was committing abominations against Him and now he was blocking me from my blessings.

God did it, just like He promised he blessed me with a house. I didn't need George's income or credit on the application after all, but I had grown accustomed to his nearly one thousand dollars a month contribution and I didn't see any point in stopping that so I moved him into my new home. By the time we had moved into the house I had sent Ciera to live with her dad and had put Ezekiel out of the house because he was now becoming a negative influence on his younger brothers by being disrespectful and using and selling drugs in front of them. I was literally drained from having to go to schools and courts on behalf of my son and trying to defend his bad behavior. So I felt like removing the negativity from my younger children meant I had to make certain sacrifices, including keeping a man in my home that God clearly didn't want there.

Before long Ciera had gotten pregnant and Chandreka was put out of her grandmother's house due to some improper things that she had gotten involved with. I was happy to move out of the projects but with just my income I was only able to purchase a small three-bedroom home. When I looked at the home and decided it was in my price range that would accommodate George, Nate, Prosper, and myself comfortably. That was all I needed to be concerned with since my other children were legally grown.

God told me he was going to begin sending my children back home to me, and unbeknownst to me He planned on doing it suddenly. Nate and Prosper and I barely had an opportunity to get comfortable before my oldest children came to live in my tiny house. So my household occupants changed from four people to eight. At this point I began to start dating once again even though George was still residing with me.

One particular person I became heavily involved with was seven years younger than me, but age was never a factor between us. Felix was probably the most emotionally invested relationship that I had in my adult life, and I knew that our love and respect for one another was mutual, however like me, he had a lot of baggage that came with his sincere desire for love. Felix was a very attractive man and finding a woman was never a problem, which explains why he had so many children with different women. He was financially handicapped, Still I chose to judge his heart rather than his circumstance and we eventually fell in love. He actually became my scapegoat from all the disrespect and chaos that had surrounded me in my own home, and although he lived with his brother he made me feel as if it were my home as well. He was protective of me, understanding and very attentive to my every need. I longed to make him my husband so much that I obsessively prayed about it.

God instructed me to begin writing down everything that He told me would transpire and when they took place I would know with assurance that he had spoken to me, which allowed my faith in Him to build over time. God also warned me that I was going to have to be trusting and obedient to Him no matter how the circumstances looked or what others thought about it. So I purchased a notebook and begin jotting down everything God spoke to me, whether I understood it or not. God began telling me that HE wanted to give me my heart's desires. My heart just so happened to be desiring Felix. Felix had been separated from his wife for quite some time and had actually gone through the process of the divorce proceedings, but there were complications which required them to refile. God told me he would get a divorce and cure his child support dilemma. I listened to outside voices who told me this man wasn't right for me since he had so many complications in his life and put their words over the infallible Word of God.

"Heed my Word and do not worry about what your ears hear or what your eyes see. Do not look to Facebook for your answers, but seek and trust in me." God would warn me, "These things are temporal and bound to change, but my Word is everlasting and forever settled in the heavens." It wasn't long before I allowed the influence of others to dilute my faith even further. I went as far as nearly stalking his Facebook page to observe what he was doing. I continued to seek others for guidance more than I sought God. I allowed them to either intentionally or unintentionally lure me away from the promises of God, yet God still wanted to prove to me that HE was sovereign and totally in control of the situation, so he allowed certain things to miraculously manifest. For instance, one day I called him out of the blue and he said he was out celebrating his divorce, just like God said.

Another time, I called the child support place for him and they notified me that they had made a mistake and had taken funds from his child support payments and given the credit to his father, who had the exact name as his, and now they had corrected the problem, bringing his child support out of arrearages up to date. Unfortunately, God revealed the flip side of not obeying him, because I went on Facebook and saw a picture of him and a beautiful young woman. I instantly became enraged and vindictive. I started posting childish intimate things about him on Facebook. It just so happened that while I was doing this I was watching a sermon on TV and the preacher said, "Don't worry about what it looks like, believe Gods word. The devil gives distractions and delusions. I heard the preacher but wasn't convicted enough to stop my childish rants until out of the blue I noticed a comment where he described this young lady as his first cousin. I felt so ashamed. I couldn't erase the post fast enough. I even had help from a close confidant who warned me several times to be obedient to what God had spoken, but my impatience, lack of trust and immaturity had gotten the best of me. Needless to say even after seeing all of the manifestations that God caused to come forth I should have never doubted his ability and should have taken a deeper look into my faith and disobedience. This was my first lesson that disobedience disqualifies one from the promises of God but God wouldn't be a good teacher if He didn't test me again.

* * *

Obedience was something I demanded from my children and being a child of God he demanded the same from me. Countless times I was warned to get the abomination out of my home, referring to George, and I chose not to obey the instructions because I wanted his money. One day we began attending a new church with Apostle Linda Thompson as its Pastor. Although she was the pastor, this day that I visited the church she had a guest speaker who considered himself to be a prophet. After the man had preached his inspiring message, he had those in need of prayer to stand in line. I was in the back of the prayer line, patiently waiting my turn, when the man suddenly stopped ministering and told me to come to the head of the line. He said, "I'm not going to openly rebuke you and call you out in front of all these people, but you know in your heart what you need to do, because God speaks to you and shows you things doesn't he? You are a prophetess," he told me. Then he took me by the hand and began walking with me across the church, and told me God desired to walk with me hand and hand. But there was something that God had been dealing with me to let go of and I had been struggling to comply. I knew what he was referring to and I began sobbing uncontrollably. Some ushers came and assisted me back to my seat and the man continued ministering to several other people in the prayer line, and once again he suddenly paused and said to me, Sister God is serious. The devil wants to destroy you if you don't remove the abomination. Then he told all of the congregation to point their hands at me and say let it go… the tears began to pour that much more.

I knew exactly what the preacher was saying and I was sad that I had frustrated God to the point that I felt like I was actually hurting him, but I didn't understand why God wanted me to put George out of my house when I was no longer intimately involved with him. I needed his income and most of my family and friends agreed with my logic. I stubbornly kept him in my home in spite of God's numerous rebukes, and I made the excuse that as soon as I got my income tax check I would put him out since it was only a few months away, but as usual God had different plans.

For the next month or so I tried to put my prayer life on the back burner. I knew what God was going to tell me and although I loved God and wanted to honor Him I was trying to borrow the time in order to get my funds together and then comply with His demand. Even though I wasn't praying at home I knew that when it was time to bring in the 2012 New Year, I was going to be in church. Just like every other church service, Apostle Linda had us to do praise and worship to usher in the spirit of God and I had gotten so deep into my worship I forgot that other people were even around me. I began crying out to God and as usual He spoke through me, loud enough for the entire congregation to hear. "Get the abominations out of your house, return to me with your full heart and trust in me for I desire to use you," God spoke to me. "Why have you hardened your heart against my word?" He said, "Repent and honor me with your heart and not your mouth". I cried out to God, pleading with him, not realizing that He was getting fed up with my stubbornness.

All the years this man and I had been together he had never stayed out all night before. But when we returned home from church he wasn't there. The next morning when I woke up, as embarrassing as this is to admit, I still ended up calling people in hopes that they would side with me against God. I wanted them to say it was ok for me to have the man God had repeatedly warned me about, live in my house just a little while longer. One particular friend who also was a member of the church and had witnessed God speak through me on several occasions, put me back in my place and told me she wasn't going to interfere with God, and that clearly God speaks to me and suggested I should consult God instead of individuals. I took her advice and went into the privacy of my bedroom and prayed to my Creator. God demanded, "Get the abomination out of your house. Choose ye this day whom you will serve and it will forever be settled in the heavens for I am a just God though I desire to use you I will not force myself upon you and I will give you your earnest desires. You cannot take this devil into your next level God warned me. Today is the day make your decision. No longer will I stand idly by and wait for you to take heed of my plea."

By the time I finished praying I was all cried out and I knew exactly what I had to do. Without taking another minute to ponder over it I began packing his clothes. I told my children what God had said, and they began assisting me with gathering his things because they had grown to know God as our only source for everything. When George returned home I informed him that he was no longer welcome at my residence and that God told me I had to make a choice that day because he was committing abominations against God. He didn't even deny it this time. He just began crying, and proceeded to the shed where we informed him his things were located. I knew then that everything God warned me about was true, but now that I was actually putting the abomination out I wasn't sure how in the world I was going to pay my bills.

* * *

When God created us He gave us the gift of free will because He is good in nature and doesn't force Himself or His ways on anyone, but He requires us to live with our choices and their consequences. My choice was laid out before me and God knew the entire time I would inevitably choose Him over anything or anyone. But now I had to choose to trust Him to sustain my seven- member household with only my income The Bible says God miraculously fed over five thousand with two fishes and five loaves of bread and right then I was counting on Him to bless my bread (money) and multiply it to meet our needs. One day while I was in prayer God told me to write down the fact that I wasn't going to lose my job, house, or car. The ink didn't have a chance to dry good before the devil began fighting me in these areas. I didn't even have time to prepare for the match before the devil began hitting me right below the belt and straight into my pockets when he ultimately began trying to take my job from me on several different occasions. Twice my job was saved just at the brink of being terminated and my faith in God soared, so I was astonished when in the next round the devil won by a TKO; I was actually terminated from my job. Confusion set in as I wondered if I had really heard from God. And did I make a mistake putting out the only source of help I had. Strange as it seems, it was my children who constantly reminded me of God's unfailing faithfulness and how He had always come through for me. I was starting to comprehend why the bible suggests we come to God with child-like faith because my eyes were blinded by my problems; but my children were walking by faith.

Luke 22:31 tells us that Satan desires to sift us as wheat. That is to say that little by little he desires to weigh us down with trials, tribulations and adversity until he has conquered our faith, which is why Jesus says in the same verse that he prayed that our faith doesn't fail us. I was in the midst of Satan's sifter and my faith was surely shaken as my bills were falling behind to the point I thought I may lose everything. Foreclosure and repossession warnings were causing me to lose my confidence, but my children kept on believing God's word. I think God acted on my children's faith as he supernaturally began answering our prayers. The first relief came when I got the news that my youngest daughter's application for an income based apartment finally came through. I was now going to be able to move four members of my crowded house into another location, but with none of them working, guess who was going to be responsible to pay for the cost of the move, furnishings, and maintaining the apartment. I wasn't sure if this really was a blessing in disguise or just another burden.

The house was a lot more peaceful when my three oldest children and my grandson moved into their own two-bedroom apartment. I made it very comfortable for them, purchasing all their necessities and paying their twenty-five dollar a month rent. I was happy to finally get my house back with just me and my two minor sons. Especially Prosper, since he had moved away temporarily and was living with close friends of ours, because our home was overcrowded with his older siblings. He was saddened by the fact that he had sacrificed his bedroom in order to offer them some stability after they were forced to come back and live with me, because of mistakes they had made in their own lives. I didn't comprehend the sacrifice that my youngest children had made until I was forced to attend a meeting with the school board concerning their attendance, it was there that I was notified about how Prosper felt about having to give up the comfort of his own bedroom to fend for grown children who he felt like weren't trying to assist me or themselves. It broke my heart to see my son break down crying because he felt like my oldest children were adding burdens to my already very complicated life and taking my time away from him.

I tried desperately hard to try to get my children to the point of independence, and although it took a while I managed to assist them in making the transition, but it didn't come until I forced myself to stop adhering to their every demand and started telling them no. I had to teach them that the same God they had grown accustomed to being there for me, wanted to be there for them as well. I had to allow them to develop their own personal relationships with Him. Meanwhile I had two minor children I needed to focus on and ensure they had a fair chance of achieving success. Every time I got one thing accomplished it seemed as if ten more things would stand up against me. I was in the process of rebuilding with my minor children when things in my life began to slowly burn away. My confidence, faith, hope, strength and joy all seemed to wither away in an invisible force that was set ablaze within a combustion of trials and tribulations. The fire would soon appear in the physical realm in an attempt to burn me and my children out of the home God promised I wouldn't lose.

Although it aggravated me to the point of losing awareness and was clearly another weapon thrown by the devil, God used it as tool to bless me. A few months prior to being terminated from my job, Prosper had accidently burned up my kitchen while trying to fry chicken. I was so upset and taken aback from all the turmoil in my life that the thought of losing my house caused me to lose consciousness in the middle of the street. I awoke to Prosper kneeling, crying and praying over me. I was so furious with him for his stupid mistake that I made him go stay with his older siblings for the night while I consulted with God. Thankfully no serious damage was caused by the fire and the insurance company settled right away for the minor repairs. Who would have guessed that the check would come at the same exact time I lost my job? So it seemed that the devil and all his tricks were no match for the Sovereign, Omniscient God, but that never stopped him from trying. Believe it or not with check in tow the devil still had more tricks up his sleeve and unfortunately I was the ignorant participate in his magic act.

The devil doesn't have any new tricks because there is nothing new under the sun. So he came at me with the same cunning games he always used and like a fool I fell for them. I don't know if it was lust or love, but I could never really manage to stay away from men, no matter how much heartache I had experienced with them. I felt incomplete without one to call my own, which is why it was easier to fall into an adulterous affair. I met Dennis in a dance club, even though I was back in church people convinced me that clubbing wasn't a sin. Like most married men he complained about how unhappy he was in his marriage and how he was seeking a way out of his failing relationship with his lazy unmotivated wife, as he would often call her. But it was his knowledge of God's word and his supposed relationship with God that grabbed my attention. I mean after all, I wanted a godly man to one day become my husband and fulfill the prophecy that God had spoken over my life so long ago about having a marriage that would prosper. If it hadn't been for his mother confirming or withholding information about him, I would have never given him an opportunity to get close to me; and cause me harm.

As I look back on it now, I couldn't tell you what I was thinking about moving this stranger into my home with me and my children. The bible studies, prayer meetings, long conversations, and good advice to my sons were very enlightening, but they were not worth the pain he caused when he stole the insurance check that came at the same time I had lost my job. I knew I wasn't going to be able to use any of those insurance funds on the actual repairs to my kitchen. My thought was that I would repair my kitchen later on and use the money to bring my house out of foreclosure, but I wouldn't get the chance to do either. You can imagine the feeling of despair and stupidity as I realized that I had allowed the devil to come in and steal the blessing that

God intended to use to pull me out of my pit. I can't say it happened without warning because I knew the adulterous affair would have its consequences. My children had told me they had witnessed Dennis snort cocaine at one point. Even his own mother had informed me about his former drug addiction that she claimed he had been delivered from. He was fully aware that I was facing foreclosure and He seemed to be very supportive of me by sharing funds when he would find odd jobs as a welder and keeping me uplifted in my spirit by speaking faith into me. But all my faith diminished when I woke up to find the money and my car gone.

***

I was robbed of more than just my money and car that day I was robbed of my good standing with God, but I knew this was a form of chastisement for indulging in the known sin of adultery. I was willing to accept my punishment but I wanted him to be punished for his part as well. I prayed constantly for his demise and I destroyed every single possession that he had in my home no matter what the sentimental value was for him, but that wasn't enough; I wanted to see him suffer. Thankfully his mother was able to contact him and convince him to return my car that he had taken out of the city to visit his daughter and take her shopping with my money. I found my car in my driveway two days later with the keys still in the ignition. Later he we would contact me to give me some bizarre story as to why he had to take my car. When I told him I didn't believe him and wanted to see him punished, he quoted a Bible verse that said I must forgive him if I wanted my own sins forgiven.

It sounded like a bunch of nonsense, although I knew that is precisely what the word of God says. I didn't want to believe it applied to me, at least not in this particular situation. Like in every other situation God would confirm this same message to me in prayer. I guess I tried to rationalize that Dennis was a willing participate in the adultery and I had nothing to do with being robbed by him. I didn't think I caused him any sort of hurt, but I neglected to think about the hurt I had unintentionally put his wife through. I wanted her to feel some sort of mercy for me when I notified her that her husband had stolen my car. In prayer God reminded me of the sanctity of marriage and the vow of no man putting asunder what He had joined together. I immediately felt remorse in my heart and repented of the sin right away and sought forgiveness from God, his wife and even him. I had once again learned to be obedient to God's requirements and God promised that He would reward me by avenging me and that I would behold it with my own eyes.

After reaching out with my apologies he began to try to contact me more by phone. I constantly blocked out random numbers that he would call me from, but it didn't sway him from trying to reach me. It seems as if adultery was something that he perfected because I soon learned that he was involved with another woman not long after that incident. The woman had contacted me once she noticed how many times he was calling me from her phone and was currently looking for him, because he had stolen her car. I informed the lady about where I knew he and his wife once resided and even agreed to take her over there to look for her car. I bonded with her over the fact that I had also been a victim of his. I vowed to help her in any way I could to get her vehicle back. One time when she and I were conversing on the phone his call beeped in on the other end. I informed her that it was him and that is when God literally placed him into a web.

He desperately wanted to see me this one day so I decided to oblige him. The only thing was that I had arranged for her and some of her family members to be waiting at a nearby gas station. She and her family wanted to cause him bodily harm. I didn't agree to those terms. I told her I also wanted him to pay for what he had done to the both of us, but I didn't want to take the law into my own hands and that I would only agree to meet up with her if the police were going to be there as well. She hesitantly agreed and so the plan was in motion. I wanted my children to witness God's promise unfold, so I stopped by my house to see if they were home. When I arrived there nobody was at my house except my nephew and I informed him about what was happening. We used the excuse that he needed to go to the gas station to get something to drink and we headed to the store where we knew the trap was set. At the gas station he agreed to fill my car with gas and buy us something to drink. While he was on the inside paying for everything the police and the lady pulled up on the other side of the building. Once he came out and proceeded to fill my car with fuel they immediately pulled up and apprehended him. God was right He did repay and I did behold His vengeance.

After that incident I got myself back into church and even though I felt like I was learning more from God in my own private Bible study and prayer times, I still felt the need to keep my children grounded in church. God was revealing things to me and would drop subtle clues about what he planned for my destiny. I knew His ultimate goal was to cause me to prosper in everything He set out for me to do as a sign He had me to name my youngest son Prosper. I raised Prosper to know that He was a true and direct manifestation of God's promise to me, and I knew that he was connected to God's plan for my life, I just didn't know how and at what cost. I assumed that because he was such a young motivated entrepreneur that he would be the business management or some sort of financial advisor for my ministry, but it seemed God had bigger plans and the closest hint I would get to these plans were revealed to both Prosper in me one day at church.

It happened on a weeknight. I had taken Prosper along with his brothers and his close friend to church with me. Apostle Linda Thompson was preaching and just like every other service nearing its end God began to use her to prophesy to members of the congregation. I wasn't surprised she had walked over to speak a word of God to me that God had revealed to her that I was also called to be a prophetess, God had begun confirming the prophecy he had spoken to me through various preachers. This specific day She spoke to all of my sons confirming their call by God and warning them of hidden dangers. Prosper was the last person she approached and to be honest it was the most dramatic. She walked over to my son and then looked at me and said "This baby is so connected to your destiny, but God can't do what he needs to do with you until he has finished and completed his assignment. She told him he was a special child of God and that his name was given to him by God. She also warned him about the company he was keeping. She said that he should be careful because people he thinks are his friends were not really his friends. Then she walked over to me and said that she saw me in a ship going across the world to do book signings. She said my ministry was going to be global and that the pain in my past was going to be nothing compared to the glory that God had for my future.

Soon after that prophecy Prosper got into trouble when he was caught riding around in a car with some friends and a gun in his possession. He was the only minor in the car and the only one to go to jail that day. I will admit that Prosper had gotten into trouble for minor things like trespassing in an old apartment complex where we had lived for five years. Unfortunately Prosper was only fifteen or sixteen years of age and very naïve thinking that this incident would end like the other misdemeanor charges where I would simply come sign my name on the dotted line and take him home. But because this was a felony charge he was now facing I knew it would not be that easy. My baby was facing serious charges and could possibly be charged as an adult where he could easily spend the next ten years of his life in an adult prison.

While my baby was facing these serious charges I decided to get closer to God. I needed to get by myself as I prayed for my son's deliverance in his case. One of the first things God began showing me was not to have any other Gods before Him, and to worship and trust Him only. God told me to turn away from celebrating pagan holidays that took the worship from him. These pagan holidays infused some deity that would cause me to unknowingly participate in idol worship. As I started learning the truth behind these holidays I felt convicted and I repented immediately from it. I revealed everything God had shown me to my children. To my amazement God had already begun revealing these truths to them and it was not difficult for us to relinquish our participation in celebrating them any longer. I can't say with certainty if this was the reason God showed mercy to my son and allowed him not to be charged as an adult, but I will say that the timing was consistent with one another.

In the end God answered my prayer and my baby was sent to do only a year in an adolescent boot camp for troubled youth. I never wanted Prosper to get away with his wrongdoings but I wanted the consequences of his actions to cause him to make better choices. So every Sunday I visited my baby and I taught him to embrace the time to make improvements in his life and view it not necessarily as a punishment. He would call every week and I would quote the scripture NO WEAPON FORMED AGAINST YOU SHALL PROSPER and convince him to recite it whenever things seemed to be going wrong. While Prosper was away God did draw both of us into a closer relationship with Him and each other. God taught us new revelations and our faith increased as we learned to stand on the faithfulness of God's word.

One of the revelations that God began revealing to me was the journey from the wilderness into the promised land where He desires to take all of His children. That is the fulfillment of God's promise and spiritual rest and happiness that we find in Jesus Christ (God's Word). The promised land stood for departing from works and entering into God's rest. I learned this principle by faithfully watching and reading the books of Joseph Prince.

I began to study the Bible. Answers came about why one generation was allowed into the promised land and the other before it was denied. I learned that just abiding by a set of laws that were created to demonstrate our need for a Savior wasn't what God required to make the journey into the promised land. It was never about one being good enough, for none of us could ever live up to perfection. The Bible declares that all have sinned and come short of the glory of God. Entry into the promised land is granted only by grace, and the belief and acceptance of God's redemption plan through His son; which can only be given by our Creator, who created the law, and the penalty for breaking the law is death. The Bible states that the wages of sin is death. So grace is not permission to break the law, it is the restitution that God paid when he sent his son to die in our place, paying our penalty, since God knew we could never keep the whole law, and because to God, breaking one law is the same as breaking all of them. Grace was the only thing that could save us.

The other thing I had learned in my study was that there were giants that were already occupying the promise land. The first generation's fear of those giants and their unbelief, disqualified them from entry into the promised land. Lastly, I learned that in order to make it into the promised land you must have a different spirit, one that is willing to trust and follow God, like sheep who follow their Shepherd.

One by one God would test me in all of these areas to see if I was qualified to make my way into what he had promised me. The first step was allowing me to go over into the promised land to scope it out. The promised land was being occupied by people who didn't have a relationship with God and for me to spy it out meant I had to affiliate myself with them. It all began during a bible study where we were studying something in the New Testament and without explanation my Bible turned to Zephaniah 3:20, where God promises to give Israel a good reputation, making it praiseworthy (the meaning of my name) among all the people of the world and restoring its prosperity (my son's name). Clearly God was giving me a sign, but just like Joshua doubt started flowing from close members of my congregation.

God says with two or three witnesses let every word be established so I asked him to give examples of people who had to step into the worldly system to achieve what God had promised them. He gave me three names that stood out in my mind. They were *Joseph* who was sold back into slavery in Egypt and became Prime minister to the pagan and idol worshipping of a self-proclaimed god, otherwise known as Pharaoh. God caused Pharaoh to favor Joseph's character and the gift of interpreting dreams that God had anointed him with. David was sent into Saul's kingdom to play soothing worshipful music whenever Saul was attacked by an evil spirit sent from the Lord. Eventually David would take Saul's place as King. Then our Lord Jesus had to come down to Earth where Satan is the ruler and defeat him to regain the authority and dominion that Adam relinquished to Satan through disobedience.

Now that God had given me the examples I was ready to go in and spy out my land. I didn't have to do much to make my way into a land where giants were roaming about caring less about the God I loved and served. Like David, Joseph, and Jesus, people began to take notice of my gifts and before I knew what was happening, different people and organizations were helping me to groom my gifts by giving me the opportunity to practice and perfect it.

Just like the Bible verse said, my name began to spread and I was sought after for my writing and speaking abilities. The thing I had to remember was that I couldn't partake in everything they did and totally turn my back on God and my beliefs. That line was very fine and I was praying every day God wouldn't allow me to cross it. My name was inspiring praise, but the devil desired to use it to glorify himself and ultimately defame my name and God. Church people thought I was being a hypocrite as I started appearing in clubs, on music video sets and in countless studios, learning the mastery of the music and entertainment business. I remember being so excited about it because God had clearly given me a sign that HE was in total control of everything that was going on in my life. Christians were making me feel guilty for listening to and trusting God, and I began wondering what god was I really listening and trusting in.

As my popularity grew people began to take notice and many sought out my talents and gifts. Most people thought that my involvement in the secular community was nothing more than for financial gain and that I was being led astray, but God continued to guide me in His usual mysterious ways. One day after discussing the possibilities of making money doing these projects I had gotten into my car when a series of songs played, one after the other. They played out each and every emotion and movement I was experiencing at that time (when I cried, a song came on about crying, when I wiped my tears a song came on about God wiping away tears) and by the time I got to my destination the person I had come to see quoted the exact words of the last song that had played on my media device. I knew this was no coincidence. God was sending me messages through these songs. I was so excited about these God's given signs and I wanted to share it with members of the new temple I recently began attending.

After I enthusiastically shared my testimony my spirit was brought down by the ridicule of the Pastor who made it a point to remind me constantly of his superior position and power over me. He made me feel no matter what revelation God gave to me if it hadn't been given to him, then I was in error. I could feel the confidence and excitement literally leave my body as my faith started to fade away. I began questioning whether I was in fact lost, or had

I been tricked once again as I'd been by the witches so long ago. I excused myself from the room and went into the restroom after relentless minutes of ridicule from him. I stared in the mirror, tears began to flow down my face as I reminded God of the promise He made to never allow me to be tricked into demonic activity again while thinking I was following him. I left the restroom, I tried to quench the spirit while walking passed the pastor, but the Holy Spirit would not be denied and I began to prophesy. "Why is your spirit heavy. Why do you doubt when you know that I speak to you as I spoke to Moses? Get your eyes off man and replace them on me," God said. Then he rebuked the pastor asking him who told him to speak those words of doubt to me and he asked him why he thought Satan was stronger than God. "Was not Satan made to be a servant of his Creator and will I not utilize who I desire to bring my plans" about said God. I went on to prophesy to several other church members including the Pastor's wife but something was different about this experience. It was the first time my spirit actually appeared before the throne of God and God anointed my vocal chords to sing.

I ended up leaving that organization as well and continued devoting myself to learning everything God wanted me to learn from the giants in the secular world. From magazine writing, to radio hosting and even movie directing. People placed me under their wings and willfully gave me their knowledge without expecting any form of payment, except my soul. My presence in the strip clubs and certain types of parties made me uncomfortable so I stopped attending them, but Satan would continuously push the envelope beyond any and every boundary that God created.

It would be dishonest to say that everyone I worked with hated God because many of the people I worked with encouraged me to keep growing in my faith. Still others tried to persuade me that the sins and abominations that they were partakers of were my only way to achieve the prosperity that God had promised. The biggest threat to my spiritual well-being came from an older, openly homosexual, talented woman in the entertainment business who took pleasure in recruiting young talent and grooming them into what the secular industry required. She was a woman of many gifts like singing, photography, graphic design, music, video, and film production. Working with her was like finding a gold mine because she had everything one needed in order to obtain success in the industry, if one was willing to pay the cost.

I was eager to work and learn from her because I felt like she was my one stop shop for success. The first time I met her was on the scene of a video shoot where I was co-hosting for a local internet show. I was instantly mesmerized by her talents and the talents of her artists as well, especially one named Novacane whom I developed a deep friendship with, and began to date over time. She had to be convinced to allow me into her tight knit organization but once she let her guard down I was welcomed into a whole new level of darkness.

It was obvious to people that God had gifted me and given me favor among men, therefore I was brought into the company for my networking and writing skills. I also decided to bring Nate into the company with me as God's gifting upon him was being realized and I wanted to help nurture it. Just as God had promised all of my children began to display creativity in the poetic anointing that is upon our lives. The only problem was that people did not want to utilize our skills to promote the Godly things that I wanted to create, instead they wanted me to assist them in making money by promoting the exact opposite. I was confused and conflicted in my emotions about doing the events that were gaining me recognition and knowledge, but pulling me away from the things of God. My son would come to me complaining about how uncomfortable it was for him to be a part of certain things that I tried to drag him into. Movies and parties that promoted the same homosexual abomination, drugs, and violence that God had demanded me to stay clear of were now the custom for this lady and most of her organization and its affiliates. What kind of example was I setting for my children, and did I cross the line into eternal damnation? I was reprimanding my sons whenever they spoke out against the vile things that I was morally against, but publically promoting. I often found myself being offended by those who suggested I had gone too far, but I summed up their open rebukes to be nothing more than mere jealousy.

Eventually I left the company when I felt like they were trying to gain control over me, and my ideas were being shunned to promote theirs, but something always drew me back. I felt as though if I could put my morals and indifferences to the side to accomplish other people's goals then they wouldn't have any qualms about doing likewise for me. Little did I know that these people I was so grateful to for helping learn the business and assisting me in grooming my gifts, were also on assignment to hinder me from achieving God's purpose in my life. That is why they were so adamant about me promoting things that I knew God would not touch nor wanted me to touch. As I began praying, God opened my spiritual eyes and ears. I remembered the prophecy pastor Greg told me that the devil wanted my gifts for himself that time when I became demon possessed, but he cannot touch God's anointed without God's permission. In essence it was God who was keeping them from tainting my God given prophecy of one day having a worldwide ministry that would help heal, liberate and encourage people. Instead the devil wanted to pollute it with a worldwide ministry that would send people further into sin and bondage.

An uneasy feeling began to settle in the pit of my stomach as I watched this woman brag about turning young girls out with the promise of fame, proudly breaking up marriages, and promoting violence and drugs through music and movies. In search of prosperity, I was in the realm of darkness and too blind to see that my baby boy Prosper, God's given symbol, was also in search for prosperity; sadly, he had entered this evil realm right along with me.

**

When Prosper was finally released from juvenile boot camp a year later my prayer was that he had learned his lesson and was ready to get his life on track. I thought I could pull him off of the street and into the entertainment field as I had with his brother. Although Prosper was not interested in it for himself, he was excited to hear about everything his brother and I had gotten involved with. He showed his excitement by listening to his brother's music almost the entire four- hour ride home. I could tell something was different about Prosper, he seemed more mature and less introverted with his family. The little boy who had hidden behind the façade of a man all of his life was ready to step into manhood and get his life together, but there wasn't a man readily available or willing to teach him how to make the transition, so once again he turned to the streets for protection, guidance, and provision.

The first thing I did when my son returned home was to put him in a special educational program that allowed him the opportunity to earn the high school credits he missed out on by skipping school and misbehaving before he had gone into the boot camp. The school was a self-serviced school that only required four hours a day of his time and I felt my son would appreciate not being in the typical public schooling that had caused him so much frustration. Unfortunately Prosper only had his mind set on becoming a merchant seaman and was only interested in attending their program which would have been a superb idea if his judge was willing to take him off his undisclosed and undetermined probation period and allow him the chance to relocate to another state to attend the program. After six months of good behavior and just weeks before his eighteenth birthday my son's probation officer came for a home visit. My son was excited to let her know that he had researched The Merchant Seaman program while he was in boot camp and was adamant about going into the program, and that he had actually been saving up to pay his own tuition for the program. I am not proud of it but I knew that Prosper had resorted to some of his old habits and began selling marijuana again. After all, selling goods like water and Gatorade had always been a lucrative business for him, so drugs seemed to be just as easy but more financially rewarding. I warned Prosper that a temporal means sometimes has lasting consequences. But he was at a loss and didn't see another way out. I wasn't getting any financial assistance from his dad and I knew I couldn't neglect my bills to pay for him to attend the program in the time frame that he was requesting, but I ensured him that if he waited six months for me to get my tax refund I would assist him with the fees, but Prosper was set on going in the next few weeks right after he turned 18.

Prosper began acting as though he was on borrowed time. I didn't pay attention to just how paranoid he was until that day that his officer came to visit us and informed us that she didn't think the judge was going to release Prosper to attend the program. My son started tearing up, although he desperately tried to conceal his tears his emotions overwhelmed him. Before I knew it he burst out in agonizing pain and his spirit was absolutely crushed. I had never seen my son cry like that before. Not since he was my little spoiled rotten baby who had attached himself to my hip and cradled in my arm, and was pulled away from my love and nurturing, had he shed tears like that. My heart broke for him and just like when he was younger I reached out to console him in my arms, but he was so embarrassed that he ran and locked himself in his bedroom. I banged on his door and tried to convince him to come out and plead his case with the probation officer, but he would only respond through the closed door. He said, "If I don't leave something bad is going to happen to me. "Yall don't care about my life he told her. Why come y'all don't want me to leave and do better. It's like y'all want something to happen to me." His words pierced my heart and I began to plead with her. I asked her to please do whatever she could so that my son could feel safe and have an opportunity to start anew. I told my son that whatever we had to do to get him in the program we were going to do.

Soon after that Prosper began requesting to go see his daddy's side of the family as his birthday gift. He was confident that he was going to have the opportunity to fulfill his dreams and he wanted to say his farewells.

Prosper was always considered a go-getter and would get on people who didn't live up to their potential and resorted to begging or bumming for a living. He didn't make excuses for those well abled individuals but wanted to help anyone he saw putting forth an effort. I had constantly reminded him that he was only a child himself and that the weight of the world was not his concern, but still he pressured himself by taking on the responsibilities of others. I began to minister to him on a one on one basis as he slowly began to open up and reveal his heart to me. I told him that he couldn't take on burdens that belong to God and reminded him that he was one of God's special children, and why I named him Prosper. To my surprise he informed me that he understood and that the people in the camp told him how much faith I had to have in him and God to give him such a significant name. He also told me that while he was away in boot camp that he began to read his Bible, pray, and eventually gave his life to God. It was evident to me that my son was maturing and wanting to live up to his name and prosper in life.

Shortly after his release Prosper had gotten into a relationship with a slightly older girl. She was a beautiful young lady who seemed just as goal oriented as my son. To be honest I wasn't ready for my baby to begin dating, but once I realized that she was keeping him home and out of trouble and was going out of her way to assist him in his transition from the street life into an honest man, I slowly began to let my guard down. Prosper kept reminding me that this girl was different and he had plans to marry her once he had become a merchant seaman. I used to laugh at him as he would fantasize about their future and always include me in it. I had to remind him that he had to build his own life, but He would become so irritated with the thought of him and I not living together forever. To him it didn't matter who either of us were married to, his destiny was attached to mine.

*　*　*

Prosper was just as overprotective of me as I was of him. He had witnessed me being beaten at the hands of men, including his dad, for most of his life when he was too young to do anything to defend me. I had been badly beaten by a boyfriend, whom Prosper never had a chance to meet, while Novacane and I were on a break from one another and Prosper was away at boot camp. By the time Prosper had come home from the program my relationship with this violent man had ended and Novacane and I had rekindled ours. Even though I was no longer with the man, that had beat me up severely in a hotel room, Prosper felt betrayed, and angry that he wasn't there to help defend me therefore his suspicions and dislikes automatically adhered to Novacane like paint on a wall.

Having my children so young caused me to have a different relationship with them than most people. Even though we didn't always attend church regularly as religion would dictate, I made certain that all my children developed their own personal relationships with their Creator. As a God-fearing woman I made certain to affirm His desire to use them for ministry, but I allowed them the freedom to be children who would live and learn from their own mistakes. Prayer was relevant in my household and my children were accustomed to hearing me pray, they knew that I had the gift of prophecy where God would speak through me. When God kept telling me that my ministry would begin in the year of 2014 I wasn't sure how He would bring it about. All I knew was that He promised to save and use me and all of my children for his glory, so I took God at His word and was certain that God's desire would over-ride any plan the devil had to destroy them before God fulfilled his promise. We lived our lives trusting that God's word would perfect and protect anything concerning this prophecy. I taught my children that no weapon formed against it should prosper, but because I had named my symbolic son of God's promise, Prosper, I imprudently only focused on the prosper part and ignored the part of the weapons constantly being thrown against me and the symbol of God's word, Prosper.

It was a Sunday, five days before my baby's eighteenth birthday. I had cooked a big meal the night before. Novacane and I woke up around noon and as usual I went into the kitchen to prepare a late breakfast for the family. To my surprise Prosper was already up and in the kitchen fixing himself a plate of leftovers. I asked him if his girlfriend was over and I reprimanded him about having her stay past the time allotted. He became frustrated and asked me how come I wouldn't let her stay over if I saw she was keeping him out of trouble. As usual I reminded him that he was just a child and needed to stay in a child's place. She wasn't there that night he assured me, so I questioned him about the amount of food on his plate and why he had prepared so much. "It's for friends," he said sarcastically. "Can I give my friend some of your food off my plate, or do you want me to pay for it?" He asked trying to be funny. I warned him not to get sassy with me and answered that I couldn't afford to take care of him and his friends and warned him not to make a habit of giving away my food. Prosper knew that I did not allow any and everybody in my home and he was just as protective himself, so I was astonished to see several young men whom I'd never seen before lingering outside.

I immediately questioned my son as to the identity of these young boys, and demanded that he remove them from my premises. Prosper knew I meant business and I trusted him to do as I told him, but I didn't realize that Prosper had left with these individuals until I had knocked on his bedroom door later that day to see if he still wanted lunch. After realizing that he wasn't home I phoned him to ask him about his whereabouts. Like clockwork he answered my call and requested I put his food in the microwave. Later on that evening he came home and approached me while I was in the bedroom. He asked about his plate and then asked if I was still mad at him from that morning. I told him no, but I reminded him that he couldn't trust just anybody enough to bring them to his home. He then apologized for getting smart with me that morning, asked for my forgiveness and told me that he loved me. He asked if I forgave him and if I loved him, I replied of course I do. Then he asked me to just come right out and say it and without hesitation I said, "Prosper I love you. You are my baby I am always going to love you." Prosper asked if I was straight or if I needed anything. I told him that I was straight. He then went right next door to his brother Nate's room and asked him to make sure that I was straight and walked out of the door.

Now that Novacane and I were back dating and working for this openly gay woman we were required to be at a meeting later on that day, concerning a new movie and single she was about to put out that made me feel so uncomfortable that I kept praying and seeking God about it. I had actually prayed less than a week before this meeting with another young lady this woman had turned out into the homosexual life style many years before, but had later gotten delivered, married, and had become a mother. The spirit of God fell into my house as God began to minister to me. Prosper who was on the phone with his girlfriend at the time and was accustomed to me prophesying, shared in the joy that I have such a unique gift and relationship with God. God spoke to me that day. Later I would find out that the devil was also listening. Although I am not prejudiced against the gay community and have friends and family that I love who are a part of it, I felt guilty promoting it when God kept telling me it was against His creative process and design. I tried to water down my decision to direct and have my impressionable son, in an ungodly movie in a desperate attempt to help God bring about the worldwide ministry and fame that God had promised. I guess I had forgotten the lesson God demonstrated when Sarah tried to help God fulfill His promise to her.

When we arrived at the meeting that was scheduled for seven p.m. I had developed a bad attitude. I couldn't put my finger on it but there was bad energy flowing all around me. The producer started the meeting off by announcing that she had made me not only the director of the movie but also her Public Relations Manager and Marketing Specialist, without first consulting me, which meant that I was going to not only direct the movie but openly promote it to the world. I became infuriated with her; and the devil that was trying to get me to further defy God and my convictions. I sat in complete silence and shock as I observed just how cunning Satan had been by luring me right back into the abominations God said I had to remove from my home if I wanted to be blessed. The devil often comes in a different manner but he still represents the same package of evil, and I knew right then and there in that moment that I was done being manipulated and neither I nor my son was ever going to be a part of anymore of her productions.

After the meeting I went home and went straight to bed. I noticed that Prosper hadn't returned home yet, but it was still fairly early and there wasn't any cause for alarm… until the very next morning.

Prosper never came home. It was unlike my sons to not contact me several times in the course of the day, therefore fear began to immediately set in, but my faith assured me that my son was safe and sound, until Nate began informing me of a rumor that my son was murdered and people thought a picture of a young man lying dead in the street may have been him. I didn't want to hear or accept any of that nonsense. I just wanted my son to answer his phone or contact me so I could fuss at him and move on. I ended up calling my job and telling them they had to cover my shift because there was no way I could work under that level of distress. I proceeded to call all of the hospitals and jails to see if they knew anything. When I called the police to report him missing they informed me that I had to wait twenty-four hours before they would take the report. I asked them about the person that everyone said was reported by the news as having been involved in some shoot out and had been gunned down in the middle of the street. The police informed me that all but one of the three victims had been identified because the last victim wasn't wearing any identification on him. I described the humongous tattoo of my name across my son's chest that he had gotten after his brothers had gotten smaller tattoos of my names on other parts of their bodies. I was proud that my son loved me so much to honor me by engraving my name on his chest close to his heart, but I never thought for a second that tattoo would be used to identify him.

He didn't leave the street life quickly enough and he ended up paying the consequence with his own life. He was the youngest victim of the three people who had lost their lives that day. My son's death was all over the news as different accusations and theories surrounding his death began to surface. Before I knew it videos praising my son and his name, for his brave act of dying while trying to assist his friend, was all over the media. Countless, times of writing down God's promises and watching them manifest made me ponder why God had not revealed my son's death to me. Had God given me signs that I didn't pay attention to. I thought back to the time I was in bible study and my bible suddenly flipped to Zephaniah 3; 19, 20 where God promises to give Israel a good reputation, making it praiseworthy among all the people of the world and restoring its prosperity. God didn't say how he would bring this about, but I knew just as my name means Praiseworthy that God was speaking to me. What I didn't know was God was also referring to my son Prosper as well. I felt with deep assurance that my son was in heaven, because I trusted God's word. But the moment I found out how brutal his death was I questioned God's love. Once I began to question God's love, my faith in his plan began to crumble and I became the biggest weapon against it…

The following is an excerpt from my forthcoming book 2:

"No Weapon Formed Against Me Shall Prosper (2)"

Believing that Prosper was now in heaven, I found myself quoting the no weapon shall Prosper verse when it came to the devil taunting me about the eternal well-being of my baby boy, but I didn't realize that weapons were now being thrown at my other baby and I hadn't even given birth to her yet. The holy spirit is so kind and patient when he is teaching us the things of God. He kept bringing things back to my remembrance. Like the time Pastor griffin said I was pregnant not only in the physical but in the spiritual realm while I was carrying Prosper. I remembered the prophecies of the world wide ministry in the form of a book. Then a verse suddenly appeared in my mind Revelations 12:4 with the story of a woman who was about to give birth and the dragon who was waiting to devour the baby as soon as it was born. Clearly God is not speaking of me or my son in this verse, but God is a God of pattern and He doesn't change His ways or Word. Everything he created was for a precise purpose. Women were created with a womb to birth things in this world and Satan desires to destroy or contaminate the fruit of our wombs.

    Satan wanted my babies and he was going to stop at nothing until he had devoured them. If I thought for a moment that the death of my son would cause him to have mercy on me, I was about to find out this ruthless, evil minded, God hating creature is incapable of such emotion. After giving birth to five children naturally and never experiencing its pain, I would have to learn to trevail through a sovereign God's spiritually induced labor. I began to wonder when God was telling Eve that she would go through tremendous pain when giving birth did He mean it in a spiritual sense as well.

Giving birth to this book was by far the hardest labor I ever experienced. From the first word to the last period I not only re-lived hell as I wrote of devastating memories, I had to wrestle with hell to do it. One thing about a prophecy is it leaves very little room for choice. There is a time period for everything and I could not stay pregnant forever. The only thing that I could do was give birth to this baby(book) and pray that the devil didn't devour it or me before it had a chance to survive. For years I would dream of having a baby and in my dreams the baby was always taken from me in some way. In my dreams the baby was always a little girl (my Destiny) and since God had spoken that Prosper was going to be a boy I never looked at my dream or prophecy from a spiritual perspective until now. Although I had visitations into the spiritual realm and dimension God wanted me to learn to abide in it. It was the only way that I was going to learn the truth of his power, sovereignty, and faithfulness. I couldn't even watch a movie without seeing it from a spiritual perspective and that was only the beginning as I would learn the Spiritual Realm is the residence of God and where God is His power is and boy was I in need of His power

I was neither, mentally, financially, or spiritually ready to bury my son and even less prepared to write a book. After almost losing my house I couldn't afford insurance and really didn't think I would ever need it since I thought I could take God at his word that he was going to use all of my children for his glory. I thought they would reach adulthood and I would witness them, first hand, ministering for the Lord so when my son's death came about I could not have been any less prepared. Thankfully God worked it out and the moment I realized I had to put a service together for my son, Pastor Eric came to my mind. He knew my children better than any other preacher whose church we had visited, because our families actually became friends outside the doors of the church. Unfortunately, Pastor Eric had moved and I didn't know how to contact him, but God allowed him to contact me and offered to have the services at his church for free.

Isaiah 54:17 had been connected to my son his whole life and I was not about to disconnect him from it now. I wasn't going to give the devil the pleasure of me throwing a sad funeral for my son. I was going to embrace the bible traditions and throw my son a music filled praise and worship, going-home-celebration. No one was allowed to wear the black color of mourning. I had gone so far as to have T- shirts made with the *no weapon* verse on it, along with my son's picture. Fred Hammond's song No "Weapon" honored my son's name and ushered in the people and presence of God. I had entertainers including Novacane, rap the lyrics of God's love and salvation to children of all ages. Pastor Eric did a beautiful job and ministered to these young people the meaning of the verse they had become infatuated with and connected to my son by having it and him tattooed on their bodies.

Through my confusion I tried to minister to young children the need of God's salvation, making wise choices, and about God's love, power and sovereignty, over the enemy that wishes to destroy us. Organizations such as Department of Juvenile Justice, Urban league, Families of Slain Children as well as social media all offered me the unique opportunity to spread God's word and redemption plan, but how could I explain his sovereignty, love or power to them when they questioned why God allowed such a horrible scene to play out in my son's tragic death; the truth is I didn't know myself.

I remember the minister telling me that my son was really connected to my destiny and that God could not fulfill it until my son's assignment was complete, but she never said my baby had to die. My mind went into a frenzy and my faith began to waiver as I became double minded and unstable in all of my ways. I wanted to continue to minister for God but not at the sacrifice of my son. If there was a choice I would have lived a life loving God but not exactly desiring to be used by him, not if it came to losing my child. My faith and hope were replaced by anger and confusion. My desire to minister left me, and now my prayers of forgiveness turned into prayers of revenge as my drunkenness from liquor replaced my drunkenness from God's holy Spirit.

Although I had been possessed by demons and contemplated suicide several times, never had my mind been so tormented. I moved all of my children away from me because I wanted them to be safe from the people who had brutally taken my son's life, but more importantly I wanted them to be safe from me. I had so much hate, anger, and disappointment from them failing me and me failing them. I couldn't take the pressure of watching the demise of another child I gave birth too. It was time that I stopped trying to be their god and allow them to develop their own relationship with Him, after all my relationship with God was now suspect.

God constantly began warning me to get out of my flesh and come up higher into the spiritual dimension. I knew I needed to get to where God was. He was elevated over the raging seas that He wanted to teach me to walk on. I could visualize Jesus walking boldly on the raging waters and calling out for me to join him. One moment I would heed his call and begin walking tall, with my shoulders back and my head held up as my faith soared higher than the treacherous waves that were trying to take me under, the next moment I would begin sinking as doubt crept in and weighed me down. As with the disciple Peter, the more I focused my eyes on the raging waters that were surrounding me, instead of focusing on God, the more I began to drown in my sorrows, resentment, anger, and confusion. I became enraged. I wanted justice for my son and I wanted God to deliver it. I no longer had control over my emotions and I could not think logically. Anything reminding me of my son would set me off and send me spiraling into rage and anyone in my path was likely to feel my wrath; even the one person who God himself, chose to take this dreadful journey with me.

Novacane was my knight in shining armor and my worst nightmare…. From the first day that he had learned of my baby's death he didn't leave my side. He sacrificed so much of himself to prove his devotion to me, but my heart rejected his devout love because after Prosper's death it could only comprehend pain. Nothing he did to help me with the grieving process, could make up for him hurting me in the past. I wanted everyone to pay for their sins against me, and who better to begin with then the closest person to me. I was honored that he had dedicated his life to me, but another sinister side of me literally wanted to take his life and Satan was honored to assist me. Novacane didn't know what to expect from me from day to day. As my faith wavered so did my emotions. The change would be so drastic and dramatic that we often ended up in verbal and physical confrontations. Everything he did was scrutinized because I had lost faith in him and all human beings in general. I wanted him to understand the level of pain I was under having my son snatched out of my life. I couldn't fathom why he didn't understand my level of distress after the sudden death of my baby boy. Slowly my knight in shining armor began to dimmer as we began rehashing all the abuse that I had gone through in my past. Novacane couldn't have been less prepared for the rage that hid behind my smiles, the violence, that laid dormant in my soft caress, or the torment that concealed itself within my vocal chords. Prosper's death introduced him to the dark side of me; writing and reliving this book made him and my ungodly side well acquainted.

* * *

I thought back to years ago when I first received the prophecy to name my son Prosper while I was pregnant with him. The devil tried to take my child's life so many times, but God had to remind me the devil is a spirit just as God is. The devil knows that the spirit realm is the realm of truth, therefore if God wants to be worshipped in spirit and truth then the devil wants to be worshipped in the flesh or natural realm and in lies. God needed to birth me through the power of resurrection, into another dimension from the natural realm of my limited knowledge into the supernatural power and wisdom of God. God needed to teach me the true meaning of the verse that I had had engraved in my son's mind. Little did I know that death was the only entryway into this new dimension and journey into the Promised Land. Death from the flesh and resurrection into the spiritual realm was the requirement for my son to enter into the ultimate promise land known as heaven, but death would also be required of me to enter into what God promised me while I was still an occupant of the Earth. Just like Joshua and Caleb I had to become spiritually minded if I wanted to defeat the giants fighting against me.

Someone should have warned me that giants come in all colors, shapes, sizes and people. From my faith, family, friends, and foes alike the battle ground was set as their fiery darts and venomous words began being thrown at me, but before God could armor me from the outward giants God had to armor me for the giants living on the inside of me the same giants I grew to love and depend on. Ready or not I was about to enter into the biggest war of my life and this time the stakes could cause me to lose Prosper forever...

Destiny

There is a baby girl inside of me longing to be birthed

She was conceived the moment Apostle McCoy spoke God's word

The moment I agreed with God she jumped inside my womb

I knew I had been intimate with God, but religion had me to assume

That relationships with God was not something of the ordinary

I search the scriptures, which is the heart of God and found it to be contrary

To what man believes; to what they were trying to teach me to receive

There laws and pagan worship cause many to have
intercourse, but unable to conceive

I've dreamed about my daughter, in all honesty
I've had constant nightmares

I would see me giving birth, hold her and suddenly she would disappear

Times I dreamt of forsaking her, her forgetting that she was even born

Flashbacks of my giving birth became my flesh's thorn

I knew I had given birth I'm in a labor room plus
my body is tired and so very weak

The nurses are cleaning up my blood I watch in
exhaustion too tired to even speak

I see my baby in the incubator, excited, my eyes
began to puff up and slowly water

I want to hold her in my arms overwhelmed
with love I ask to hold my daughter

Immediately she's placed in my arms and I'm
consumed in personal satisfaction

This is where it gets confusing because I leave the hospital
without her and not knowing what happened

Still in the dreams I find myself pondering; did I ever really give birth

I call back to the hospital and ask that they do a complete and vital search

My baby is missing or maybe giving birth was all in my mind

I seek reassurance, but doubt and confusion is all that I find

I wake up asking God what you are trying to say to me

Kindly he speaks "your daughter represents your destiny

You will give birth for no one can be pregnant forever

Only you have the power to abort, which is why
the wiles of Satan are subtle and clever

But you should watch and pray who you allow in your delivery room

Was that really a nurse he asked or did you just assume

I thought back to the dream and could now
see the darkness in the nurse's eyes

More important was the name tag that read," Lucifer in disguise

Oh my God! My heart dropped suddenly to the floor

I knew demise had found my baby I would see her no more

Panicked I prayed, sickened by the devil's scheme,
wishing I could do it differently

I would pay closer attention and watch who I let get close to me

The pregnancy I complained about with its symptoms always bothering me

Now I would do anything to put my daughter back inside of me

The labor that took so much blood symbolic of my sacrifice

My weak and tired body was evidence of the heavy price

That I paid, but paying without praying voids our discernment

In a dream God showed it so in reality I would learn this.

Each and every one of us has a destiny that has to be birthed

It's vital we realize its magnitude and treasure its worth

For Satan desires to devour it and will use anybody to fill his mission

But would I take heed to God's warning and unmerited wisdom…

About the Author

WHILE MANY WERE trained in their profession, others were created for it. Such is the case with Tonya Love, writer/poet, extraordinaire. Born in the country hills of West Virginia on June 30th on her mother's birthday, Tonya was undoubtedly perceived as a precious gift, but no one could imagine the gifts that laid dormant inside of her. That is until her second grade teacher took notice of her very creative and descriptive style of writing.

As the charismatic prophet's life accelerated from childhood to adolescence her gifts would become more proficient and profound as life developed her character and trained her with its experiences, her gifts would blossom and flourish into a ministry of faith, healing, and encouragement. There are no formal educational institutes or teachers to which she attributes her gifts. Her talents were given to her by her Creator and anointed by the Holy Spirit that dwells on the inside of this prophetic poet. The world became her institute and the Holy Spirit's revelation and the infallible Word of the Sovereign God became her instructor. Although trials and tribulations were sent to destroy her, God allowed them to become her lessons in the subject called life. Writing became her weapon of choice and with it the multifaceted story teller, song writer, poet, director, and actor captivates her readers with her unique ability to illuminate both the spoken and written word.

* * *

Like the children of Israel, Tonya Love was enslaved to a bondage of sin, religion, and abuse. After an attempted suicide and an angelic visitation when she was seventeen years old, God spoke to her through an Apostle of a promise land consisting of a true and intimate relationship with Him and a worldwide ministry. But first she had to be willing to cross over the spiritual Red Sea and dwell in the wilderness where God would develop her character, build her faith, and teach her His commandments. As a prophetess, God began speaking to her and giving her dreams, visions and revelations concerning His kingdom and the enemy that opposes it.

God planted a seed in Tonya during her seventh pregnancy and instructed her to name her son Prosper; as a sign that He was going to fulfill His promise to her. The kingdom of darkness continuously, through weapons of warfare against her and her seed, ultimately took his life when he was only seventeen years of age. When her symbol of God's promise died Tonya felt that her promise died right along with him. Her mind went into torment as she began to question her faith and everything she thought she knew about the God who had delivered her from witchcraft, abuse and even death. Though her son was now deceased, God ensured her that his death was all a part of His sovereign plan and that her son had stepped over into his own Promise land (Heaven) and encouraged her to continue on her journey and step over onto the other side of the Jordan where she would finally possess her Promised Land. Giants opposed her, rage consumed her, doubt delayed her, death discouraged her, and religion denied her, but Her Father promised her...

NO WEAPON SHALL PROSPER

PROSPER NA'TRON JOHNSON

#7 REPRESENTS COMPLETENESS AND PERFECTION

HE WAS MY 7TH PREGNANCY

HE WAS BORN IN THE 7TH HEBREW CALENDAR MONTH

HE DIED IN 2014 THREE 7's

EACH OF HIS NAMES HAS 7 LETTERS OR SYMBOLS

HE DIED ON THE 7OO BLOCK AROUND 7 PM

I WAS WITH HIS DAD FOR 7 YEARS

WE HAD BEEN SEPARATED FOR 14 YEARS WHEN HE DIED

#17 IS COMPLETE VICTORY OVER THE ENEMY

I WAS 17 WHEN I FIRST RECEIVED THE PROPHECY

PROSPER WAS 17 WHEN HE DIED

THE NO WEAPON VERSE IS THE 17TH VERSE

OTHER SIGNS AND WONDERS

PROSPER DIED OCTOBER 5TH THE SAME DAY MY FATHER DIED, 26 YEARS LATER TO THE DAY

HE DIED ON THE DAY AFTER YOM KIPPUR (ATONEMENT)

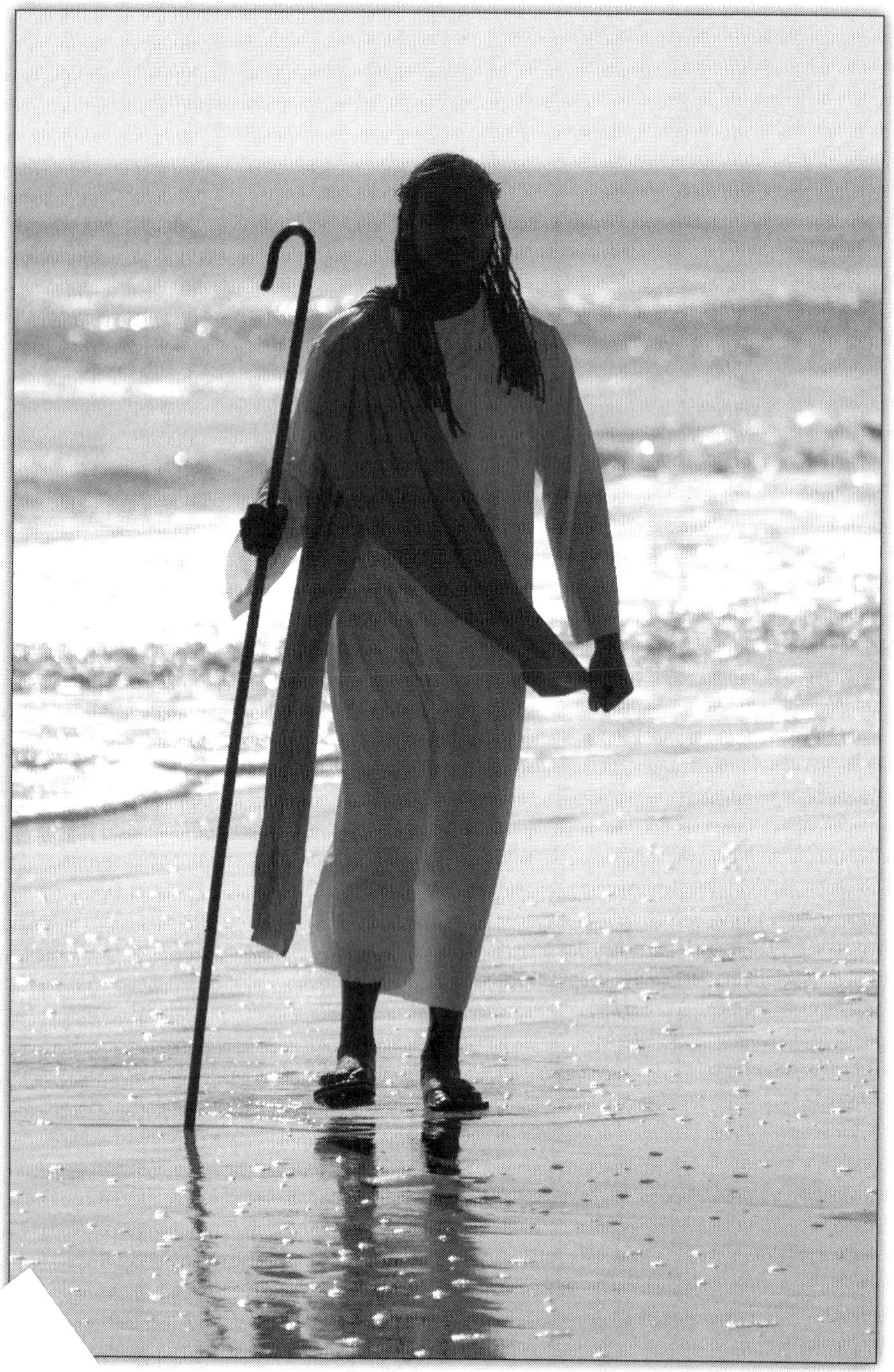

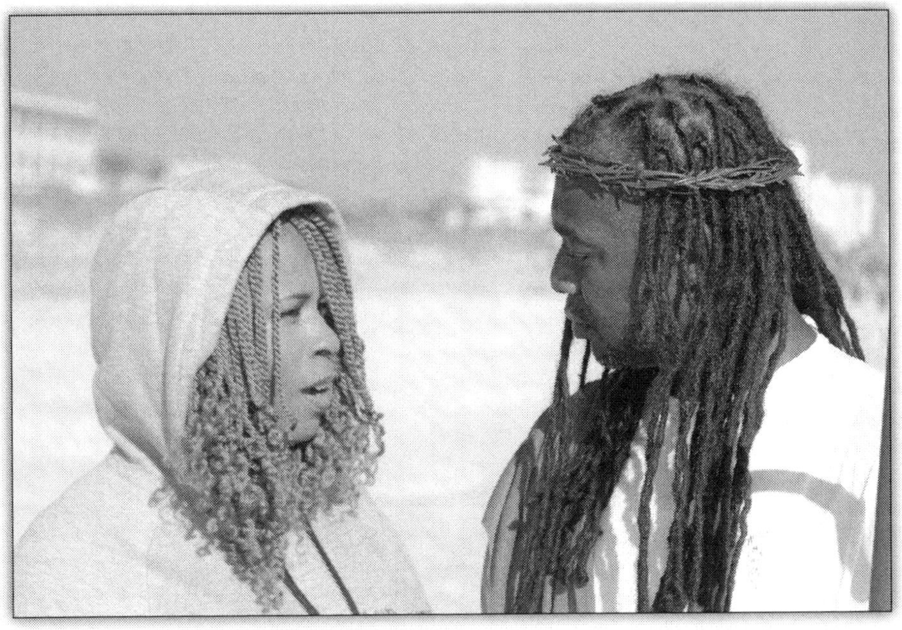

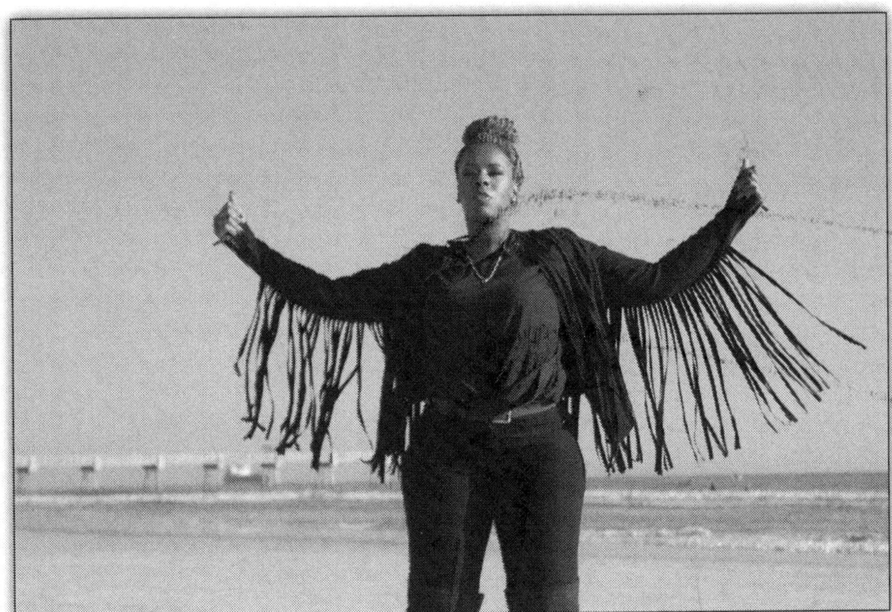

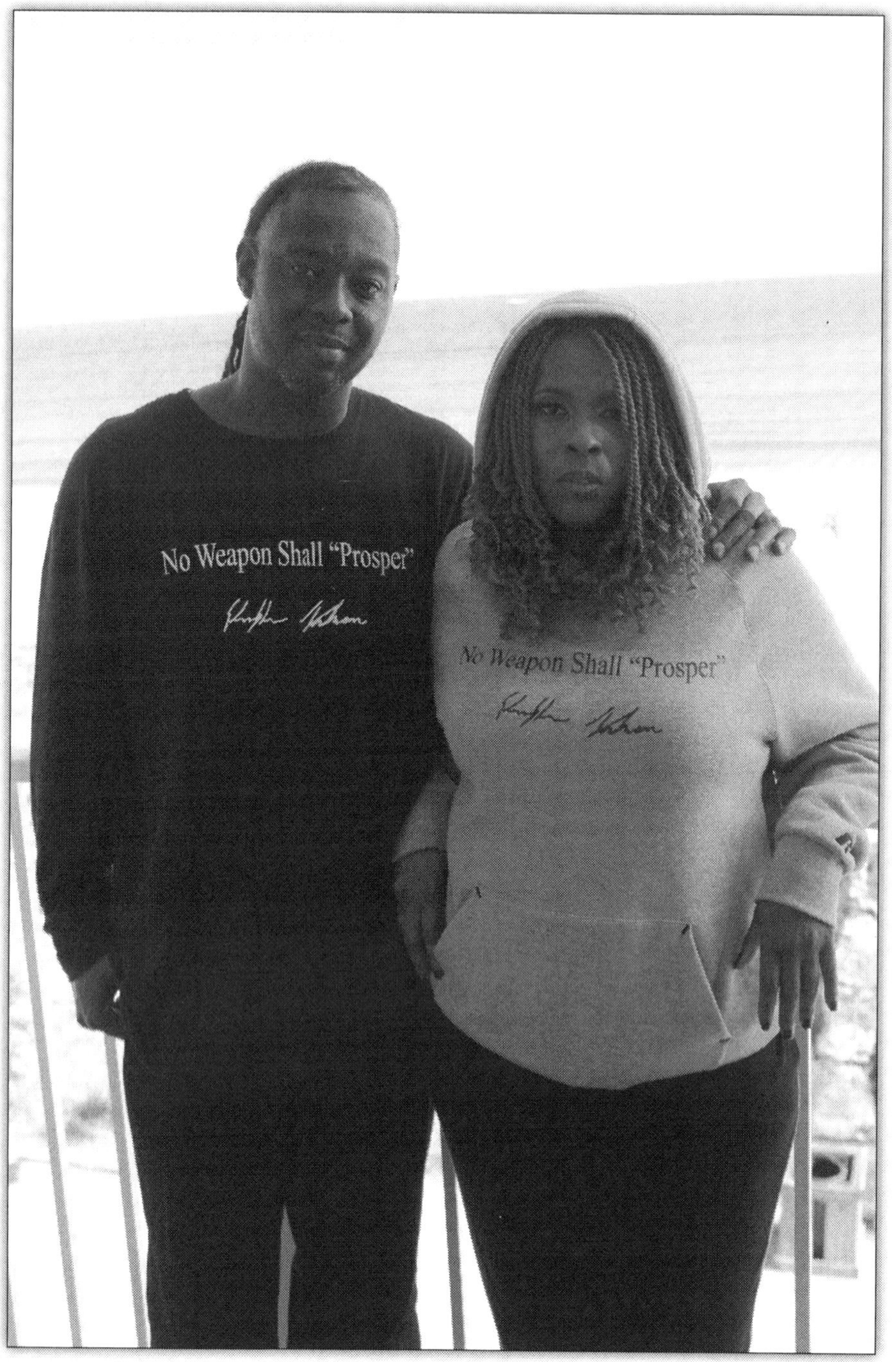
No Weapon Shall "Prosper"
No Weapon Shall "Prosper"

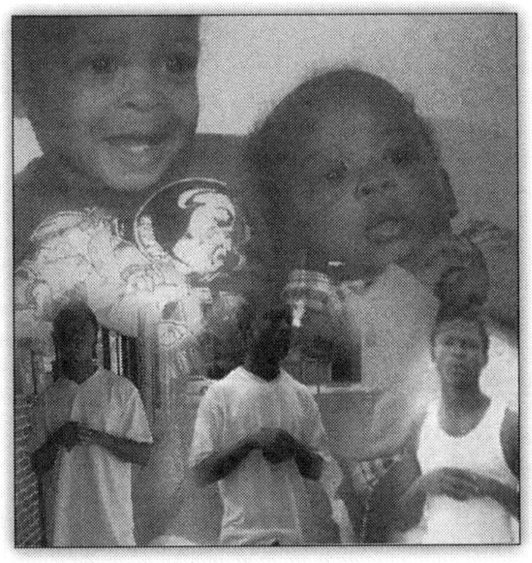

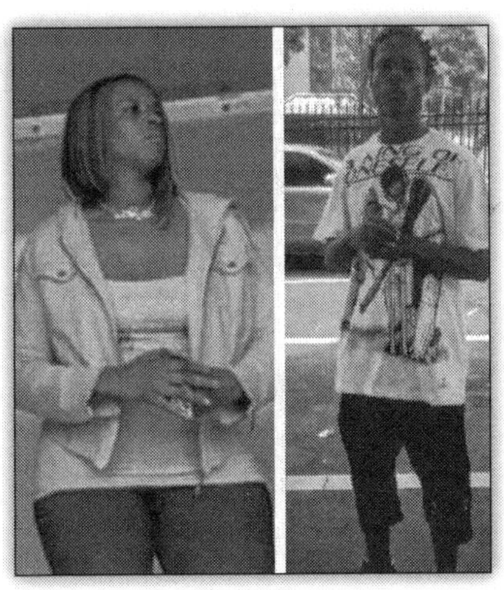

TRL
TONYA REPS LOVE

Made in the USA
Columbia, SC
20 August 2019